Cognitive Capitalism, Welfare and Labour

This book deals with the transformations of both accumulation process and labour in the transition from a Fordist to a cognitive capitalism paradigm, with specific regard to Western economies. It outlines the advent, after industrial capitalism, of a new phase of the capitalist system in which the value of cognitive labour becomes dominant. In this framework, the central stakes of capital valorisation and forms of property are directly based on the control and privatization of the production of collective knowledge. Here, the transformation of knowledge itself, into a commodity or a fictitious capital, is analyzed.

Building on this foundation, the authors outline their concept of "commonfare." This idea of commonfare implies, as a prerequisite, the social re-appropriation of the gains arising from the exploitation of those social relations which are the basis of accumulation today. This re-appropriation does not necessarily lead to the transition from private to public ownership but it does make it necessary to distinguish between common goods and the commonwealth. This book explains this distinction and how common goods and the commonwealth require a different framework of analysis.

This volume will be of great interest to all scholars and researchers, as well as a more general readership, who wish to develop a critical thinking of the mainstream analysis of this topic. Contributing to the "Marxism-heterodox" approach using rigorous theoretical analysis and empirical evidence, it is aimed at all those who act socially and aspire to a better understanding of the development and the contradictions of contemporary capitalism.

Andrea Fumagalli is Associate Professor of Economics at the Department of Economics and Management at University of Pavia, Italy. He also teaches at IUSS Pavia and his research focuses on issues of labour precarity, on basic income and transformations of contemporary capitalism.

Alfonso Giuliani is a Research Fellow at Centre d'Économie de la Sorbonne, Université Paris 1 Panthéon-Sorbonne, CNRS UMR 8174, France. His research focuses on issues of institutional economics, political economy of commons, cognitive capitalism, monetary theory of production and history of economic thought.

Stefano Lucarelli is Associate Professor in Economic Policy at University of Bergamo, Italy. His research projects include institutional economics, cognitive capitalism, monetary theory of production, financialization, stock-flow consistent models and complementary currencies.

Carlo Vercellone is Full Professor at Université de Paris 8, France, Department of Culture and Communication. He is also a member of Centre d'Études sur les Médias et l'Internationalisation (CEMTI), Associate Researcher at CNRS-Centre d'Economie de la Sorbonne (CES) and Sophiapol (Université Paris Nanterre). His research focuses on the knowledge economy, cognitive capitalism, welfare state and basic income.

Routledge Frontiers of Political Economy

251. Commodity
The Global Commodity System in the 21st Century
Photis Lysandrou

252. Uncertainty and Economics
A Paradigmatic Perspective
Christian Müller-Kademann

253. Discourse Analysis and Austerity
Critical Studies from Economics and Linguistics
Edited by Kate Power, Tanweer Ali and Eva Lebdušková

254. A Macroeconomic Analysis of Profit
Andrea Carrera

255. The Dark Places of Business Enterprise
Reinstating Social Costs in Institutional Economics
Pietro Frigato and Francisco J. Santos Arteaga

256. Economic Woman
Gendering Economic Inequality in the Age of Capital
Frances Raday

257. The Economics of Military Spending
A Marxist Perspective
Adem Yavuz Elveren

258. Political Pluralism, Disagreement and Justice
The Case for Polycentric Democracy
Julian F. Müller

259. Nonviolent Political Economy
Theory and Applications
Edited by Freddy Cante and Wanda Tatiana Torres

260. Cognitive Capitalism, Welfare and Labour
The Commonfare Hypothesis
Andrea Fumagalli, Alfonso Giuliani, Stefano Lucarelli and Carlo Vercellone

For more information about this series, please visit: www.routledge.com/books/series/SE0345

Cognitive Capitalism, Welfare and Labour

The Commonfare Hypothesis

Andrea Fumagalli, Alfonso Giuliani, Stefano Lucarelli and Carlo Vercellone

With the participation of Stefano Dughera

Postface by Antonio Negri

Routledge
Taylor & Francis Group
LONDON AND NEW YORK

First published 2019 by Routledge

2 Park Square, Milton Park, Abingdon, Oxon, OX14 4RN
605 Third Avenue, New York, NY 10017

Routledge is an imprint of the Taylor & Francis Group, an informa business

First issued in paperback 2020

British Library Cataloguing in Publication Data
A catalogue record for this book is available from the British Library

Library of Congress Cataloging-in-Publication Data
A catalog record has been requested for this book

ISBN: 978-1-138-65430-3 (hbk)
ISBN: 978-0-367-72809-0 (pbk)

Typeset in Times New Roman
by Taylor & Francis Books

Contents

Illustrations

Figures

Tables

Introduction[1]

After the post-Fordist period, started in the mid-1990s, a new paradigm has emerged in a sufficiently hegemonic and pervasive way in a large part of the globe. Some scholars (including the authors of this book) have thus begun to speak of cognitive capitalism, a term which, as is well known, has conveyed a lot of controversy, especially within orthodox Marxist approaches that still consider Fordist ways of extracting surplus value as dominant. According to this view, real subsumption, the sharp separation between machines and humans, between productive waged labor and tendentially unproductive (residual) labor that incorporates cognitive and relational/intellectual activities still represented the basis for defining the nature and form of exploitation within the capital–labor relation.

First the crisis of the net-economy (2000), then the subprime crisis (2007–2009), have made this "continuist" reading even more obsolete. There are several reasons that justify this statement. The first concerns the nature of the accumulation and valorization process that followed the financial and GDP collapse in the two-year period from 2008 to 2009.

The subprime crisis can be read as the result of a deviation between a process of exploitation of a labor activity, however internal to the labor market governance (which caused an increasingly precarious and compressed remuneration) and a process of financial valorization characterized by a private ownership structure that wanted to be increasingly widespread even if increasingly impoverished.

The profits of large multinational companies only partially derived from the direct exploitation of labor, and if this happened that was the exploitation of some parts of the entire cycle of subcontracting and production: in particular, the nodes not directly concerned with the core production and technology. Despite the increase in the intensity of exploitation (high precariousness, reduction of previously acquired rights, decomposition of work, incapacity and often connivance of trade unions), this basis for extracting surplus value was no longer sufficient when confronted to the spread of global competition and the redefinition at the global scale of the geo-economic structure, with the emergence of new capitalist economic powers. Capitalism thus needed new value-sources. Financialization, on the one hand, and commodification of territories and natures alike, on the other, could provide an adequate response. However, that has proved insufficient.

Hence the need to include the life of individuals in the process of financialization in an ever-more pervasive way through the becoming-rent of increasing portions of wage (especially the deferred one, due to the dismantling of the welfare system in Europe or its extension in financial terms, as happened with the Obama health reform in the USA). The financial securitization of living conditions through the development of derivatives (from houses to intellectual property rights, to health insurance, social security, education, etc.) had to compensate in some way for the possible crisis of realization due to the increase in the concentration of incomes following a process of labor exploitation that had reached limits that could no longer be surpassed.

In other words, with the diffusion of the paradigm of cognitive capitalism, a process of self-valuing money—money (M-M′) was "tested," mediated by the exploitation of physical labor (logistics), and, to an increasing extent, of cognitive labor within productive sites, which, breaking the boundaries of the traditional factory, innervate the space of human action to an ever-more pervasive extent, to the point of creating its own virtual space.

This first phase of cognitive capitalism, a hybrid in which traditional forms of work coexisted, some even pre-waged, with new forms of work, especially in immaterial productions, went into crisis in the second half of 2000s since the basis of its accumulation proved too narrow for the needs of exploitation, against a composition of intangible capital that still manifests itself mainly as constant capital (as a machinery).

In Marxian terms, we could say that in this first phase of cognitive capitalism, the organic composition of capital grows faster than the rate of exploitation, creating the bursting of the financial bubble as a site, predominant but uncertain, of valorization of surplus labor.

According to Fumagalli's interpretation, the financial crisis of cognitive capitalism paves the way for bio-cognitive capitalism to emerge. The prefix *bio* is, in this case, decisive. It indicates that the current phase of capitalist accumulation is identified with the exploitation of life in its essence, going beyond the exploitation of productive labor certified as such and therefore remunerated. Value-labor leaves more and more room for value-life (Morini and Fumagalli 2011).

This process is both extensive and intensive. Extensive because life as a whole, in its singularity, becomes an object of exploitation, even in its simple everyday life. New productions are taking hold. Social (re)production, which has always operated in the history of mankind, becomes directly productive but only partially waged; the genesis of life (procreation) is transformed into business; free time is boxed, like friendly and sentimental relations, inside tracks and devices that, through algorithmic technologies, allow the extraction of surplus value (network value); the human body in its physical and cerebral components becomes the raw material for the production and planning of health and life extension, due to new bio-medical techniques.

Intensive, because these processes are accompanied by new technical and organizational methods and new processes of commodification. Life put into production and therefore into value manifests itself in the first place as an undertaking of human and social relations. Social cooperation, understood as a set of more or less hierarchical human relationships, becomes the basis of capitalist accumulation. But this is not enough, as underlined by the research of Melinda Cooper and Catherine Waldby (Cooper and Waldby 2014); the human body itself, and its parts, become more and more the object of commodification and direct production of exchange value.

Recent debates, especially within Autonomous Marxism, have identified in *the common* a new mode of production (Negri 2016; Vercellone et al. 2015; Vercellone et al. 2017). This is an important aspect for understanding the forms of productive organization, of firm management and of labor.

The second reason to justify the structural change in the accumulation regime after the crisis of Fordism is based on the observation that bio-cognitive capitalism is accompanied by an acceleration of technological progress. There is no certainty that a new technological paradigm is under way, yet a number of trends seem to confirm such a hypothesis. What emerges is a progression in the hybridization between machines and humans in a direction that involves at the same time experimentation with forms of complete automation aimed at replacing the human being in some of their functions, on the one hand; and the becoming-machine of the human body, on the other. The fields of artificial intelligence, biotechnologies, nanotechnologies, the construction of human tissues with genetic experimentation,[2] neurosciences, the industry of processing masses of increasingly complex and individualized data (big data), show a distinct process in which the becoming-human of the machine is combined with the becoming-machine of the human. Regardless of the future dynamics that these trajectories will take, although the construction of a "post-human" seems inevitable,[3] what we are interested in observing is how the separation between human and machine is lacking. Not only does the relationship between abstract labor and concrete labor (Fumagalli 2007) undergo a twist, but also the relationship between constant and variable capital, between dead labor and living labor tends to change more and more, to the point of engendering a metamorphosis of the capital–labor nexus.

This dynamic poses a series of important theoretical and empirical problems. First, there is a structural change in the form of capital. In large US companies (listed on the Standard & Poor index), it is since the end of the twentieth century that the share of intangible capital (consisting mainly of R&D, brand, communication, and training) has exceeded the tangible one. The composition of investments has changed accordingly. The term *human capital* has become commonplace. Now the same investment in constant capital has increasingly involved the *bios*, to the point of making the traditional notion of fixed capital obsolete. Second, these transformations pose measurement problems that cannot always be defined, despite the fact that new indicators have been created, and it is not by chance that they are increasingly correlated to the dynamics of the share value of capital listed on the financial markets.

The third reason concerns the investigation of the new social composition of labor that has resulted from it. We are witnessing the subjective growth of multiple and differentiated works that makes it impossible, in the current state of affairs, to identify a homogeneous social class composition. The coexistence of non-waged forms, of unpaid forms of work (Armano and Murgia 2016; Coin 2017), of forms of semi-slavery, of forms of emotional-cerebral involvement, of direct heteroforms, of forms of third-generation autonomous work (Fumagalli 2015), of forms of self-realization and self-entrepreneurship (for example: the makers) make it difficult to codify both the technical and political composition of labor, provided that these two key expressions of the Autonomist literature still make sense.

The crisis of wage-earning labor, however, does not open up prospects of overcoming the working condition. On the contrary, it further fragments it and depresses it. Symptomatic in this regard is the current tendency to erase the monetary remuneration of a growing number of directly productive work performances that cannot be assimilated to the archipelago of voluntary and "free" work. The spread of unpaid labor does not imply that there is no longer any remuneration or that there is a theft of wages, but rather a new form of remuneration that is not defined by the wage form. We are thus witnessing new ways of labor remuneration, characterized by increasingly symbolic, relational, and immaterial elements.

These dynamics lead us to reconsider the concept of technical composition of labor, especially within a process that moves in the direction of overcoming the human–machine dichotomy. Does this tendency mean that the capital–labor relationship is no longer present? We strongly disagree with that. What is emerging, as is usual in when the dominant technological paradigm changes, is a new configuration of this relationship, where the material element and, consequently, its measure in terms of monetary remuneration, loses its effectiveness to the benefit of a new capital–labor relationship, even more imbued with subjective elements than it previously was.

Current capitalist valorization is increasingly based on the production of subjectivity. Fixed capital hybridizes with variable capital, dead labor with living labor and vice versa. The challenge facing us is not only the reappropriation of our fixed capital but also, and perhaps above all, the capacity for self-managing our variable capital.

Methodology

The various contributions in this book aim at analyzing the main characteristics of the process of accumulation and enhancement of contemporary capitalism, based on a distinctive methodological approach. The theoretical research in this book moves, in fact, along the lines of the (neo)-workerist methodology, a methodology that takes root in co-research on the working condition of the mass-worker, at the beginning of the 1960s in Italy.

Today we live in structurally different times and face very different theoretical problems and empirical analyses. However, there is a methodological element that links those times to today with a thin red thread. It is the intuition, provided by the militant journal *Quaderni Rossi*, that the capital–labor relationship involves conflicting subjectivities: different subjectivities that move on different and asymmetrical planes. We can translate this intuition in the terms used by Mario Tronti (2019) in *Operai e Capitale*, namely in the simple and enlightening observation that labor expresses its own subjectivity (composite, and therefore worth of analysis) which can in any case operate without capital; the same cannot be said of capital, whose existence depends on the relationship with labor and for this reason this latter needs to be subordinated. This book aims to analyze the evolution of this relationship between a full subjectivity (living labor) and a maimed subjectivity (capital's dead labor), in a historical phase where living knowledge embodied in the *general intellect* has become, today more than ever, the pivot on which valorization revolves. And there is more: the force of invention and the potential autonomy of labor cooperation also lead to processes of exodus from the wage condition and to the experimentation of alternative forms of self-organization of production based on the common.

All authors argue that an emphasis on this experimental attitude is the shared element of a consistent number of studies on the transformations of the capital–labor relation in the past thirty years, namely since the first researches on post-Fordism were published in the early 1990s. It is a line of research that, today as in the early 1990s, looks with distrust at a sociological approach to the analysis of class conflict, often stiffened in an idea of "class" historically determined and unable to grasp its evolution, which is visible through its subjective changes.[4]

Today, we speak of "neo-workerism" precisely to underline this methodological red thread. It seems to us that this term is more explicit and theoretically coherent than the term, often used (especially by the adversaries), of "post-workerism," which carries the typical ambiguity and approximation of all terms that begin with the prefix *post-*.

The concept of neo-workerism allows us to underline the substantial continuity of a methodology based on the driving role of labor subjectivity, "within and against capital," despite the changes that have taken place in the object of analysis, that is, the transformations that occurred in the class composition and in the regime of accumulation of capital between the Fordist age of the first workerism of the 1960s and that of cognitive capitalism.

It is clear that the term "neo-workerism" no longer refers to the centrality of the mass-worker of the 1960s or to its evolution into the term "social worker" of the 1970s. But it is precisely this method of research that allows us to say that today "the" central subject of reference of social conflict in industrial capitalism has disappeared.

Precisely for this reason, neo-workerist thought is also anything but homogeneous and cohesive. Consonance with a method of analysis does not directly imply a single theoretical elaboration and a single interpretation of the capital–labor relationship, a relationship always object of metamorphosis (as Marx's method taught us) and, consequently, political proposals can vary while referring to a common root. The counterproof of this is the current debate between the different analyses on the concept of subsumption: subsumption of the general intellect for some, life subsumption for others, to the point of fearing the uselessness of such a concept in the current capitalist phase.

The structure of this book

The index of the book (largely composed of unpublished contributions)is designed precisely to allow the reader to reconstruct the main hypotheses shared by neo-workerist approaches, without however concealing hesitations and doubts, as well as some real differences of analysis regarding the origins, meaning and stakes of the current mutations of capitalism.

In the first chapter, some central hypotheses for a neo-Marxist approach to the thesis of cognitive capitalism are proposed. They are based on an interpretative grid in which the transformations of the role of knowledge in the economy are grasped on the basis of the key role of antagonism between living knowledge of labor and dead knowledge of capital. In this perspective, Vercellone and Giuliani start from a critique of the knowledge-based economy, then show how the thesis of cognitive capitalism constitutes a renewal of the research program of the French Regulation school. Finally, they proceed to the elaboration and interpretation of the main stylized facts that make it possible to diagnose the passage from industrial capitalism to a new phase of capitalism, i.e. cognitive capitalism.

In the second chapter, Vercellone and Dughera specify this research agenda both at the level of its Marxist theoretical foundations and at the level of the main characters of new capitalism. The aim of this contribution is to clarify with precision the logical and historical meaning of the crisis of the law of value founded on labor time and to put it in relation with the tendency of "becoming-rent of profit". This analysis addresses to two necessities. The first, within the theoretical development of the neo-workerist approach, is to show the close link that unites the theses on the general intellect and the crisis of the law of value, on the one hand, and the analysis of the transformation of the rules of distribution between wages, income and profit, on the other. The second necessity is to put an end to the many misunderstandings that the expression "crisis of the law of value" has caused in hasty readings of the approach of cognitive capitalism, to the point of assimilating it to an abandonment of the Marxist foundations of value and surplus-value theory.

The third chapter by Andrea Fumagalli tries to clarify an issue that has provoked much debate in the past few years, especially in the field of heretic and heterodox thought, that is to say, the analysis of the salient characteristics of the current phase of capitalism. In the past two decades, innovations in the fields of transportation, language, and communication started to gather around a new single paradigm of accumulation and valorization. The new capitalist configuration tends to identify in "knowledge" and "space," conceived of as productive factors, a new foundation for accumulation. Fumagalli defines the contemporary form of capitalism as *bio-cognitive capitalism*. Independently of the dominant convention, contemporary capitalism is always in search of new social and vital circles to absorb, and of new means of production to commodify, involving more and more the bare vital faculties of human beings.

Following this reasoning, in Chapter 4, new form of valorization and exploitation in contemporary capitalism are analyzed. Capitalist exploitation is described by Marx with two forms of subsumption: "formal" and "real," as outcome of the historical evolution of capitalism and the continuous metamorphosis of the capital–labor ratio. Those two subsumptions refer to two different concepts of surplus value: absolute and relative. Nowadays, in time of bio-cognitive capitalism, we see a new metamorphosis of the capital–labor ratio and the emergence of a new form of subsumption, which Fumagalli proposes to define life subsumption, as a result of the entire life (body, soul, brain) being put to work, then to value.

In the fifth chapter, Fumagalli and Lucarelli provide a theoretical framework to describe the shift from a monetary production economy to a financial production economy. In accordance with the Schumpeterian perspective, this framework points to both the monetary-financial nature *of*, and qualitative changes *in*, the capitalist system. The financialization of the monetary economy of production can be better explained if we understand the shift to a new technological paradigm as a general outlook on the productive problems faced by firms, whereby the relevance of the so-called immaterial production takes on greater importance.

Chapter 6, written by Fumagalli and Lucarelli, describes the main features of the accumulation paradigm in cognitive capitalism. It provides a theoretical framework of it and discusses the conditions of stability and instability of the model. In cognitive capitalism instability turns out to be structural. Once competition has become a specific productive factor, new light can be shed on the uncertainty which characterize economic activities. Such light can then better explain the causes of systemic instabilities.

In the seventh chapter, Vercellone and Giuliani go back to the contradiction between cognitive capitalism and the knowledge-based economy in order to show how it generated the development of a new "mode of production" founded on the common. A twofold process must be highlighted: while traditional and more distributive forms of capital–labor antagonism seemed to be decreasing in their intensity, the development of a collective intelligence disclosed a new conflict zone directly on the ground of the development of productive forces. Both its size and penetration in different sectors would be unimaginable in a Fordist context. Politically speaking, however, a wide variety of scenarios can be envisaged. The extreme plasticity on which the resilience of capitalism depends (Braudel 1967) and its ability to integrate "*artistic criticism* and *social criticism*" as an engine of its development (Boltanski and Chiappello 1999), have already allowed it to subsume within its logic of enhancement consistent forms of production based on the common.

Notes

1 This introduction is the result of a common work by the authors.
2 The mapping of the human genome can mark a technological and social leap similar to that derived from the periodic table of elements of Mendeleev in 1869, with the possibility no longer remote to create artificial living material and no longer just artificial natural material (birth of inorganic chemistry).
3 The debate on post-humanity has been going on for a few decades now. Initially, it analyzed the evolution of the human being, nature and technology relationship (Pepperell 1995, Pepperell and Punt 2003) then more directly on the process of transformation of the human being (Braidotti 2013).
4 In the Anglo-Saxon debate, this line of theoretical elaboration was (and it is) called "autonomist Marxism," precisely to emphasize the diversity of traditional "scientific" Marxism, which developed during the twentieth century.

References

Armano, E. and A. Murgia (eds.) (2016) *Le reti del lavoro gratuito, Spazi urbani e nuove soggettività*, Verona:Ombre Corte.

Boltanski, L. and E. Chiapello (1999) *Le Nouvel Esprit du capitalisme*, Paris: Gallimard.

Braidotti, R. (2013) *Posthuman*, Cambridge: Polity Press.

Braudel, F. (1967) *Civilisation materielle et capitalisme (XVe–XVIIIe Siecle)*, Paris: Armand Colin.

Coin, F. (ed.) (2017) *Salari rubati: economia politica e conflitto ai tempi del lavoro gratuito*, Verona: Ombre Corte.

Cooper, M. and C. Waldby (2014) *Clinical Labor: Tissue Donors and Research Subjects in the Global Bioeconomy (Experimental Futures)*, Durham, NC: Duke University Press.

Fumagalli, A. (2007) *Bioeconomics and Cognitive Capitalism: Towards a New Accumulation Regime*, Rome: Carocci.

Fumagalli, A. (2015) "Le trasformazioni del lavoro autonomo tra crisi e precarietà: il lavoro autonomo di III generazione," *Quaderni di ricerca sull'artigianato*, 2:225–254.

Fumagalli, A. and C. Morini (2011) "Life Put to Work: Towards a Theory of Life-Value," *Ephemera*, 10(3–4): 234–252.

Negri, A. (2016) *Il comune come modo di produzione*, available at www.euronomade.info/?p=7331, June (accessed December 2018).

Pepperell, R.(1995)*The Posthuman Condition: Consciousness Beyond the Brain*, Portland, Oreg.: Intellect Books.

Pepperell, R. and M. Punt (2003) *The Postdigital Membrane: Imagination, Technology and Desire*, Portland, Oreg.: Intellect Books.

Tronti, M. (2019) *Workers and Capital*, London: Penguin.

Vercellone, C., F. Bria, A. Fumagalli, E. Gentilucci, A. Giuliani, G. Griziotti, and P. Vattimo (2015) *Managing the Commons in the Knowledge Economy*, Report D-CENT Project, available at www.nesta.org.uk/report/d-cent-managing-the-commons-in-the-knowledge-economy/ (accessed March 25, 2019).

Vercellone, C., A. Giuliani, F. Brancaccio, P. Vattimo (2017) *Il comune come modo di produzione*, Verona:Ombre Corte.

1 An introduction to cognitive capitalism

A Marxist approach

Carlo Vercellone and Alfonso Giuliani

Introduction

This chapter outlines some elements of a research program organized around the thesis of cognitive capitalism, a project that insists upon rereading the historical development of the capital–labour relation from the point of view of the knowledge economy. This research program is a product of the particular historical and theoretical context that has emerged since the crisis of the Fordist growth regime.

Since the Fordist crisis, capitalism has entered a period of major transformation that has affected the modalities of valorisation, the forms of property and the division of labour. This "new capitalism" has called into question many of the most essential aspects of the logic of development that emerged after the first industrial revolution. At the heart of this transformation is the growing importance of knowledge and the immaterial. This is not to say that the centrality of knowledge to capitalism is in itself new. Rather, the question we must ask is to what extent we can speak of a new role for knowledge in the economy and, more importantly, how we can conceive its relationship to transformations in the *capital–labour* relation.

The thesis of cognitive capitalism has been developed in response to a double imperative: the need for a critique of the theorizations of the *knowledge-based economy*, and, above all, the elaboration of an approach that considers the meaning of the contemporary transformation, taking as a starting point the centrality of the capital–labour antagonism as it relates, to borrow an expression from Marx, to the mastery of the "intellectual powers of production."

The first part of the chapter outlines a method of analysis in terms of cognitive capitalism by insisting on the critique of conventional theories of both the *economics of knowledge* and the *knowledge-based economy*. This is done in order to explain the role of knowledge in the long-term development of capitalism, while providing a Marxian theoretical map of historical time in the process.

The second part of chapter will be devoted to explaining the methodological choice in favour of an approach that combines theory, history, and transformations of social relations and shares a central concern with the initial research program of French Regulation School.

We will make clear our theoretical position vis-à-vis the Regulation School approach. Particularly, we will highlight the heuristic value of new intermediate categories of the analysis of capitalist dynamics and of its "major crises" and phases of historical transformation. These categories will allow us to propose a periodisation based upon the identification and succession of three "historical systems of accumulation": mercantile capitalism, industrial capitalism, and then cognitive capitalism.

The third part of the chapter dedicated to providing an historical perspective for the crisis of industrial capitalism and the transition towards cognitive capitalism. Our thesis is that the "nature" of the Fordist crisis is not simply one of a "major crisis" of *transformation* internal to industrial capitalism. The crisis of Fordism, usually characterised as a crisis of the mode of development, corresponds in fact to a higher level of crisis affecting some of the most essential aspects of industrial capitalism itself. Finally, by cognitive capitalism we mean the emergence of an "historical system of accumulation" in which the cognitive and intellectual dimensions of labour become dominant and the central stake over the valorisation of capital become directly related to the transformation of knowledge into a *fictitious commodity*, in the sense of Polanyi.

From knowledge-based economy to cognitive capitalism

To understand the specificity of the cognitive-capitalism thesis, we must first of all dissipate the theoretical misunderstanding that assimilates it to a variation on the theories of the knowledge-based economy. To do so, in this section we will begin by characterising certain limitations of the contemporary theorisations of knowledge, limitations we consider fundamental. We will then show that the thesis of cognitive capitalism rests on a method of analysis that is able to perceive the meaning and stakes of the current mutation of the place of knowledge in the economy, on the basis of the primary role played by historical transformations in the capital–labour relation.

Limitations of the contemporary theories of knowledge

Contemporary theory perceives knowledge either as the object of a new subdiscipline (the economics of knowledge) or as the index of a shift to a new stage of economic development (the knowledge-based economy). Two series of closely associated critiques can be addressed to these theorisations.

The first critique concerns the tendency to approach the question of knowledge by starting from general theoretical models that would be valid at all times and in all places and are founded on a separation between the economic domain and that of social relations. This tendency to reject the historicity of economies is particularly clear in Howitt's work. In his view (Howitt 1996, 2004) nothing really new characterises the place of knowledge in economic growth. The only real novelty resides in the current capacity of theory to better discern its functions and primary role, neglected by former theories of growth. In short, the historical novelty is not to be found in a new phase of capitalism or even in the shift to a knowledge-based economy. It is to be found exclusively in the formation of an economics of knowledge, that is, of a subdiscipline of the science of economics specialized in the study of the mechanisms governing the production, distribution, and appropriation of knowledge. This is the way Howitt interprets the birth and development, through gradual improvements, of the theories of endogenous growth, without any reference to the historical transformations in the accumulation of capital and the wage relation. In this kind of conception, the theoretician seems to ignore or deny the importance of the underlying structural changes that provide the foundation for the emergence of a new field of research.

The second critique concerns the reductive vision of the place of knowledge and its new role, a vision on which most interpretations of the emergence of a knowledge-based economy are founded. These approaches have the unquestionable merit of foregrounding the idea of a historical break, and for that reason they will receive the most attention in the rest of this subsection. However, their conception of historical time skips over the transformation of social relations and relations of knowledge and power that structure the development of the productive forces, both material and immaterial.

The origin of a knowledge-based economy is essentially explained as a change in the magnitude of the phenomenon, a kind of Hegelian shift from quantity to quality. It is seen as the result of the encounter or indeed, the clash, between two factors: (1) a long-term trend towards a rise in so-called intangible capital (education, training, R&D, health) which from the mid-1970s onward (in 1973 in the USA, for example) has overcame the percentage of "material" capital in the stock of capital and now asserted itself as the key variable in growth; and (2) the sweeping change in the conditions of the reproduction and transmission of knowledge and information resulting from the "spectacular spread" of the information and communication technologies (ICT) (Foray 2006).

Finally, for the hard core of this vision, today broadly shared by the theorists of the knowledge-based economy and by numerous international institutions (OECD, EU), the rise of a knowledge-based economy is still essentially considered as an effect of crossing a threshold. The social determinants that are at the origin of the social crisis of the Fordist model and on the historical bifurcation towards an economy founded on distribution and the primary role of knowledge remain largely hidden. More precisely, in our opinion two obstacles keep the theories of a knowledge-based economy from accounting for the new and contradictory place of knowledge in the "new capitalism."

First, the reductive nature of a characterisation of the knowledge-based economy centred on activities devoted to the deliberate production of knowledge. Thus, for example, the research of the OECD (1996) remains essentially anchored in the "Fordist" conception that emerged from of Arrow's model (1962), where the production of knowledge is the privilege of elite R&D workers, scientific research, and the knowledge industries.

This interpretation obscures the most important phenomenon to have taken place since the crisis of Fordism, namely the return in force of the cognitive dimensions of labour, which are apparent at almost every level of production, material and immaterial alike.

The technological determinism that lends ICT a primary role in the shift to the "*mass production*" of knowledge and immaterial goods, adopting a mechanistic theory similar to approaches which, according to Thompson (1963), made the steam engine into the vector of the first industrial revolution, leading to the formation of the working class and the mass production of material goods.

Let us note that this tendency towards technological determinism and the underestimation of social causalities is also found in analyses that nonetheless develop a wider vision of the knowledge-based economy, integrating the problem of non-deliberate forms of knowledge production (Foray and Lundvall 1997). Despite the sophistication of such work, the principal explanation of the growing importance taken on by these non-deliberate forms still appears to rest in fact on the primary role of ICT. The latter is in effect understood as the major vector for the effectuation of mechanisms of horizontal coordination and networked organisation at the origin of historically unprecedented modes of "collective invention."

Despite changes in detail, the shift towards a knowledge-based economy is always conceived via an interpretative grid that casts it as the product of a happy encounter between the information revolution and a long-term trend towards the increase of intangible capital.

In this way, even the most highly articulated theories of the rise of the knowledge-based economy are led to omit certain elements necessary for understanding what we see as the origin, the meaning, and the stakes of the current transformation of capitalism. A few preliminary observations will allow us to measure the breadth and importance of these omissions.

No real reference is made to the social conflicts at the origin of the crisis of Fordism and the transformations of the relations of knowledge and power that structure the division of labour and the regulation of the wage relation. The interpretation of the stylised fact relative to the primacy of the new so-called intangible capital, embodied for the most part in human beings, systematically ignores a key element: this dynamic is linked above all to the development of collective services furnished historically by the welfare state. To forget the largely non-commodified nature of these collective services and their role as a motive force in the new capitalism of knowledge is all the more astonishing when the institutions of the welfare state are now being powerfully destabilized by austerity policies and falling prey to creeping privatisation.

In our view, it is not so much in ICT as in the development of a diffuse intellectuality that one should seek the primordial factor of the transition towards a capitalism founded on knowledge and towards new forms of the division of labour. We will advance this hypothesis: the departure point of the formation of cognitive capitalism is to be found in a process of the diffusion of knowledge, engendered particularly by the development of mass education and a formidable rise in the average level of training. What is more, this phenomenon, which has played a key role in raising the percentage of so-called intangible capital, does not only correspond to the slow deployment of a long-term trend. Instead it is a historically accelerated process driven to a large extent by the social demand for the democratisation of the access to knowledge conceived at once as a means of self-realisation and of social mobility for the popular generations of the baby boom.

The constitution of the figure of a diffuse intellectuality, which finds its first form of social expression in the events of 1968, not only precedes the "information revolution" from the logical and historical point of view but is also partially at its origin. It is enough to consider the fact that some of the major innovations of the aforementioned "revolution" come out of the ideals and practices of the protest culture of the years 1960–1970.

Moreover, where ICT is concerned, one must also make two other remarks. On the one hand, ICT can only function correctly on the basis of a living knowledge capable of mobilising it, because it is *knowledge* that governs the treatment of information: otherwise it remains a sterile resource, like capital without labour. On the other hand, its role can be profoundly ambivalent depending on its use and on the technical support structures into which ICT is integrated, favoring either the operation of neo-Taylorist forms or a requalification and de-hierarchisation of labour relations.

Finally, the technological determinism of the theorists of the knowledge-based economy refers back to a positivist conception of science, knowledge, and technological progress. This perspective leads to the abstraction of the social relations and conflicts surrounding the question of the control of the "intellectual powers of production" that have marked the entire history of capitalism. Indeed, the proof of this is the recourse to the colourless notion of the knowledge-based economy, to which one could apply the same remark made by Gailbraith (2004) when, in his last work, he stigmatised the "lie" that consists in speaking of a *market economy* instead of capitalism, with the aim of erasing the power relations which the latter word conveys.

Ultimately, these approaches overlook the fact that the novelty of the contemporary historical conjuncture does not involve the simple creation of a knowledge-based economy. The meaning and stakes of the current transformation of capitalism are not to be found, in fact, in the simple constitution of an economy founded on knowledge but in the formation of a knowledge-based economy framed and subsumed by the laws of capital accumulation.

The approach of cognitive capitalism vis-à-vis mainstream theorizations of the *knowledge-based economy* constitutes a double reversal at both the conceptual and methodological levels.

On the one hand, the neutral concept of the knowledge-based economy is justly replaced by that of cognitive capitalism. This concept throws into relief the historical dimension and conflictual dialectic between the two terms of which it is composed. The term "capitalism" indicates the permanence, beyond all variation, of the *invariants* of the capitalist system; in particular the determining role of profit and the wage relation or, more precisely, the different forms of labour on which the extraction of surplus value rests. The term "cognitive" brings to light the novel nature of the labour, the sources of value and the forms of property that support the accumulation of capital and the contradictions that this engenders. These contradictions are made manifest both in the relationship between labour and capital (in the sphere of production and circulation) and in the increasingly acute antagonism between the social nature of production and the private nature of appropriation.

At the methodological level, the approach of cognitive capitalism places knowledge at the heart of the concrete historical development of conflictual relations of knowledge and power that have forged the development of the capitalist division of labour and the transformation of the wage relation.

Knowledge and the dynamics of the capital–labour relation: a Marxian approach

To better understand this problematic, it is important to recall that for Marx, labour as a cognitive activity—understood as the inseparable unity between thought and action—is the very essence of man (*Capital*, Book I, chapter 7). It seems to us that the crucial point is the following: if the cognitive dimension of labour is the very essence of human activity, awareness of this might be understood as an impediment to the capitalist control of production and, therefore, accumulation. From this, it is clear why the relationship between knowledge and power constitutes an essential element in the class struggle resulting from the organization of production. This struggle is articulated around two central points. First, those who master and dictate the forms of labour are also masters of the intensity and the quality of labour. To the extent that the buying and selling of labour-power affects the availability of a quantity of time and not the effective labour of salaried workers, this results in structural uncertainty. Here we have an area that Taylor, for example, explicitly attacked when he analyzed the causes of failure on the job. He deduced that through scientific studies of time and movement it is necessary to bring to light and expropriate the tacit knowledge of the worker, in order to convert it into the codified knowledge possessed by management and then return it to workers in the form of timed schedules for the labour process. The second reason, which is even more fundamental, regards the fact that those who possess this knowledge might aspire to manage production, that is to say to define the organization of labour as well as the social ends of production. In fact, a large body of work has shown that the diffusion of Fordist and Taylorist methods of organising labour and production are not only restricted to the logic of mass production. This results in the necessity of undermining, of *destructuring* (in the sense of the Italian operaista term *destrutturare*), the composition of the professional working class who, most notably with the workers council movement between the wars, have struggled for the direct re-appropriation of the means of production in the face of a labour process that was not yet entirely subjected to and molded by capital into the form of an objective armature independent from the workers.

Finally, the relations connected with control over the intellectual power of production explains why the development of the capitalist division of labour, in the wake of the industrial revolution, consisted of trying, as much as possible, to empty labour of its cognitive dimension and to transform it into its opposite, a mechanical and repetitive activity. Here we have the origin of the tendency that Marx characterised as the passage from the formal to the real subsumption of labour by capital. However, this tendency, which finds its historical fulfilment in the model of Fordist growth, will remain imperfect and unachieved. It is always new types of knowledge that tend to reconstitute themselves at the highest levels of the technical and social division of labour, much as Marx had already envisioned in his hypotheses about the *general intellect* and the crisis of the logic of real subsumption (Vercellone 2007).

We are referring to those passages in the *Grundrisse* in which Marx develops, after the stage of real subsumption, the hypothesis of the *General Intellect*, which anticipates the coming of an economy founded on the diffusion and centrality of knowledge, in addition to the increasing dominance of the productive value of scientific and intellectual labour (Negri 1997). Framed in this way, the law of value founded on abstract labour time where value is expressed as a definite quantity of simple and homogeneous unskilled labour enters into crisis. This does not mean that the law of value disappears entirely, because capital continues to maintain control through force. Nor does this situation mean that labour, notably in its cognitive dimension, loses its centrality as the source of the creation of value and surplus value.

Regulation theory and cognitive capitalism thesis

The methodological choice in favour of an approach that combines the theory, history and transformation of social relations shares a central concern with the initial program of Regulation School political economy, whose goal was to elaborate a series of intermediate tools and categories in order to make sense of the temporal and spatial variability of social and economic laws and dynamics (Lipietz 1993).

Breaking with conventional Marxism and its stress on the forms of competition, the Regulation School placed at the center of its historical analysis of growth and crises the key role of the transformations of the wage relation, in order to characterise, "the mutual relations between different kinds of organization of labor, ways of living and modes of waged labor's reproduction" (Boyer 1986: 49).On this basis, regulation theory has brought a fundamental contribution to the elaboration of an alternative macro economy, combining theory and history to understand historical change using three central concepts: *regimes of accumulation* and *modes of regulation*, whose intersection defines the *mode of development* or growth regime (Boyer 2004). Modes of development are particular forms in which capital organises and expands for a period of time, exhibiting some degree of stability.

Another fundamental contribution has consisted precisely in showing how each mode of development has corresponded to a specific form of "major crisis." Thus, regulation has extended to industrial capitalism one of the major lessons of the *Annales* school of history, by developing the hypothesis that each economy has the structural crisis of its social and institutional configuration.

Through this analytic perspective, the Regulation School has furnished an original periodisation of the major structural and institutional changes, which, in the most developed countries, have led from the industrial revolution to Fordism, placing a particular accent on the specificity of the factors at the origin of the rise, then of the crisis of each mode of development.

However, the theoretical tools and intermediary categories forged by the Regulation School to characterise the dynamics of industrial capitalism now appear insufficient, in our eyes, to account for the breadth of contemporary transformations of capitalism. Indeed, we are confronted with mutations concerning the dynamic of the division of labour and of the role of knowledge which throw into doubt certain structural invariants within the very logic of industrial capitalism.

In a more general way, let us also note that the use in economics of such fuzzy categories as "post-Fordism" or "post-industrial society" seems to bear witness to this difficulty. Indeed, these terms present the great limitation of characterising the current transformation by stressing what it no longer is, instead of defining the new nature of capitalism. The research program around cognitive capitalism emerges from the observation of a crisis that has extended over the past thirty years and that has disavowed all the scenarios of a neo- or post-Fordist recomposition of the regulation of capitalism. It also emerges from a reaction, as we have seen, to the looseness of concepts like "post-industrial society" and "knowledge-based economy," when they are used to characterise the meaning and the stakes of the current transformation of capitalism.

In the face of this challenge, the approach of cognitive capitalism has developed a theoretical reading which can offer two major contributions to the enrichment of the analytical categories of the French regulation theory. The first contribution concerns the periodisation of capitalism through the development of intermediary categories that are able to test the hypothesis of an exit from industrial capitalism. In this respect, as we have mentioned, the Regulation School focused its analyses within a particular configuration of capitalism, industrial capitalism, whose transformations it characterises by identifying the historical succession of different modes of development based on the particular association of a regime of accumulation and a mode of regulation.

In particular, two theoretical difficulties result from an approach that focuses exclusively on the internal transformations of industrial capitalism. First, it pays insufficient attention to what Marx called the processes of primitive accumulation and the way in which these processes are structurally produced in time and space in novel forms that today find their essential dimension in the privatization of knowledge and life itself. Second, it fails to produce any intermediary concept between the "mode of production," which designates the most fundamental invariants of capitalism, and the "mode of development," which designates a specific stage in the development of industrial capitalism itself.

In noting these problems, we are drawing upon one of the major lessons of the work of Fernand Braudel (1979), according to which the history of capitalism both precedes and goes beyond the industrial revolution, and can also be linked to different forms of surplus-value extraction and capital accumulation. Therefore, we believe that the periodisation of capitalism (and of the major crises that characterize its transformations) must take into account the historical succession of different dominant configurations of capital accumulation.

We have chosen to describe this intermediary level between the "mode of production" and the "mode of development" using the concept of the "historical system of accumulation" (Lebert and Vercellone 2004; Paulré 2004). In the history of the capitalist mode of production, this concept designates a dominant logic of accumulation that orients, over the long term, the tendencies inherent in the valorisation of capital, the division of labour, and the reproduction of the most fundamental aspects of social relations. According to this perspective, mercantile capitalism was succeeded by industrial capitalism, which has itself now entered a new transitional phase towards the historical system of accumulation called cognitive capitalism.

We note that the concept of the "historical system of accumulation" also introduces the possibility of a crisis at a higher level to that recognized by the regulationist concept of the *major crisis of the mode of development*. According to the thesis of cognitive capitalism, the significance of the crisis in the Fordist mode of development is not simply one of a *crisis of transformation* internal to industrial capitalism. Rather, the crisis of Fordism has affected some of the most essential aspects of industrial capitalism itself. To summarise, the thesis of cognitive capitalism would signal the exhaustion not only of a mode of development specific to industrial capitalism, but the tendential crisis of some of the more structural invariants in the dynamics of the long period opened by the first industrial revolution.

We want to be clear that this hypothesis does not suggest that history is a linear process. Rather, it proceeds by means of overlapping and hybridisation; moreover, in the same manner that a mode of production is never present in an absolutely "pure" state but is articulated with and subsumes other modes of production, likewise a new historical system of accumulation, such as cognitive capitalism, does not completely supplant its predecessor, but reassembles and rearticulates it within the framework of a new logic.

The second contribution concerns the attempt to forge a few analytical categories aiming specifically to circumscribe the historical transformations of the place of knowledge in relation to that of the wage relation and of other institutional forms of capitalism. To do this, we began with an observation.

Knowledge has always played a primary role in the development of capitalism. The roles and forms of knowledge, however, have varied across both time and space. It is important, therefore, to specify the nature of the transformation that is today affecting the relationship between knowledge and capitalism, and that allows us to speak of the crisis of industrial capitalism and the transition towards a new historical system of accumulation. With the goal of gaining a greater insight into the historicity of the phenomenon of "knowledge," it seems useful from a heuristic point of view to emphasize three complementary dimensions from which the place of knowledge in the development of capitalism can be understood.

The first dimension concerns the capital–labour relation and is related to the often conflictual relationship between two inseparable aspects of the knowledge economy: (1) knowledge incorporated and mobilized by labour, the description of which is reliant on the forms of the technical and social division of labour and the socio-institutional mechanisms that regulate access to knowledge and determine the general level of education of the working class; and (2) knowledge incorporated into capital in the form of fixed physical capital or immaterial assets. The relation between these two aspects is at the heart of the historical characterisation of the different configurations of the capital–labour relation. This relation plays a central role in the production of knowledge and innovation, as well as in the determination of value and the competitivity of firms and territories. This fact is primary since it orients and overlaps with the two other dimensions of the problem.

The second dimension relates to the question of the regulation of the forms of access, diffusion, and appropriation of knowledge. To simplify somewhat, this is the way in which knowledge is guaranteed as a common good, exempt from the logic of the market or, at the other end of the spectrum, constituted as a scarce resource allowing for its private appropriation and its transformation into what Polanyi would call a fictitious commodity. The study of this dimension raises crucial questions that are today at the centre of unresolved debates and conflicts, in particular those regarding intellectual property and the institutional regulation of relations between the *open* and *closed* models of scientific research.

The third dimension concerns knowledge as a central factor in the determination of competitivity at the micro-, meso- and macroeconomic levels. As a result, knowledge plays an essential role in the historical analysis of forms of competition and modalities of entry into the international division of labour.The interrelation of these dimensions gives us a relatively coherent logic to describe the regulation and production of knowledge that is dominant in a particular historical system of accumulation.

From industrial capitalism to the transition towards cognitive capitalism: elements for an historical perspective

We are now going to develop the thesis of cognitive capitalism by placing it in the context of the long-term history of capitalism. According to this periodisation, we will give an important place to the forms of the division of labour and the regulation of the relations between knowledge and power, at the expense of other dimensions that might equally deserve to be considered. Furthermore, given the limited space of this introductory chapter, we will focus exclusively on the transition between industrial and cognitive capitalism.

The knowledge economy in industrial capitalism: some stylised facts

The emergence of industrial capitalism corresponds to the opening of a particular path in the regulation of the knowledge economy. This regime is based on three main tendencies: the social polarisation of knowledge, the separation of intellectual labour from manual labour, and the incorporation of knowledge as fixed capital. These processes are supported by a logic of accumulation based first on the centrality of the large Mancunian firm, and second on the Fordist model for the mass production of standardized durable goods. This model makes the development of fixed capital the fundamental object of property and the principal form of technical progress. In industrial capitalism, the centrality of material labour goes hand in hand with the establishment of norms for value creation inherent to economies based on homogenous time and bulk productivity.

The wage relation and the knowledge economy in industrial capitalism

In the dynamics of technical progress driven by the first industrial revolution, the search for increased productivity is inseparable from and subordinated to the lessening dependence of capital on the know-how of workers, compared to its importance in the pre-industrial organisation of production (Dockès and Rosier 1983; Marglin 1974). The development of industrial capitalism rests on a process of progressive expropriation of the knowledge of workers and their incorporation into an increasingly complex system of tools and machines. This tendency towards the real subsumption of labour to capital is made concrete in the separation and opposition of knowledge and collective labour.

According to this logic, the principal criterion for economic effectiveness in industrial capitalism is the search for homogenous temporal economies. This criterion, which is also one of the fundamental aspects of the relation between value and labour time, is made manifest in the organisation of the labour process in terms of prescribed tasks and operating times. This logic is likewise at the origin of a rupture in the social representation of time. This rupture opposes directly paid labour time, which is considered as the only productive time, to other "non-productive" social times dedicated to the formation and reproduction of labour power.

In many ways, the polarising logic of knowledge in industrial capitalism reaches its pinnacle in the Fordist model. In terms of knowledge economies, this model is based on the hierarchy between two starkly divided levels in the division of labour. At the level of the workshop, the scientific organization of labour seeks to remove all intellectual elements from the act of production; labour, in the sense used by Marx, becomes more and more "abstract," not only in its form but also in its content, as management centralises the knowledge that was previously in the possession of labourers. This separation of labour from the subjectivity of the worker results in the objectification of labour itself within the ensemble of describable, measurable, and timed tasks. Innovation is chased out of the workshop and the work of conceptualisation becomes the exclusive domain of small groups of workers restricted to the offices of industrial engineers and R&D centres. Let us also note that all the elements in this logic of the specifically capitalist development of the division of labour rest on the fact that the greatest part of value creation is found in the sphere of direct material production where the activity of the worker's labour consists principally in acting on inanimate material by means of tools and machines, according to a paradigm of energy expenditure. This centrality of material labor encourages the respect of two central conditions of the canonical definition of the wage relation, which are: (1) the renunciation, in exchange for the wage, of the worker's share of any claim on the ownership of the product of their labour, to the extent that this product is physically separated from the worker's labour and appropriated by the employer; and (2) the fact that in industrial capitalism, the wage is effectively exchanged for the purchase by capital of a determinate fraction of human time, placed at the disposal of the corporation. The productive time of labour in the paradigm of energy expenditure corresponded to the time executed and remunerated inside the factory according to the dispositions established by the work contract. On the contrary, the respect of these conditions, as we will see, is often destabilised today by the rise of the immaterial and cognitive dimension of labor.

Knowledge, innovation, and the determinants of competitivity

In industrial capitalism, the competitive capacity of an economic system is determined by the degree of development of a sector of material equipment goods. The specialisation of countries in this sector is the primary means for mastering the evolution of the norms of production that are incorporated in fixed capital and that dictate the hierarchy of the international division of labour (Mistral 1986). In particular, during the golden age of Fordism, it was thought that the large corporation could plan space with the same efficiency as the time and motion engineers applied the "scientific organization of labour" on the shop floors. The regional and international division of labor thus appeared as a variable that the large firms could, to a large, submit to their strategy of valorization. This vision of the international division of labour, responding to a dynamic logic of comparative advantages, was expressed very well by the theory of the product cycle (Vernon 1979) and in a more sophisticated way by the theory of the Fordist branch circuit (Lipietz 1983). The latter stressed the hierarchical organization of spaces according to the more or less strategic nature of the productive activities that they hosted, with a fracturing of production ranging from engineering and design to the most routinized activities of fabrication.

The driving force of tangible capital and the cycle of innovation native to industrial capitalism (which is marked by short periods of radical innovation followed by longer periods of incremental innovation) help to explain the mode of regulation for research and industrial property during this period of development.

Intellectual property and the regulation of research in industrial capitalism

Since the beginning of the twentieth century, the mechanisms for the deliberate production of knowledge have rested on two specific systems of regulation:

1 A public system of research and higher education whose essential function is to produce and transmit free basic knowledge according to the model of so-called "open science." In this system, research is financed by subsidies on the condition that the results are shared freely and without cost, and that the primary motivation of the research is not profit, but recognition by one's peers.
2 A system of R&D centers managed by large firms, in which scientific knowledge, specifically related to technology, is internally produced. It is characterised by goals that are clearly specified by the firm and controlled in a vertical manner.

The rules of intellectual property are in accordance with a logic of capital accumulation and private appropriation of knowledge that are ultimately reliant on active materials. The patenting of inventions must be justified by their incorporation into a technical industrial apparatus, that is to say they are connected to creative human labour and not nature. These norms trace a clear border between true innovation and discovery.

Furthermore, in industrial capitalism the patent system is inscribed in regimes of accumulation that are essentially national in nature. Therefore, the patent is limited not only in time but also in the territorial domain of its application, namely the nation-state. The pillars of this system today are called into question with the displacement and internationalization of the borders of traditional intellectual property rights according to the model used in the USA.

The crisis of industrial capitalism and the transition towards cognitive capitalism: its origin and meaning

The origin of the transformation of contemporary capitalism can be found most clearly by calling into question the long-term trend towards the polarisation of knowledge characteristic of industrial capitalism. This reversal corresponds to a crisis in the logic of real subsumption, at least from the viewpoint of production. It translates into the recognition of a great number of new kinds of living knowledge, which are incorporated and mobilised by labour, as compared to formalised knowledge, which is incorporated into fixed capital and the organization of firms. It is in the recognition of this new hegemony of the knowledge of living labour in relation to the dead knowledge of capital that we can find the central framework for the hypothesis of cognitive capitalism. In sum, knowledge and intellectual labour are no longer, as Smith (1970: 14) suggested, "like every other employment, the principal or sole trade and occupation of a particular class of citizens." Knowledge begins to be dispersed across society, a diffusion that will become progressively more apparent at the very heart of organisations and the relations between firms.

This evolution has its roots in three processes at the heart of the social crisis of the Fordist wage relation:

1 *The refusal of atomised labour and the rise of demands for autonomy among waged workers.* This has caused a crisis in the scientific organization of labour, even if this evolution did not signify the end of neo-Taylorist research programs for the rationalisation of labour (including intellectual labour). This process of social transformation has moved beyond the limits of the factory and destabilised, in a more general manner, the ensemble of institutions of the disciplinary society, in Michel Foucault's sense, upon which industrial capitalism was founded.
2 *The constitution of a diffuse intellectuality developing from the "democratisation of education" and a rise in the general level of training.* It is this new quality of labour power that has led to the rise of immaterial and intellectual labour and the calling into question of the kinds of division of labour and technical progress that characterised industrial capitalism.
3 *The expansion of the collective services and insurances of welfare.* This process has long been interpreted as a single factor in the crisis of Fordism that reverses "the long-term tendency for the reduction of the social cost of the social reproduction of labour power" (Aglietta 1976: 326). In contrast to this position, we believe that the expansion of welfare also offered two essential conditions for the emergence of an economy based on knowledge and characterised by a logic that in many respects could constitute an alternative to the contemporary regulation of cognitive capitalism.

Two main considerations support this third claim. First, the social conditions and the real driving force of an economy founded on knowledge are not found in the private laboratories of R&D centres, but in the institutions and collective productions of the welfare state (health, education, public research institutions, etc.) that result in the *human production for and by humans* (Boyer 2002; Monnier and Vercellone 2007). These are activities in which the cognitive and relational dimension of labour is dominant and could be the vector of an alternative model of development founded on the primacy of collective services provided outside the logic of the market.

Second, during the 1970s, the expansion of social wages (pensions, unemployment insurance) allowed for an attenuation of the constraints on the wage relation and promoted independent mobility between different kinds of labour and activities (in contrast to current forms of *précarisation*). This corresponded to a freeing-up of time (subtracted from capital) that, from the point of view of the development of the knowledge economy, presented itself as an immediately productive force (to borrow Marx's description of the General Intellect). In this respect, it is necessary to highlight an essential argument concerning the genesis of the new capitalism. The installation of the conditions for an economy based on knowledge and the centrality of immaterial and intellectual labour precedes, both historically and logically, the genesis of cognitive capitalism. The transition towards cognitive capitalism is the result of a process of restructuring through which capital attempts to frame and control the collective conditions of knowledge production and stifle the emancipatory potential inscribed in the emergence of a diffuse intellectuality.

It is this context that explains much of how cognitive capitalism (under the aegis of finance capital and neo-liberal policies) has pushed towards a new process of desocialisation of the economy, one that aims for two objectives (which also work against the development of institutions and social conditions that might have allowed for the efficient management of the knowledge economy): (1) the goal of enlarging the space of the market by progressively colonizing the institutions of the welfare state and the common goods represented by knowledge and life; and (2) the accentuation of precarity and individualization in the wage relation through a return to competition. This is because the reinforcement of economic constraints on salaried workers is an essential condition for controlling and putting back to work labour power that is increasingly autonomous within the production process.

In sum, we recognize that the contemporary regulation of cognitive capitalism depends on a logic that is capable of drawing from the collective sources of knowledge production. In order to better grasp the meaning and contradictions of the passage to cognitive capitalism we will now examine its relationship to the three levels of knowledge suggested above.

Changes in the division of labour and the wage relation

The principal source of value now lies with the knowledge mobilised by living labour and not in the resources of material labour. In fact, in the new capitalism, the labour of a growing part of the population increasingly consists in working with information, producing knowledge, and engaging in service relations based on the exchange of knowledge, communication, and *human production by humans*. The importance of routine productive activity and manual labour, consisting in the transformation of material with the help of tools and machines, has given way to a new paradigm in which labour is at once more immaterial, intellectual, and communicational. From this position, we can affirm that information and codified knowledge now constitute the principal material being transformed in production, and that tacit knowledge, which resides in the brain, stands as the principal tool allowing for the processing of this material, that is to say its transformation into new products and new knowledge.

The rise of the cognitive and immaterial dimensions of labour are at the origin of two major mutations in the organization of production and the wage relation, both of which break with the tendencies of industrial capitalism.

The first concern is the movement from a Taylorian to a cognitive division of labour. In other words, the structuring principle of the division of labour in the workplace moves from a technical logic based on the decomposition of tasks to a logic of apprenticeship and specialization across a field of competencies (Mouhoud 2003). The efficiency in this form of labour division no longer rests on the labour time linked to different tasks but on the cumulative nature of knowledge that assures the maximisation of the capacity for learning and innovation. This evolution tends to break down the once strict borders between conception and execution, and allows the power of innovation to return to the workshop from which industrial capitalism had hoped to banish it. In sum, as Philippe Lorino (1993) suggests, "productive science is no longer 'encapsulated' in the form fixed by machines." It increasingly resides in the responsive nature of labour power, capable of sharing generic and decontextualized knowledge and open to multiple uses in different fields (Veltz 2000). This change in the wage relation brings new tensions to the surface. In particular, the new importance of knowledge incorporated in labour poses the unforeseen problem of measurement, since the productive cooperation of waged workers can develop autonomously in relation to the management of the enterprise. In this movement, the Taylorist control of labour tends to be replaced by the "control of subjectivity" (Clot 2002: 78). This demands that workers apply themselves to their labour by putting their creativity at the service of the enterprise as though it were a species of free and independent activity. This attempt to respond to the crisis of the real subsumption of labour, at the level of the labour process, with the subsumption of the subjectivity of labourers itself runs into two major contradictions. In reality, the control of subjectivity corresponds to a "double bind" that consists of demanding something and its opposite at the same time. It results in a "crack in the self" that threatens to affect the capacity for workers to learn and, as a result, the ability of enterprises to change. Moreover, the control of subjectivity is most often carried out by means of individual incentives that work against the collective cohesion of labour upon which the accumulation of knowledge depends.

The second change concerns the crisis of the Fordist-industrial model regarding bulk -productivity and the organisation of time based on the clear division between labour and non-labour, the productive sphere and the sphere of reproduction (Vercellone 2007). The industrial criteria for evaluation of efficiency are also called into question: references to homogenous time are no longer able to either describe or organise labour, nor are they reliable measures of the value or costs of production. In particular, in the knowledge-intensive sectors of the economy, labour time directly devoted to productive activity during the official working day constitutes merely a fraction, and frequently not the most important part, of the social time of production. Cognitive labour, due to its very nature, stands as a complex combination of the intellectual activities of reflection, communication, sharing, and elaboration of knowledge that are carried out as much outside as within the framework of immediately productive labour.

Let us note that the rise of the cognitive and immaterial dimension of labour is, potentially, at the origin of a double destabilization of the terms of the canonical wage relation on which the work contract rested in industrial capitalism:

First, in the activities in which the cognitive and immaterial dimension of labour is dominant, the renunciation by the workers, in compensation for the wage, to any claim on the property of the product of their labour is no longer guaranteed. In cognitive labour, which is productive of knowledge, the result of labour remains incorporated in the brain of the worker and thus inseparable from their person. Together with other factors, this helps to explain the pressure exercised by enterprises in order to attain a strengthening of the rights of intellectual property and to re-enclose the social mechanisms at the basis of the circulation of knowledge, in a new phase of the primitive accumulation of capital.

Second, in industrial capitalism's paradigm of energy expenditure, the wage was exchanged for the purchase by capital of a clearly determined and limited fraction of human time, inside the enterprise. Within this temporal framework the employer then had to find the most efficient ways to make use of this paid time in order, as Marx would say, to extract from the use value of labour power the largest possible quantity of surplus labour. Thanks to the expropriation of workers' knowledge and to the strict prescription of operational times and modes, Taylorism was in its day a response to this decisive question. In the Fordist factory, effective labour time, productivity and the value and volume of production appeared to be perfectly predetermined in a scientific way, even if in reality the assembly line could never have functioned without an important gap between prescribed and real labour.

But everything changes when work, as it becomes increasingly immaterial and cognitive, can no longer be reduced to a simple expenditure of energy carried out during a given time period. By its nature it implies both a qualitative dimension and an involvement of the workers, mobilising their subjectivity and all their knowledge. Thus the effective time during which labour power is placed at the disposal of the employer exceeds and overflows the strict and official framework of the labour time foreseen by the contract, to the point where it encompasses all of social time. The result is a rise of unmeasured labour, which is very hard to quantify according to the traditional criteria for its measurement.

Finally, in cognitive capitalism, the increasingly social and intellectual character of the labour determines, in our view, a displacement of the concept of productive labour as well as that of exploitation. Precisely due to the crumbling of the traditional frontiers between the sphere of reproduction and that of direct production, the exploitation of the use value of labour power is expanded to the totality of social time.

The move towards a regime of permanent innovation and an international division of labour based on cognitive principles

The acceleration of the rhythm of innovation is another distinguishing trait of the transition towards cognitive capitalism. We are witnessing the installation of a "regime of permanent innovation" (Paulré 2000: 37) in which the principal source of competition is no longer found in the incorporated knowledge technologies of fixed capital, but in the abilities of a labour force capable of mastering the dynamics of continuous change and the ceaseless renewal of knowledge that quickly becomes obsolete.

Within this framework, a break occurs with the linear model of programmed innovation and the rigid hierarchy of the Fordist division of labour theorised by the model of the branch circuit. Indeed, the shift to a regime of permanent innovation goes hand in hand with a socialisation and decompartementalisation of the production of knowledge. This development reinforces the hypothesis which holds that the essential trait of the shift from industrial to cognitive capitalism is linked to a radical change in the mode of knowledge production, the latter being more and more collectively distributed. This socialisation of knowledge production and innovation is manifest at several levels: within firms, through the decompartmentalisation of R&D and production activities; at the level of inter-firm relations, where the network becomes the dominant model of organisation and where knowledge production is characterised by an intensification of cooperative relations between enterprises, but also between enterprises and different research institutions; and finally, in the proliferation of "knowledge-intensive communities" outside the logic of the market, which constitute one of the most powerful expressions of a dynamic of distribution and production of knowledge that overflows the framework of the corporations, even to the point where it appears as an alternative form of organization with respect to both hierarchy and market as forms of coordination.

This evolution has a crucial impact of the location of firms and the genesis of international specialisation. Also, the hegemony of intellectual labour and the primacy of cognitive labour in the new international division of labour are attested by the mobility of capital. The places currently in the most difficulty are often neo-Taylorist, since they are the most vulnerable to the extreme volatility of capital. In contradiction to this, knowledge-intensive activities are more territorially rooted since, in this case, it is capital that depends on a pool of intellectual and immaterial labour that pre-exists the activity of corporations and is most notably concentrated in cities. In sum, in the new international division of labour, itself based on cognitive principles, the long-term competitivity of a territory depends increasingly on the "stock" of intellectual labour that can be mobilized in a cooperative manner. In this way, "the logic of the exploitation of comparative advantages is replaced by the retention in a territory of monopolistic elements or absolute advantages over specific areas of competence" (Mouhoud, 2003: 128). The emergence of cognitive capitalism goes along with a strong tendency towards the polarisation of the geography of development between regions and nations. It threatens to condemn a certain number of developing countries that are least able to provide qualified labour, to a veritable "forced disconnection."

This tendency is growing stronger as the ability to patent living material and the biotech revolution now allow corporations in the North to appropriate freely the genetic resources and traditional knowledge of the South, replacing with "new commodities" the number of products traditionally imported by developing countries. Certainly, we are not faced with an irrevocable process. In the same way that certain phases of production can be relocated to developing regions, certain functions of control and conception have been relocated to the countries of the global South or the former Socialist bloc, such as India and China, taking advantage of an important reservoir of intellectual manpower. In this way a logic of delocalisation based on the reduction of labour costs combines with the new logic of the cognitive division of labour (Lebert and Vercellone 2004).

The refoundation of intellectual property rights and the innovation and accumulation of knowledge: a contradictory logic?

The emergence of cognitive capitalism turns on its head the foundation of the intellectual property-rights system and the regulation of research inherited from industrial capitalism. This development is favoured by two major trends. The first relates to the erasure of the line between pure and applied research, which is most prevalent in the software and biotech industries. This development makes previously unthought-of forms of privatised knowledge and life a condition for the general expansion of criteria for what can be patented, most notably allowing for a blurring of the boundary between discovery and invention (Coriat 2002).

The second relates to the way that in an economy based on diffuse intellectuality the usage of communications technologies destabilizes the system of intellectual property rights in numerous domains. At the same time, it favours the emergence of horizontal forms of cooperation and knowledge exchange based on non-market logic, such as the example of free/open source software. The question of the reinforcement and extension of the system of intellectual property rights into the domains of pure research and even life itself are the decisive aspects of the contemporary regulation of cognitive capitalism.

The reformulation of intellectual property rights is justified by the argument that in knowledge-intensive sectors of the economy, costs are fixed and centered on investment in R&D. In reality, however, these policies often correspond to the creation of *positional rents* and a strategy focused on the exploitation of public-sector research by the private sector and the logic of the market. This is much more important than the claim that patents are the best way to stimulate the production of knowledge since this claim has never been verified. In fact, it is more often the case that the enforcement of intellectual property rights acts as a brake on innovation and the cumulative aspects of the knowledge-based economy. Three main arguments confirm our interpretation:

1 The majority of fixed costs for research are related to R&D centres. In fact, the conditions of research and innovation are increasingly collective and ultimately depend on the quality and the density of labour power produced by the public education system. Moreover, a large number of patents held by corporations are not the immediate result of their research efforts, but are developed from research done at public institutions or, in other cases, come from preying on the knowledge of traditional communities (Shiva 1997).
2 It is erroneous to act as though the inventions and patented "discoveries" would not have seen the light of day without the protection of patents (Mansfield 1986). Moreover, many patents have no other function than to impede rival research and innovation in certain areas of activity. This strategy, called "saturation" or "flooding," relies on the multiplication of patents, which sometimes cover basic forms of knowledge. It results in "situations of excessive privatization, in the sense that it affects even the most minor uses of knowledge, slowing the rhythms for creating new knowledge and the creation of dominant positions that have anti-competitive effects" (CGP 2002: 155).
3 There exists no proven correlation between the existence (and breadth) of intellectual property rights and the stimulation of innovation. In fact, the decisions to re-enforce intellectual property regulations in the USA during the 1980s reduced innovation (Clement 2003) and translated into a decline in R&D in the industries and corporations that were most active in patenting their work (Bessen and Maskin 2000). At the same time, in the pharmaceutical industry, the principal reason leading to demands for increased production was the need to increase profits in a context marked by a declining rhythm of innovation since the mid-1970s.

The reinforcement of the system of intellectual property, even as the race to patent is seen as a question of survival for some corporations, in many ways constitutes a blockage of circulatory movement for the production of knowledge.

Conclusion

The emergence of cognitive capitalism corresponds to a rupture in a number of tendencies that formerly characterised the regime of the production and regulation of the *knowledge economy* that issued from the first industrial revolution. This transformation could be characterised by an almost term-by-term opposition of the pillars of the "new capitalism" and those of industrial capitalism:

- Knowledge and the immaterial become the principal source of value, replacing the criteria of output productivity and of direct labour time proper to industrial capitalism.
- The varieties of knowledge incorporated in labour take a preponderant place with respect to those incorporated in fixed capital, pushing for a recomposition of the tasks of design and execution, the activities of manufacture and innovation.
- A regime of permanent innovation replaces the sequential regime of industrial capitalism, a development going hand in hand with the installation of a new international division of labour founded on cognitive principles.
- An increasingly close intertwining of basic and applied research, which occurs particularly in the software and biotech industries, gives rise to a new paradigm of innovation. Its social output depends closely on the system of intellectual property rights associated with it.

These major changes in the wage relation and in the regime of knowledge production are associated with new mechanisms of regulation which, in many domains, block the circulation of knowledge and the collective dimension of knowledge accumulation. In particular, precarious labour conditions and the individualisation of the wage relation, the destabilisation of the collective services of the welfare state and the excess privatisation of knowledge linked to the reinforcement of intellectual property rights tend to make the current regulation of cognitive capitalism into a potential obstacle to the development of a knowledge-based economy as we shall see in the chapter seven dedicated to these topics and their relationship to the common and commons.

References

Aglietta, M. (1976) *Régulation et crises du capitalisme*, Paris: Calmann Lévy.

Arrow, K. (1962) "Economic Welfare and the Allocation of Resources for Invention," in R. Nelson (ed.), *The Rate and Direction of Inventive Activity*, Princeton, NJ: Princeton University Press.

Becker, G. S. and K. M. Murphy (1992) "The Division of Labour, Coordination Costs, and Knowledge," *Quarterly Journal of Economics*, 107(*4*): 1137–1160.

Bessen, J. and E. Maskin (2000) *Sequential Innovation, Patents and Imitation*, Working Paper, MIT Department of Economics, 00-01.

Boyer, R. (1986) *La Théorie de la régulation: une analyse critique*, Paris: Agalma.

Boyer, R. (2002) *Croissance, début du siècle*, Paris: Albin Michel.

Boyer, R. (2004) *Théorie de la régulation: 1. Les fondamentaux*, Paris: La Découverte.

Braudel, F. (1979) *Civilisation matérielle, économie et capitalisme, XV–XVIIIeme siècle*, 3 vols., Paris: Armand Colin.

Commisariat Général au Plan (2002) *La France dans l'économie du savoir*, Paris: La Documentation Française.
Clement, D. (2003) "Du mythe de la nécessité des brevets pour susciter l'innovation," *L'Economie Politique*, 19:9–24.
Clot, Y. (2002) *La Fonction psychologique du travail*, Paris: Presses Universitaires de France.
Castells, M. (1996) *The Rise of the Network*, Oxford: Blackwell Publishers.
Castells, M. (1998) *La Société en réseaux*, Paris: Fayard.
Coriat, B. (2002) "Le Nouveau Régime américain de la propriété intellectuelle," *Revue d'Economie Industrielle*, 99(2): 17–32.
Coriat, B. and G. Dosi (1998) "Learning How to Govern and Learning How to Solve Problems: On the Co-Evolution, Conflicts and Organisational Routines," in D. Chandler, P. Hagström, and Ö. Sölvell (eds.), *The Dynamic Firm: The Role of Technology, Strategy, Organisation, and Regions*, Oxford: Oxford University Press, pp. 103–133.
Dockès, P. and B. Rosier (1983) *Rythmes économiques: crises et changement social une perspective historique*, Paris: La Découverte.
Foray, D. (2006) *The Economics of Knowledge*, Cambridge, Mass.: The MIT Press.
Howitt, P. (1996) *The Implications of Knowledge-Based Growth for Microeconomic Policies*, Calgary: University of Calgary Press.
Howitt, P. (1996) "On Some Problems in Measuring Knowledge-Based Growth," in P. Howitt (ed.), *The Implications of Knowledge-Based Growth for Micro-Economic Policies*, Calgary: University of Calgary Press, pp. 9–29.
Howitt, P. (2004) "Endogenous Growth, Productivity and Economic Policy: A Progress Report," *International Productivity Monitor*, 8:3–15.
Lebert, D. and C. Vercellone (2004) "L'Économie de la connaissance et de l'immatériel, entre théorie et histoire: du capitalisme industriel au capitalisme cognitif," *Cahiers Lillois d'Economie et de Sociologie*, 43–44:17–41.
Lipietz, A. (1983) *Le Capital et son espace*, Paris: Maspero.
Lipietz, A. (1993) "From Althusserianism to 'Regulation Theory'," in E. A. Kaplan and M. Sprinker (eds.), *The Althusserian Legacy*, London and New York: Verso.
Lorino, P. (1993) "Au risque de l'éclatement social," *Le Monde Diplomatique*. Available at https://www.monde-diplomatique.fr/mav/18/LORINO/55004 (accessed 24 March 2019).
Lucarelli, S. and A. Fumagalli (2008) "Basic Income and Productivity in Cognitive Capitalism," *Review of Social Economy*, 69: 14–37.
Lucas, R. (1988) "On the Mechanism of Economic Growth," *Journal of Monetary Economics*, 22(1): 3–42.
Mansfield, E. (1986) "Patents and Innovation: An Empirical Study," *Management Science*, 32(2): 173–181.
Marglin, S. (1974) "What Do Bosses Do? The Origins and Functions of Hierarchy in Capitalist Production," *Review of Radical Political Economics*, 6(2): 60–112.
Marx, K. (1993) *Grundrisse: Foundations of the Critique of Political Economy*, London: Penguin Books.
Mistral, J. (1986) "Régime international et trajectoires nationales," in R. Boyer (ed.), *Capitalismes fin de siècle*, Paris: Presses Universitaires de France, pp. 167–202.
Monnier, J.-M. and C. Vercellone (2006) "Crise et réforme du système de protection sociale à l'heure du capitalisme cognitif: la proposition du revenu social garanti," in

A. Dang, J.-L. Outin, and H. Zajdela (eds.), *Défis et mutations des relations emploi-protection sociale*, Paris: Editions du CNRS, pp. 199–217.

Monnier, J.-M. and C. Vercellone (2007) "Travail, genre et protection sociale dans la transition vers le capitalisme cognitif," *European Journal of Economic and Social Systems*, 20(1): 15–35.

Mouhoud, E. M. (2003) "Division internationale du travail et économie de la connaissance," in C. Vercellone (ed.), *Sommes-nous sortis du capitalisme industriel*, Paris: La Dispute, pp. 121–136.

Negri, A. (1997) "Vingt thèses sur Marx," in M. Vakaloulis and J.-M. Vincent (eds.), *Marx après les Marxismes*, Tome 2. Paris: L'Harmattan, pp. 333–372.

OECD (1996) *The Knowledge-Based Economy*, Paris: OECD.

OECD (2003) *Science, technologie et industrie: tableau de bord*, Paris: OECD.

Paulré, B. (2000) "De la New Economy au capitalisme cognitif," *Multitudes*, 2(2): 25–42.

Paulré, B. (2004) "Introduction au capitalisme cognitif," Working Paper, *Workshop Gres–Matisse–Isys*, Université Paris 1 Panthéon-Sorbonne, Paris.

Romer, P. M. (1990) "Endogenous Technological Change," *Journal of Political Economy*, 98(5): 71–102.

Shiva, V. (1997) *Biopiracy: The Plunder of Nature and Knowledge*, Boston, MA: South End Press.

Smith, A. (1970) *The Wealth of Nations*, London: J. M. Dent and Sons. First published 1776.

Thompson, E. P. (1963) *The Making of the English Working Class*, New York: Vintage.

Veltz, P. (2000) *Le Nouveau Monde industriel*, Paris: Gallimard.

Vercellone, C. (ed.) (2006) *Capitalismo cognitivo: conoscenza e finanza nell'epoca post-Fordista*, Rome: Manifestolibri.

Vercellone, C. (2007) "From Formal Subsumption to General Intellect: Elements for a Marxist Reading of the Thesis of Cognitive Capitalism," *Historical Materialism*, 15(1): 13–36.

Vernon, R. (1979) "The Product Cycle Hypothesis in a New International Environment," *Oxford Bulletin of Economics and Statistics*, 41(4): 255–267.

2 Metamorphosis of the theory of value and becoming-rent of profit

An attempt to clarify the terms of a debate

Carlo Vercellone and Stefano Dughera

Introduction

The purpose of this chapter is to define, within a neo-workerist theoretical framework, the logical and historical meaning of the Marxian law of value in the transition from industrial to cognitive capitalism. The reason for pursuing this purpose is mainly twofold: on the one hand, with respect to the development of the neo-workerist approach, it aims at showing the tight bond linking the thesis concerning the crisis of the theory of value and that of the *becoming-rent of profit*. On the other hand, it intends to reply to the multiple misunderstandings that the expression "crisis of the theory of value" arose in some hasty readings of the cognitive-capitalism approach, to the point where this was understood as abandoning the Marxian labour theory of value.

The analysis will be developed into three parts. In the first section, we shall recall how Marxism encompasses two different—and to some extent, even antithetic—conceptions of the labour theory of value. In order to do so, we will outline how the *law of value/labour time* and its articulation have to be related to the theory of surplus value, to which the former is a historically determined dependent variable. We will label such articulation as the *theory of value/surplus value*.

The second section discusses the historical consistency of the *theory of value/surplus value* within the realm of industrial capitalism, where the primacy of material capital over living labour supported a logic of real subsumption. In such situation, *profit prevailed over rent*, thus fulfilling the role that, whether right or wrong, Marx bestowed upon capital. Indeed, in his understanding, capital was conceived as a mean for fostering the development of the forces of production. In the third section we shall refer to some "stylised facts" in order to analyse the symptoms of utmost importance that unveil the crisis of the law of value in cognitive capitalism. Such a crisis, as we shall argue, mirrors a "non-correspondence" situation of increasing tension between the social relations of production and property as these are imposed within the framework of cognitive capitalism, and the productive forces of a knowledge-based economy which are "naturally" addressed towards those productions "*de l'homme par l'homme*" (as Boyer [2014] calls them),[1] tension whose conditions of existence are "too narrow to comprise the wealth created by them" (Marx 2007: 15). This very situation goes hand in hand with the tendency that we label as the *becoming-rent of profit*.

Two conceptions of the labour theory of value

Within the Marxist tradition cohabits, as recalled by Negri (1992), two conceptions of the theory of value. The first insists on the quantitative issue related to the determination of the magnitude of value. This conception conceives the labour-time as a criterion for measuring the value of commodities. This is related to what we call *law of value/labour time*. This first understanding is well defined by P. Sweezy, precisely when he states that in a capitalistic-mercantile society abstract labour is abstract only in the quite straightforward sense that all special characteristics which differentiate one kind of labour from another are ignored. Abstract labour, in short, is, as Karl Marx's usage quite clearly attests, equivalent to "labour in general"; it is what is common to all productive human activity (Sweezy 1942: 30).

From this viewpoint, the law of value is essentially conceptualised as a non-historical law of measure and equilibrium which governs the allocation of resources. The notion of abstract labour then becomes a quasi-natural category, nothing more than a mental abstraction deprived of all those features which instead qualifies it as a specific trait of capitalism itself, whose historical peculiarity is to be related to that "estrangement inherent in the nature of labour" (Marx 1988: 73) which concerns both the separation of the worker from the products of their work, and the dispossession of the knowledge which constitutes the condition of existence of their own labour. Here, we are confronted with an approach towards the labour theory of value which is more Ricardian than Marxian, according to which the historical genealogy of the law itself would refer to a hypothetical "simple-commodity mode of production" (*einfache Warenproduktion*) which only subsequently would have extended to capitalism.

This conception of the theory of value entails three major shortcomings—both theoretical and political—tightly entangled with one another. The first is precisely to consider the abstraction of labour as a theoretical product of the economic science, rather than conceiving it as a concrete fact implemented within the framework of a salary-based capitalistic society. This abstraction equally deals with the content of labour and with the meaning of the working activity, which, hetero-determined in its own ends, is reduced to a simple mean to make a living. This is the reason why one should carefully avoid to conceive exploitation at the only level of distribution, as it is not limited to the extraction of labour, but it also and mainly determines the alienation of labour itself with respect to its content and to the social purposes of production. Thus, this addresses the antagonistic crux concerning the absence of democracy within the capitalistic organization of production, relocating those questions so long evaded by political economy at the core of the debate: *How and what to produce? Whom for and to satisfy which needs? According to which norms wealth is distributed?*

The second issue is to cancel out from the representation of the operational rules which govern a capitalistic economy, that subject/object overturning which derives from the commodity fetishism capable of transfiguring relationships among people into relationships among things (Roubine 1972; Napoleoni 1972). In this respect, once that such an operation is carried out, market laws appear to be the expression of some natural and objective constraint exogenously imposed on human societies rather than being conceived as those historical and therefore modifiable devices produced by societies themselves.

The third issue is to consider the heuristic capacity of the theory of value as if its main intent would consist in the elaboration of a micro-economic explanation of relative prices rather than considering it as *macro and monetary theory of exploitation*. By doing so, one does slip away from the ground of the critique of political economy as to approach a new form of economics that would derive the scientific soundness of the Marxist theory of value from the formal coherence of the solution of the "transformation problem," landing onto a ground quite analogous and in direct competition with mainstream economics.[2] With respect to this micro-economic formalism—which loses touch with the profound essence of the theory of surplus value—it becomes quite easy to proclaim the failure and therefore to abandon the theory of value itself.

The theory of value as a macroeconomic theory of exploitation

The second conception conceives the theory of value as a macroeconomic theory of exploitation, insisting on the qualitative dimension of the social relation between capital and labour, a relation that entails the transformation of labour power into a commodity.[3] This is what we label the *theory of value/surplus value*, wherein abstract labour is understood as the substance and source of value within a capitalist society. Its development, in turn, is supported by the expansion of mercantile relationships and by the exacerbation of the capital/labour conflict. Let us stress—as far as this last issue is concerned—that in Marx the labour theory of value is directly conceived as a function of the theory of surplus value and hence it is not autonomous from it, i.e. from the law of exploitation. In this respect, it is noteworthy to stress that the Marxian highly controversial choice of taking up his analysis from the study of the commodity in the first chapter of *Capital* has nothing to do with the idea of a simple-commodity society that would have presumably preceded capitalism. On the contrary, it stems from the need to show how the transformation of labour power into a commodity can explain the mysterious origin of profit—and thus the articulation between its exchange value and its use value (labour itself). At any rate, in Marx there is no fetishism regarding the *law of value/labour time*, nor is this ever depicted as a law of exchange between equivalents that would turn it into a sort of structural invariant of the functioning of the economy. On the contrary, the *theory of value/surplus value* has to be primarily understood on a macroeconomic level where social capital and the collective worker are juxtaposed rather than being minimized to an issue concerning the measurement of the value of the single commodities. This very reading—so it seems—is much more appropriate in so far as Hai Hac observes: "capital is indifferent to the value of the commodities that it produces, because all that it is interested in is the surplus value of which value is the bearer" (Hai Hac 2003: I, 265).

From the law of surplus value to the law of value/labour time

The sequence belonging to the Engelsian tradition leading from a simple-commodity mode of production based upon the creation of use values to the capitalistic mode of production based on the creation of surplus values has somehow to be reversed. One has to begin from the *theory of value/surplus value* in order to get to the generalisation of *law of value/labour time* in order to understand the very meaning of their mutual articulation.

Indeed, we will be precisely referring to such an approach while trying to characterize the historical genesis and the development of the *law of value/surplus value* in order to capture the profound meaning of its own crisis with respect to a *knowledge-based economy.*

In order to better understand the meaning of this articulation it may be useful to recur on the definition of the law of surplus value. Hence, the law of surplus value conveys the economic rationality of capitalism itself, its own essential kernel, prior and independent of its historically determined forms: namely, a system oriented towards the unlimited accumulation of capital. One can retrace this intuition in the well-known formula contained in *Capital* (M-C-M′), according to which the valorisation of capital is an unbounded process, as its goal is neither consumption nor the production of use values, but rather the accumulation of abstract wealth represented by money. As far as capital *per se* is concerned, commodities and production are nothing but mere means employed as to achieve the only purpose of incessantly increasing the command-power over society and labour (the source and substance of value) that money confers to capital by allowing it to seize on surplus value (either directly or indirectly). In this respect, following Negri (1979), one can affirm that the law of surplus value is to be incontrovertibly understood as a *law of exploitation and antagonism*. Both from a historical and a logical viewpoint, it precedes that law of value which sets abstract labour time as the measure of labour and therefore of the value of commodities. Considering the aforesaid, one should understand the reason according to which we do state that the *law of value/labour time* is to be conceived as a dependent variable of the law of surplus value. The origin and the historical meaning of the *law of value/labour time* is strictly connected to the configuration of the capital/labour relationships as this was established and developed throughout the first industrial revolution. It is precisely within this historical juncture that the economic rationality of capital—namely, the law of surplus value—gives up controlling the manufacturing production "from the outside" (Braudel 1979), seeping through it and progressively taking its direct control. Its hegemony is thus established, both in the realm of labour organization and with respect of the satisfaction of material needs, fostering a rationale of mass consumption centred on the production of standardised commodities. This process was developed within the knowledge/power relationships, structuring a dynamics which led to the preeminence of real subsumption over the formal one.

It is within this very framework that the *law of value/labour time* rooted itself (even before classical political economy developed the labour theory of value) as the concrete expression of those managerial practices aimed at the "rationalisation" of production. Indeed, these practices abstracted labour from its very content and turned the clock's time (and then the chronometer's one) into the favourite means employed for quantifying the economic value of labour, prescribing its modes of operation as to increase its productivity.[4] Hence, within the firm, the homogenisation of work that stems from its fragmentation into several elementary tasks fulfils a twofold role, serving simultaneously as a device for its control and as a basis for the economic calculus. This, in turn, permits the optimization of the input/output relationship by measuring both in "men and machines" labour-times, while paying—as Charles Babbage already underlined—the lowest wage to each and every task. At the same time, the *law of value/labour time* ensures—with respect to the socially necessary labour time—the a-posteriori regulation of the relationships of competition related to the decentralised activity of several units of production independent from one another.

The economic rationality of capital and the law of value/surplus value within the realm of industrial capitalism

On these bases, we are now able to precisely characterise the economic rationality of the *theory of value/surplus value* which marked the entire development of industrial capitalism. Generally speaking, this economic rationality rests on a purely quantitative notion of growth and productivity. It can be defined as a rationale consisting in manufacturing and selling commodities with the aim of maximising profit, as to produce always more with always less (Gorz 1989). For this reason, as Marx (1993b: 706) already noted in the *Grundrisse*, "capital itself is the moving contradiction, [in] that it presses to reduce labour time to a minimum, while it posits labour time, on the other side, as sole measure and source of wealth," which is to say that "as surplus value grows with the development of the productive power of social labour, so does value decrease, therefore the very same process reduces the value of commodities and increases the surplus value that it bears" (Hai Hac 2003: I, 265).

At any rate, it is the very development of this rationality that, pushed towards the limits of its own rationale, endogenously leads to a crisis whose main features and causes are precisely those that characterise the crisis of cognitive capitalism.[5]

The dynamics of surplus value and the real subsumption of society and labour under capital

To be more precise, to conceptualise the economic rationality of the *theory of value/surplus value*, one needs to conceive it from two qualitative and complementary perspectives, the exhaustion of both being at the core of the ongoing crisis.

The first dimension defines the law of value as that social relationship which extends the logic of profit and commodity up to the point where this becomes the key and progressive criterion for the development of social wealth and the satisfaction of needs. We would like to stress that this rationale entails a political, social and economical ambivalence, as argued by Gorz (1988), that nurtured that ideology of progress typical of industrial capitalism. This, in turn, granted industrial capitalism the endorsement of a consistent share of the workers and a socialist movement that led to the definite abandon of any critique concerning the capitalistic division of labour and the alienation that this brings along both in the realm of labour and in that of consumption. What does this ambivalence consist of?

It consists of the fact that the constant diminution of the labour time necessary to the mass production of material goods—together with the symmetrical and correlated fall of their unitary value—has been presented as that tool capable of freeing "humanity from scarcity," satisfying in this way an increasing mass of needs—regardless of their real or superficial nature. This "progressive" feature of the rationality of capital and of the dynamic of the surplus value was also presented—at least potentially—as the means by which it was possible to gradually reduce the time dedicated to work and therefore as a tool to improve the conditions of life of the working class. At any rate, within this logic one can find that *utopian* dimension—the development of the productive forces as a tool for struggling against scarcity—upon which industrial capitalism was able to build a sort of historical legitimacy.

The second dimension of the economic rationality of the *theory of value/surplus value* concerns its application to the organisation of production. In this, one may retrace the origin of the norm which, according to Marx, would have turned abstract labour time—measured in units of simple, unqualified labour—into the substance of the value of commodities and, simultaneously, into the instrument to evaluate, control, and prescript the content of the working performance. To fully understand the introduction and the progressive enforcement of this norm it is necessary to begin from the structural uncertainty that characterises the capital–labour exchange. Indeed, the buying and selling of labour power is based on making available a quantity of time rather than an effective content of labour. This aspect of the Marxian analysis is expressed in an extremely consonant manner by Paolo Virno (2008) through the distinction between the Aristotelian concept of *power* and that of *act*. This distinction allows us to understand the two key reasons whereby the knowledge–power relations located at the core of the organisation of production constitute an essential element to understand the antagonism between capital and labour. The first one is manifested within the abilities of those who are able to control the intensity and quality of labour in virtue of the asymmetrical retaining of some knowledge or *savoir faire*, whose possession entitles the person who owns them to dictate the times and modes of operation. The second one deals with the fact that those who possess the *intellectual power of production* can also aspire to manage its collective regulation, and therefore define the organisation of work as well as the social ends of production.

We are confronted here with a crucial question that was already at the heart of the reflections of the early great theoreticians of the industrial revolution such as A. Ure (1835) and C. Babbage (1835). This reflection would have been recovered and systematised by F. W. Taylor (1911) when he dealt with the power of the class composition of the professional workers employed in the driving industries of the second industrial revolution. Whilst recognising that "knowledge is the most precious commodity" owned by workers in the face of capital, Taylor explicitly targeted his analysis towards those systematic practices through which workers used to slow down the pace of production. The need to bring out and expropriate the workers' *tacit knowledge* would have been derived from this, in order to convert it—through the study of time and motion—into codified knowledge acquired by the management who in turn could possibly use it against the workers themselves as a strict prescription of the timing and procedures of their operations. Taylor thus believed to have laid the irreversible foundations of a *scientific organisation of labour* that would have suppressed all uncertainty over the execution of the employment contract, granting capital the *ex-ante* planning of the *theory of value/surplus-value.* By doing so, in the Taylorist factory the measure of labour and its productivity—just like the volume and value of production—were theoretically programmed and known beforehand by means of those time and methods studies performed by the engineers.

The whole of these indicators could thus be connected to a known and homogeneous unit of calculation that could also provide a relatively precise index for the rate of exploitation. Furthermore, the industrial norm of time—as well as the conceptualisation of abstract labour—embodied the capitalistic utopia of a productive organisation capable of depriving labour of all its autonomy and cognitive elements. Hence, labour seemed to have been revolted into its opposite, that is to say, into a purely mechanical, repetitive and impersonal activity totally subservient to the science incorporated within fixed capital.

Within this twofold dimension of the economic rationality of the *theory of value/surplus value* we can retrace what Marx characterised as the logic of the real subsumption of labour and society under capital. It is not by coincidence that Marx strictly linked the concept of real subsumption to that of relative surplus value, which directly indicates the simultaneous upheaval of the norms of production and of those rules related to the consumption of workers, more and more integrated within capital's circuit of accumulation.[6]

Predominance of the logic of profit over that of rent

It is noteworthy to point out that this tendency towards real subsumption also actualises the two fundamental criteria by which means it is possible—according to Marx—to clearly differentiate the category of profit from that of rent, which, in turn, would permit the distinction between the remuneration of the capital employed in the production from that sum paid for the remuneration of rents, which are to be conceived as withdrawals performed from an outer position with respect to the organisation of production (Vercellone 2008b).

In this respect, one needs to keep in mind that both profit and rent belong to an inner distribution stemming from the expropriation of surplus labour. It is also because of this reason that the criteria which allow one to clearly distinguish between profit and rent are far less evident than what one may think and thus constitute one of the main crux of both classical and neoclassical economics. Indeed, whether one embeds the classical definition of profit, profit is defined as the remuneration of capital and it consists in obtaining a revenue almost proportional to the capitals invested in the production. In this form—and Smith (1976: 127–141) himself had already underlined this very issue—profit has nothing to do with the retribution of the coordination and monitoring functions eventually implemented by the entrepreneur or either the manager of the firm. In this respect, one may consider the remuneration of capital as quite analogous to the remuneration of land, as he who owns capital is rightfully entitled to furnish the means of production without fulfilling any direct role regarding their enactment. Being confronted in this very inconsistency of classical political economy, the two major criteria developed by the following economic theory in order to manage a rigorous distinction between profit and rent seems to have been derived—as we will try to outline—from Marx himself and they would have found their proper actualisation in the realm of industrial capitalism. The first criterion affirms that profit—differently to rent, which is based on the exploitation of some real or artificial scarcity of a resource[7]—is essentially stored within the form with the scope of being subsequently reinvested. Therefore, it plays a major role in stimulating the accumulation of capital and hence in developing the forces of production, laying the ground for the passage leading *from the kingdom of necessity to that of freedom*. The second criterion underlines the way in which profit—distinguished from rent—effectively mirrors an inner and necessary function carried out by the productive capital in managing and organising labour by virtue of its control over knowledge and technology. From the very same viewpoint, in the third book of *Capital* Marx (1993a: 458) distinguishes between an outer and passive "property capital" and an inner and active "functioning capital," from which "the division of profit into interest and profit of enterprise" is to be derived.[8] This inner and active nature of the latter typology of capital—conceived as a necessary condition for organising labour—is based on a twofold representation: on the one hand, we are confronted with a sort of "entrepreneurial capital," whose depiction unifies the figures of the capitalist with that of the entrepreneur (the most common situation at the time of the redaction of *Capital*). On the other hand, we have a sort of "managerial capital," whose representation is perfectly depicted by the Chandlerian "visible hand" or by the Galbraithian "technostructure": the juxtaposition of its role to the passive property of shareholders—as this is depicted by Berle and Means (1967)—is performed by stressing its importance in programming innovation thus expanding the potential of production. Incidentally, let us note that in both cases the inner position of capital presumes a process of polarization of knowledge which contrasts the intellectual and conceptual activity—attributed directly to capital or to its functionaries—with the trivialised operative one belonging to labour. In conclusion, profit is clearly differentiable from rent in as much as (1) the real subsumption of labour under capital expresses a true primacy of the productive knowledge incorporated into constant capital; (2) the managerial organization of the firm predominates over the living knowledge incorporated and mobilised by labour.

Indeed, within this framework, the two functions of productive capital linked to the capitalistic process of production seem to confuse one another.[9] Hence, while trying to conceptualise the role of capital in the organisation of production, it becomes impossible to distinguish *a purely despotic and coercive figure* related to the process of valorisation from another figure, namely that of a sort of "orchestra leader" capable of assuring the coordination of the working activities as to foster the production of use values. The contradictory nature of the unity of these two functions seems thus to fade away. Capital fashions the productive process in its own image, disguising its command in the semblance of some natural law inscribed within the materialness of the productive forces. In this sense, capitalists—or at least, industrial capitalists—did appear to Marx (1960: 458) not only as "necessary functionar[ies], but the dominating functionar[ies] in production" who do not simply seize on surpluslabour , but who eventually *gives birth to this very surplus labour*. The landlord, in contrast intervenes only "post-festum": he "is completely useless." Given all these reasons, profit might have appeared back then as a form of surplus value stemming from the process of production, contrarily to rent which constitutes "a form of distribution pure and simple" (Marx 1993a: 1023).

Nonetheless, as far as the viewpoint of Marx is concerned, this configuration of the capital–labour relationship had no character of irreversibility and was confronted by powerful counter-trends, the first of which dealt with the manner in which the limited companies would have led to an increasing separation between the property and the management of capital. Thus, the management would have been handed to a class which, although it does not "possess capital under any title, takes care of all real functions that fall to the functioning capitalist as such, [so that] there remains only the functionary, and the capitalist vanishes from the production process as someone superfluous" (Marx 1993a: 512). Such a perspective entails a tendential overturning within the knowledge–power relationships, which eventually may have led—according to Marx himself—the "capitalist [to] become just as superfluous as a functionary in production as he himself, from his superior vantage-point, finds the large landlord" (1993a: 511).

In this respect, at the end of Book III, chapter 23, Marx adduced the simultaneous "proof" of cooperative firms by depicting them as a first example of some possible self-management of labour capable of reaffirming the autonomy of the process of production over that of valorisation, so quitting the capitalistic rationale. Despite this quite sharp insight, his own main hypothesis actually referred to the possibilities intrinsic to a development of what today we call a *widespread intellectuality* or a *collective intelligence*. Indeed, quoting T. Hodgskin, Marx recalled the way in which "the wide spread of education among the journeymen mechanics of this country diminishes daily the value of the labour and skill of almost all masters and employers by increasing the number of persons who possess their peculiar knowledge" (Hodgskin quoted in Marx 1993a: 513).

In this framework, Marx said, while being confronted with a productive cooperation capable of organising autonomously to capital, that the very functions of directing the production previously related to the manager's role becomes useless, hence unveiling their purely despotic nature. Thus, "the last pretext for confusing profit of enterprise with the wages of management was removed, and profit came to appear in practice as what it undeniably was in theory, mere surplus value, value for which no equivalent was paid, realized unpaid labour." (Marx 1993a: 514).

In conclusion, profit, even that related to the aforesaid "functioning capital," arises from a mere expropriation of surplus labour performed—as for the rent—without fulfilling any role in the organization of labour cooperation. Hence, it is designed, for capital itself, that kind of evolution which led "the landowner, such an important functionary in production in the ancient world and in the Middle Ages, [to become] a useless superfetation in the industrial world" (Marx 1969: 458).

Hence, we can retrace in Marx a theory of the *becoming-rent of profit* which captures the substantial euthanasia of the role of productive capital itself, according to a thesis that would find its logical/historical coherence and topicality if related to the General Intellect hypothesis and therefore, to the hypothesis of the crisis of the law of value within cognitive capitalism.

The crisis of the law of value/surplus value in cognitive capitalism

The trend towards real subsumption, which did find a quasi-perfect historical accomplishment in the Fordist growth models and in the figure of the great modern corporation, is doomed to remain unfulfilled. A new kind of knowledge is always bound to establish at an upper level of the division of labour.

Marx himself had well identified the realm of real subsumption as fundamentally related to the exacerbation of those conflicts located at the core of the knowledge–power relationships. Indeed, he did discuss the nature of those conflicts linked to the control of the *intellectual forces of production*, especially in a very well-known passage of the first book of *Capital*—added to the first French edition—where he argues

> That monstrosity, the disposable working population held in reserve, in misery, for the changing requirements of capitalist exploitation, must be replaced by the individual man who is absolutely available for the different kinds of labour required of him; the partially developed individual, who is merely the bearer of one specialized social function, must be replaced by the totally developed individual, for whom the different social functions are different modes of activity he takes up in turn.
>
> (Marx 1991: 618)

We may retrace in here a key aspect, considered from the perspective of living labour, belonging to the Marxian hypothesis of General Intellect and therefore to the crisis of the law of value as this was developed in the "Fragment on Machines" of the *Grundrisse.*

With the occurrence of the crisis of Fordism, this dynamic was manifested in those conflicts which led to the substantial formation of a *widespread intellectuality* and to the development of collective welfare services (healthcare, education, research) which arose beyond the compatibilities of the Fordist regulation. This evolution broke the quasi-exclusive bond that industrial capitalism—especially the Fordist capitalism of mass—established between the dynamics of relative surplus value and the production of standardised commodities destined for the private consumption of householders. A twofold consequence resulted, locating itself at the core of the Fordist crisis and thus of the metamorphosis of current capitalism.

On the one hand, as argued by M. Aglietta (1976), a severe increase of the social costs related to the reproduction of the labour force occurred both because of a great rise in the socialized share of wages and because of the progression of the collective consumptions in those sectors that we call *productions of man for man* (healthcare, education, research). This critical factor was amplified, in Europe, by the fact that these services are to be produced by the welfare institutions, according to a non-mercantile rationale based on the employment of a mass of labour which does not produce any surplus value. On the other hand, thanks to the aforesaid widespread intellectuality and to the rise of the welfare state, the institutional and productive bases for the rising of a knowledge-based economy were laid (Vercellone 2007). The enhancement of a knowledge-based economy precedes and opposes, both from a logical and from a historical viewpoint, the establishment of cognitive capitalism. The latter results from a reorganization through which capital tries to absorb and subsume, parasitically, the collective conditions of the production of knowledge, hindering the potential of emancipation inscribed within the General Intellect society. Cognitive capitalism is a *historical system of accumulation*, [10] subsequent to mercantile capitalism and to the industrial one, wherein the cognitive and the relational dimension of labour becomes dominant with respect of the production of both wealth and value. Within such a framework, the main form of capital is the so-called *immaterial* or *intellectual* capital, a concept which truly constitutes an oxymoron (Gorz 2003). At the same time, the primacy of the production of material standardised commodities destined to the private consumption of householders—typical of industrial capitalism—is replaced by those *productions of humans for and by humans* and by the production of informational goods. Both these categories play a major role in fostering a knowledge-based economy, despite the fact that they largely rely on an economical and social rationale quite opposite to that of capital. Indeed, the core mechanism of the reproduction process in cognitive capitalism becomes more and more based—through an eminently contradictory dynamics—on the control of those collective conditions by which knowledge is produced, transformed into a commodity and then into capital.

This metamorphosis coincides with the exhaustion of the economic rationale of the *theory of value/surplus value*, on which—as previously argued—industrial capitalism established its control over labour. To be more precise, the crisis of the *theory of value/surplus value* has a twofold character, involving the simultaneous dissolution of those criteria on which the net distinction between profit and rent was founded. The first one is related to a crisis of the measurement and control of labour which undermines the very same mechanisms wherein—in industrial capitalism—the inner and necessary role of productive capital was rooted, as far as the organisation of the working activity was concerned. Hence, one may consider this crisis as symptomatic in order to stress how the fundamental categories of the political economy born within the realm of industrial capitalism—with particular respect to that of constant capital—may have changed meaning or eventually, even lost their historical relevance.

The second one deals with an increasing divorce between the rationale of value and that of wealth underlying "the crisis of capitalism in its epistemic foundations" Gorz (2004: 214).

A crisis of measure and control of labour

The major transformation that—from the crisis of Fordism onwards—signals an exit from industrial capitalism, is very much found in the forceful return of the cognitive and intellectual aspect of labour. At the very core of this dynamics one can find the meeting between a widespread intellectuality and the informational revolution which opened the path to brand-new forms of horizontal coordination of labour and of re-appropriation of the means of production.

It must be noted that this emergence of cognitive labour is far from being the privilege of an elite of R&D workers operating in those sectors characterised by a high intensity of knowledge and information. Instead, it is manifested in every productive activity, both material and immaterial (as these two realms are often inextricable); it also concerns mansions that are not highly technological, as demonstrated by the growth of those indicators that measure the autonomy of labour and the enlargement of the functions of the production of knowledge and information in the economy as a whole. These functions spread over the entire society, transforming the organisation of the firms as well as its relationships with the surrounding environment. The very dynamics of the production of knowledge and innovation cannot be conceived—likewise the dominant paradigm in the Fordist era used to do—as the result of a single detached sector specialized in the production of knowledge on the basis of a production function which would combine highly qualified labour with capital.[11] Nowadays it is increasingly escaping the main places where it used to be produced by means of new decentralised and autonomous forms of organisation, quite different from those embedded in the hierarchic/administrative norms of public and private research. This evolution is translated—within the firm as well as within society as a whole—in a new qualitative preeminence of living knowledges—embodied *in* labour and mobilised *by* labour—over those formalised skills belonging to fixed capital and to the managerial organisation of modern corporations.

Two main stylised facts depict the quantitative and qualitative magnitude of this transformation.

From the hegemony of a technical division of labour towards a cognitive one

The first stylised fact concerns the transition leading from the hegemony of a technical division of labour towards a cognitive one. Sure enough, counter-tendencies do exist: history is not a linear process but proceeds in leaps and bounds. Therefore, the tendency towards a new cognitive organisation of production does not mark, *ipso facto*, the end of Taylorism, not even in the realm of intellectual labour. Capital will always make every effort to limit as much as possible the actual control that workers exert over their labour. In this new phase of capitalism, different productive models will continue to co-exist and intertwine. Nevertheless, as shown in a recent inquiry carried out by the European Foundation for the Improvement of Living and Working Conditions, it is a cognitive organisational model (the so-called *discretionary learning organization*) that plays both a qualitative and a quantitative hegemonic role with respect to the productive process on which the valorisation of capital and the competitiveness of the economic system depend (cf. exposure index in Table 2.1).

Despite some significant spatial differences, the discretionary-learning-organization model corresponds to 39.1 per cent of salaried workers, followed by the lean production Toyotist model (28.2 per cent), which may be defined as a hybrid between the technical and the cognitive division of labour. In the

Table 2.1 National difference in forms of work organisation

Country	*Percentage of employees by country in each organisational class*			
	Discretionary learning	*Lean production*	*Taylorist organisation*	*Traditional organisation*
Austria	47.5	21.5	13.1	18.0
Belgium	38.9	25.1	13.9	22.1
Denmark	60	21.9	6.8	11.3
Finland	47.8	27.6	12.5	12.1
France	38.0	33.3	11.1	17.7
Germany	44.3	19.6	14.3	21.9
Greece	18.7	25.6	28.0	27.7
Ireland	24.0	37.8	20.7	17.6
Italy	30.0	23.6	20.9	25.4
Luxembourg	42.8	25.4	11.9	20.0
Netherlands	64.0	17.2	5.3	13.5
Portugal	26.1	28.1	23.0	22.8
Spain	20.1	38.8	18.5	22.5
Sweden	52.6	18.5	7.1	21.7
UK	34.8	40.6	10.9	13.7
EU	**39.1**	**28.2**	**13.6**	**19.1**

Source: Eurofound (2000). For the exposure index, see Lundvall and Lorenz (2009).

Note: The exposure index, as calculated by Lundvall and Lorenz (2009), is an index concerning the degree of exposition to international competition as far as the openness of emergent economies is concerned.

last position, one can find the Taylorist model, which includes less than 14 per cent of the labour force.

Because of these transformations, the organisation of the productive activities located at the core of the valorisation process is increasingly less dependent on the technical decomposition of production in elementary and repetitive tasks prescribed by the management of the firm. Indeed, it is increasingly rooted in a cognitive organisation of work based on the polyvalent complementarity of different lots of knowledge collectively mobilised by workers in order to achieve a productive goal, which in turn have to be adaptable to a dynamics of perennial change with respect to the interaction with customers within a relation of co-production of services. In this framework, the static economies of scale typical of Fordism are replaced by some learning by doing and network-based dynamical economies (Fumagalli and Lucarelli 2011). At the same time, the industrial criteria for measuring efficiency no longer stands: any reference to a homogeneous time of production—as far as a great deal of situations are concerned—becomes void, being incapable either of organising labour and of measuring value and production costs (Zarifian 1995; Veltz 2000). This evolution is also quintessential to conceive some recent transformations within the automatised firm wherein labour is more and more related to monitoring activities connected to the interpretation of the information running from terminals to computers rather than dealing with any direct action aimed to transform inanimate materials. Thus, the greatest increases in efficiency have nothing to do with a reduction of the time necessary to carry out each and every single operation, but rather it deals with the optimization of the man–machine interface as to avoid any anomaly or damage capable of disturbing the fluidity of production. Therefore we observe that the *law of value/labour time* loses its pertinence if understood as a criterion for "rationalizing" the capitalistic production using the norm of abstract unqualified labour as the combined tool to simultaneously evaluate the productivity of labour and hence—by this very mean—to control it within a framework of real subsumption. More precisely, the increase in power of the cognitive dimension of labour gives this exhaustion a double meaning.

First of all, it does mean a *crisis of measure*, in so far as cognitive labour is an activity developed across the whole time of life by thinking, communicating, and sharing knowledge. The unity of time and place belonging to the Fordist wage regulation is profoundly altered. The time spent and certified in the enterprise is only a fraction of the actual social time spent "working." This dynamic is translated into an increase in that share of labour which is not easily measurable—if it is at all—according to the traditional measurement criteria.[12]

In the second place, the crisis of measure is duplicated by a *crisis of control*. The old dilemma concerning the control over the worker turns back up differently fashioned. Not only does capital depend again on the knowledge of workers, but this very knowledge, in order to be fully productive, has to be mobilised through a thorough commitment towards the goal by the workers themselves. Cognitive labour hence possesses a "genetic" capability of self-organizing its cooperation, both within the firm and within society as a whole. Thus, one may observe a growing tension between the attempt of capital of subsuming the whole of social times under the heteronomous rationale of their valorisation and the tendential autonomy of cognitive labour as a result of a potentially conflictual dynamics capable of challenging the very social ends of production. This dynamics, either spontaneous and hidden or explicitly affirmed, may take different forms both as far as the wage regulation is concerned and with respect to the division of labour, through mechanisms that all express a profound destabilization at the level of the power/knowledge relationships which entangle one another with respect of the social organization of production.

We believe that two main aspects are crucial to understand how the tendency towards a becoming-rent of profit affects productive capital itself. Hence, within the firm, the Taylorist managerial model of prescription of tasks gives way to new practices based upon (1) the *prescription of subjectivity*; (2) the *management of projects*; (3) the *commitment to result*. [13] The disciplinary power characterizing the scientific organization of labour is thus replaced by a "managinaire"[14] power based upon psychic mobilization obtained by the internalization of the values of the firm by the employee, whose ideal ego is captured by the entrepreneurial one. The point then is no longer to make "corpses" useful, submissive, and productive as it was within the realm of Taylorist organization but rather to transform the libidinal energy into labour force (Gauliac and Mercier 2012).

As for the production of value, the control over work increasingly shifts ever more before and beyond the productive activity itself. Within such a framework, it is labour itself that has the duty of finding how to achieve the goal set by the management of the firm, often in a quite deliberately unrealistic manner.[15] The purpose is to push workers towards a complete mobilisation of their knowledge in order to reach given goals while simultaneously making them internalize the guilt of being unable to fully accomplish them. The whole work is actualised by the multiplication of a panoply of tools used to evaluate the subjectivity of the worker and their conformity to the values of the firm. This often leads to structure a system of *paradoxical injunctions*, which involves both the ethical values and the fulfilment of irreconcilable tasks (quantity/quality; loyalty towards the firm/commitment towards the client; competition/solidarity among the colleagues and so forth). The individualization of the salary relationship and the fostering of competition among workers goes hand in hand with a destabilization of the working team wherein the most suitable and effective forms of cognitive cooperation should take place. In this respect, we can generally affirm that we are now observing a new qualitative leap in the historical process which has led to an increasing separation between the property and the management of capital. Indeed, the cognitive-capitalism era does not simply ratify the irreversible decline of the idyllic Weberian entrepreneur who simultaneously embodies the twofold figure of the owner and the manager of the firm. This additionally entails—which is even more significant—the end of the Galbraithian techno-structure which derived its legitimacy from its role in organizing labour and in programming innovation, according to a rationale which finds its main personification within the figure of the engineer working in the methods and times office (Negri and Vercellone 2008). These managerial figures, born and raised within the cult of technical competence and technological knowledge, give way to a new class of managers trained in the great business schools, embedded in a culture that is completely extraneous to that of production. Their major competence consists in exercising financial functions and in developing a rhetoric at the service of the creation of value for shareholders, while, as previously argued, the real functions connected to the organization of production and to the fulfilment of productive goals are more and more delegated to the workers. In this respect, as far as many forms of cooperation of cognitive labour are concerned, the very same *visible hand of manager* is getting more and more weightless, boiling down to a *useless superfetation*. Whether one may have explained the reason why property capital was located outside the productive process by juxtaposing its passive role to the necessary and active role played by the operative capital, in cognitive capitalism this is no longer possible, being these two characters gradually converging and confusing one another. As previously argued, this is to be conceived as a result of that loss of legitimacy which would stem from the fact that productive capital does no longer exercise its hegemony over productive knowledge and therefore on innovation.

This latter thesis acquires an additional clarification whether one takes into consideration the complex strategies the great *high-tech* firms of cognitive capitalism were—and still are—forced to pursue in order to face the challenges raised by the *commons of knowledge*, moving from an openly conflictual phase to the development of some sort of compromise, ending up with a partial absorption of the commons rationale within their models of business.[16] Indeed, one of the most significant expressions of the formation of a widespread intellectuality and of the development of the informational revolution consists in the proliferation of communities that intensely produce knowledge (David and Foray 2002). They do give birth to horizontal forms of cooperation and to self-reinforcing new forms of property based on the commons rationale, designing models alternative both to the public one and to the private one, to the state and to the firm. The free software experience and the copyleft invention—as far as the legal devices are concerned—are surely the most widely known expressions of this tendency, even if they do not represent but the tip of that "commons iceberg" which is to emerge.

The awareness of such a fact pushed several great corporations working in the field of bio-technologies and digital economies to experiment an *open-innovation* model of organization in order to try to cope with the most evident inefficiencies belonging to the property model. Such an open-innovation model mainly tries to integrate from the outside the innovative force of the commons as to put it at the service of the cycle of valorisation. We shall insist in more detail on the strengths and limitations of this capitalist strategy. As for now, we would like to stress that this politics of absorbing and capturing the autonomous creative force of the commons may be the most significant expression of the tendency towards the *becoming-rent of profit*, unveiling the vanishing role of capital in the production of knowledge and innovation.

Generally speaking, many other forms of *rentier* accumulations—in which the surplus value is expropriated from a position located outside the management of labour—are located at the very core of the business model followed by the main oligopolies of the Internet economy. Finally—as this is properly witnessed by the *digital free labour* [17]approach—the outsourcing of entire phases of the productive cycle towards the *prosumers* [18] did become a routine quite common both to the new and to the old economy. It entails a logic which does apply to very simple and repetitive tasks—as the simple production of data and the on-line purchase of a single ticket—as well as to complex activities which deal with the conception of the product itself. Indeed, the importance of these practices within the surplus value chains led a careful observer as G. Tiffon (2013) to build a new surplus-labour theory based on the importance of the new productive work carried out by the consumers themselves.

The new centrality of immaterial capital: oxymoron and/or crisis of the notion of constant capital?

The twofold crisis of measure and control of labour is also mirrored by the destabilization of another fundamental category of the political economy of industrial capitalism: that of constant capital. In order to better comprehend the meaning of this statement, it is useful to start back from a stylised fact which has often been recalled as to characterise the rising of a knowledge-based economy (Foray 2009). Indeed, this has been referred to the historical dynamics through which that share of capital called *intangible* (R&D, healthcare, education) overcomes that represented by material capital within the global stock of capital *tout court*, becoming the determining element for growth and competition (Kendrick 1994). This evolution means that the determining factor in the social organisation of production is now fundamentally the intellectual and creative skills of the labour force. One may affirm that the notions of intellectual or immaterial capital are symptomatic for understanding the crisis of the category of constant capital itself as this was established during industrial capitalism, wherein *c* (constant capital) used to represent that share of dead labour crystallized in the system of machines capable of imposing its dominion over living labour. Nowadays, these notions are unable to express the preponderant role that the living knowledges incorporated into the labour force plays in the social organisation of production, a role that overshadows that fulfilled by the dead knowledges incorporated into constant capital and into the management of the firm. From this viewpoint, the very same historical issue concerning the re-appropriation of the means of production is significantly ambushed with respect of the industrial capitalism era. As for today, it increasingly deals with the democratic re-appropriation of the welfare institutions which only permits the reproduction and the development of the so-called immaterial capital and therefore of a knowledge-based economy as a whole.[19]

We consider it necessary to remind how the so-called immaterial capital now represents the most considerable portion of the financial capitalisation.[20] It was estimated that the immaterial assets of the 500 greatest US corporations in their financial capitalisation would have grown from 15 per cent to 85 per cent between 1975 and 2005 (Figure 2.1).

Indeed, this capital labelled as "immaterial" ends up escaping any objective measure in terms of "historical costs" (and therefore in terms of the labour time necessary to its production). Its value can only be the expression of the subjective evaluation of estimated profits carried out by financial markets as to hoard rents. This contributes to illustrate why the stock-market value of this capital is essentially fictitious and subject to great fluctuations (Gorz 2003). It is based on that self-referential rationale typical of finance which feeds speculative bubbles irredeemably doomed to bust, dragging the whole credit and economic system into deep recessions. The impossibility of determining an objective and reliable measure of

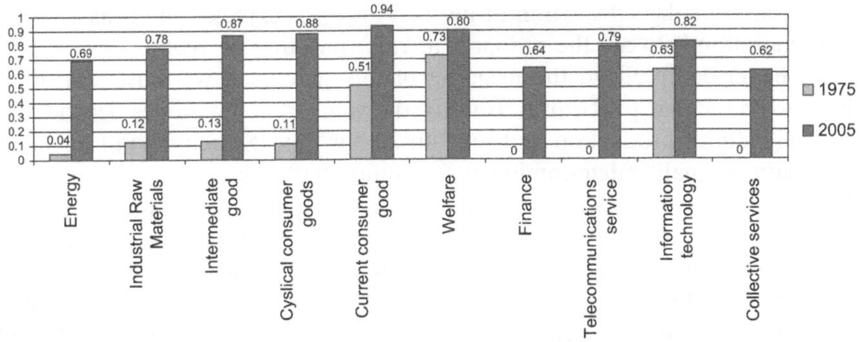

Figure 2.1 The share of intangible assets in the market capitalization of large listed companies, by sector of activity (percentages)

Note: List of S&P 500 companies in the United States. Data: Ned Davis Research, Inc. Source: Keith Cardoza et al. (2006), quoted in Centre d'analyse stratégique (2008: 2).

immaterial capital is also confirmed by the controversy on the origin of the famous accounting concept of *goodwill* (which designates the growing gap between the companies' market value and that of their tangible assets): the main immaterial asset on which the surplus value embodied by the *goodwill* depends is actually nothing but the "intellectual capital" represented by the competence, experience, tacit knowledge, and ability to cooperate of the labour force. In other words, despite the twists at work in the concepts of intellectual or human capital, this is not capital but rather the intellectual qualities of the labour force that by definition (unless they are reduced to slavery) constitute an asset which by definition is non-negotiable on the market. This is why, as Halary (2004) notes, the attempt to explain the *goodwill* through the presence of *non-classified immaterial assets* falls prey to a circular argument that does not allow for the elimination of the indeterminacy of the value of these immaterial assets. Why circular? Because the answer to the question "What does *goodwill* depend on?" is "On the human capital of the enterprise"; and to the question "And how is the value of human capital determined?" is "By *goodwill*!" This means that the measure of capital and the foundation of its power over society depend less and less on past labour and on the knowledge incorporated in constant capital, while they are now mainly founded on a *social convention* that finds its main impulse in the power of finance.

The exhaustion of the economic rationality of capital and the dissociation of value from wealth

The second facet of the crisis of the law of value/surplus value recalls the exhaustion of that social relationship which turns the logic of commodity and profit into the key and progressive criterion for the development of social wealth and for the satisfaction of needs. This crisis expresses itself as a growing separation between the rationale of *value* and that of *wealth*.

To better comprehend the meaning of this statement, we must remember how, to Marx (but to Ricardo as well), the value of commodities depends on the difficulty of production and thus on labour time. Scarcity is not an inner and natural quality determining the commodities' value. It is merely a historically determined necessary condition for their production, production that ought to be conceived as that actual tool for reducing scarcity whereof the socially necessary labour time is nothing but a rough measure. The concept of *value* is therefore completely different to that of *wealth*, which instead depends on abundance, on use value (as opposed to exchange value), and therefore on gratuity. Hence, these two concepts must not be confused, as neoclassical economics does, whose foundation rests properly on the denial of the distinction between wealth and value according to an epistemological position that plays an increasingly relevant role within a historical framework wherein the distance keeping apart the value and the wealth rationale is more and more alarming.

Sure enough, the capitalist rationale of mass-producing standardised commodities had found, as we have seen, a sort of historical legitimacy in the realm of industrial capitalism, being this capable of fostering wealth, producing ever more commodities with less work, thus with ever lower overall prices, and allowing for the satisfaction of an ever growing mass of needs. In contrast, in cognitive capitalism, this positive association between value and wealth, between commodity production and satisfaction of needs, is broken. This implies that the law of value now survives as an empty shell deprived of what Marx considered the progressive function of capital, which is to say its role in enhancing the development of the forces of production as a tool employed in the struggle against scarcity, which, in the long run, would have favoured a leap from the *kingdom of necessity* to the *kingdom of freedom*.

Several evolutions of cognitive capitalism illustrate this *disassociation between value and wealth* that expresses—in what is most essential to it—the progressive loss of power of the *theory of value/surplus value* and thus the impossibility of establishing around it any struggle–development dialectics. They refer back to the fundamental contradiction between the valorisation rationale of cognitive capitalism and that of a knowledge-based and "man for man"-oriented economy which is intrinsically non-mercantile.

The first evolution concerns a formidable process for enforcing and extending intellectual property rights which pushed itself up to the point where the very same boundaries between innovation and invention on the one hand, and basic and applied research on the other hand are being discussed. The patents boom started in the 1980s witnesses such a dynamics.[21] Two main factors strictly entangled to one another can explain the extension of the process of the privatization of knowledge with respect to the crisis of the law of value and to the tendency of the *becoming-rent of profit*.

In the first place, the same movement by which the automation of production reduces the immediate labour of fabrication to "as an, of course, indispensable but subordinate moment, compared to general scientific labour" (Marx 1993b: 700), it simultaneously dislocates the core of the valorisation process in the conceptual phase, wherein the main input is knowledge itself and thus they who control it. Knowledge as such, together with its transformation into a commodity and then into capital, tends to become an entire section of the accumulation process. In this respect, it is sufficient to keep in mind that the management of a portfolio of patents became a key element in the struggle for competition to a several enterprises, often used as to blackmail innovative start-ups and free-software-based projects by the threat of starting a lawsuit for the violation of some intellectual property.

This process exacerbates the contradiction between the logic of *value* and the logic of *wealth*, which is to say, to the under-usage of knowledge due to an excessive reinforcement of intellectual property rights. In fact, the attempt to turn knowledge into a fictitious commodity gives rise to a paradoxical situation whereby the more the exchange value of knowledge artificially increases, the more its use value decreases, precisely because of its privatisation and rarefaction. In other words, cognitive capitalism can only reproduce itself by placing obstacles to the objective conditions and the creative capacities of the agents which constitute the very basis of the development of a knowledge-based economy.

More generally, let us note that when it comes to many goods with a high knowledge content (software, digitalised cultural goods, drugs, etc.), the labour time and thus the costs of reproduction are extremely low and sometimes even close to zero. Therefore, the value-labour time of these commodities would have to translate into a drastic reduction of their price, of the monetary value of production, and of associated profits.

Following the developments of the IT automation, we are closing in towards the fulfilment of the tendency Marx described in the *Fragment on Machines* where he outlined how "as soon as labour in the direct form has ceased to be the great well-spring of wealth, labour time ceases and must cease to be its measure, and hence exchange value [must cease to be the measure] of use value" (1993b: 705).

Thus, capital is increasingly led to develop a new politics for reinforcing intellectual property rights as to foster an increase in prices which artificially leads to the rarefaction of supply, in the attempt to forcibly maintain the primacy of exchange value and safeguard profits. In this way, the very principles upon which the founding fathers of political economy used to justify private property as a mean to struggle against scarcity are being violated. Nowadays, it is the extension of the private sphere which generates scarcity. In some sense, one may thus affirm that the very attempt of forcibly maintain the primacy of the exchange value is actually leading capital to try to emancipate itself from the *law of value/labour time*. An increasingly severe contradiction between the social character of production and the private character of accumulation is thus generated and enforced, manifesting a major issue in order to understand the crisis of the law of value in cognitive capitalism.

The last but not least important manifestation of the exhaustion of the rationality of capital and then of the divorce between *wealth* and *value* is that the crisis of the law of value in cognitive capitalism does not only consist in an artificially created scarcity of resources that are in themselves abundant and free. It is also expressed in the acceleration of a predatory logic of rarefaction of natural non-renewable resources. As a matter of fact, cognitive capitalism does not suppress the productivist rationale of industrial capitalism. It actually redevelops and reinforces it, especially thanks to a subordination of science to capital whereby, as in the case of genetically modified foods, new technologies are at the service of a strategy of standardisation and commodification of life which accentuates the dangers of destroying biodiversity and thus destabilising the ecology of the planet. It is also expressed within the acceleration of that rationale that aims at the predation and rarefaction of non-renewable resources. The intrinsic deviation which divides the unlimited horizon of the accumulation of capital and the finiteness of resources is thus manifested in the ecological crisis which witnesses the harshness of a growing entropy which is threatening the very same survival of the planet.

Conclusions

The whole of the subjective, objective, and ecological contradictions crossing cognitive capitalism—stressing the crisis of the *theory of value/surplus value*—are so acute that they recall a situation Marx described in the fifty-first and penultimate chapter of the third volume of *Capital* when he affirmed:

> The sign that the moment of such a crisis has arrived is that the contradiction and antithesis between, on the one hand, the relations of distribution, hence also the specific historical form of relations of production corresponding to them, and, on the other hand, the productive forces, productivity, and the development of its agents, gains in breadth and depth.
>
> (Marx 1993a: 1024)

Located at the very core of this crisis one can find the exhaustion of the propulsive force of the *theory of value/surplus value*, which goes hand in hand with the crumbling of the traditional boundaries which used to separate the category of the profit from that of the rent. To sum up, two major tendencies allowed us to characterize the connection between these evolutions. The first one refers to the way in which the growth of the cognitive dimension of labour determines the crisis of the industrial norm which, within a real subsumption framework, used to employ abstract labour as a joint tool for measuring and controlling the output of the working activity. Indeed, in the

General Intellect era, the subsumption of labour under capital is becoming formal again. From a Marxist perspective, this means that this does not rest any longer on the capitalistic control of knowledge. As it was at the early beginnings of capitalism itself, the constriction bounding the worker to the wage relationship essentially depends on some financial and institutional mechanisms of "dispossession" of the commons which allow capital to extract surplus value from a co-operation which pre-exists it. Nonetheless, this analogy between the era of a first capitalism based upon formal subsumption and the *General Intellect* epoch entails a major distinction: at the current historical level of complexity of the social division of labour, capital is no longer able to reproduce, with respect to a *widespread intellectuality*, that process of expropriation of artisan knowledges which led from formal to real subsumption.

In this respect, the twofold crisis of measure and control of labour is strictly connected to the tendency of the *becoming-rent of profit*. This concept does not simply apply to the development of some "classical" rentier forms—e.g., patents, financial rent, real-estate rent—wherein the capture of surplus value is executed from a clearly outer position with respect of the realm of production; it entails that this outer position is now typical to a configuration wherein productive capital itself does not play any role as far as the organisation of labour and the knowledge management is concerned. The orchestra-leader figure disappears or becomes more and more useless. Hence, capital can only exercise its hierarchical and despotic functions connected to the valorisation process, most of the times not only fulfilling a useless role but even playing a destabilizing one, undermining some principles that may assure a more efficient coordination of the cognitive working activity. To sum up, profit, like rent, tends to become a pure distributional relationship, given that capital seizes surplus value, performing—in the majority of cases—"no function in the production process, at least not in the normal case" (Marx 1993a: 1023).

The second tendency is linked to the exhaustion of the law of value conceived as the social relationships which employ the logic of commodity as the key and progressive criterion for fostering the production of wealth and use values and, therefore, for implementing the satisfaction of needs. In a knowledge-based economy, the *immediate labour time* necessary to the production of a great deal of commodities and services is an all-time low, which may lead to a drastic fall in the costs of production and therefore to a simultaneous shortage of the correlated profits. As a result, capital, while trying to forcibly maintain the primacy of commodity and the safeguard profits, is brought to the development of some *rentier* mechanisms which rarefy supply, imposing barriers to access the market and thus creating an artificial scarcity of resources. Furthermore, this divorce between value and wealth is not narrowed to those areas where the passage towards an economy of abundance is potentially achievable. It is also manifested through a productivist rationale that leads to the predation of rare resources, while the austerity policies and the "mercantilisation" of welfare institutions jeopardize the most essential conditions of the reproduction of a knowledge-based economy

Finally, we have unambiguously demonstrated that the tendencies characterizing the crisis of the law of value does not imply that labour is no longer the substance and origin of the creation of value and surplus value. They simply entails that the law of surplus value, like the law of exploitation, survives as an empty shell, deprived of what Marx—rightfully or not—believed to be the progressive functions of capital, which is to say its active role in the organisation of labour and in the development of the productive forces as a mean to leap from the *kingdom of necessity to the kingdom of freedom.*

On the contrary, one may affirm that within the great crises interregnum—those historical bifurcations where "the old is dying and the new cannot be born" (Gramsci 1971: 276)—capital tries to escape from the crisis of the law of value simultaneously operating a sort of leap ahead in the fulfilment of its own logic, through an intensification of the times of production—and through the commodification of the whole of social times.

In this respect, cognitive capitalism is not only, as Gorz (2003: 81–82) rightfully affirmed, the way in which capitalism perpetuates itself when its own categories lost their historical coherence, but it represents the exacerbation of capitalism *tout court*: it survives as a *walking dead*, but, paradoxically, it looks like a corpse in optimal health.

Notes

1 In the following text we have chosen to translate this expression with the formula "production of humans for and by humans" to eliminate any connotation of gender.
2 Following a similar line of reasoning, M. Montalban (2012) illustrates the logic which led several economists from the Regulation School to abandon the labour theory of value.
3 For a definition of the theoretical groundings of this second conception see Bellofiore (2004).
4 To be more precise, according to Marx (1991: 467), "early in the period of manufacture, the principle of lessening the labour-time necessary for the production of commodities was consciously formulated and expressed."
5 A viewpoint already marked by A. Bordiga (1976) and P. Naville (1963) in their early readings of *The Fragment on Machines.*
6 In this respect, see also Aglietta (1976).
7 Real, as for natural and non-renewable resources, artificial as in the case of the monopolization of the resource obtained through the reinforcement of property rights.
8 Contrary to what was affirmed by C. Serfati (2011), according to whom the distinction between *property capital* and *functioning capital*—and therefore the distinction between interest and entrepreneurial revenue—is of a purely technical and accounting nature.
9 The analysis of the dual face of the capitalistic process of production and of the organizational functions of capital is developed by Marx in Chapters 5 and 11 of Book I of *Capital.*

10 For a detailed discussion of this concept and its relationship with a hypothesis concerning a superior level of *great crisis* see also Chapter 1.
11 To borrow the canonical definition of K. Arrow (1962). For an in-depth analysis of the crisis of the Arrow and Merton knowledge paradigm, see Chapter 8.
12 On this aspect, see also Chapter 1.
13 For the analysis of the managerial revolution occurred following the crisis of Fordism, see Boltanski and Chiappello (1999) and De Gaulejac and Mercier (2012).
14 This term is a contraction of "*management*" and the French word "*imaginaire.*" It is also labelled *management par l'illusion* (management by illusion).
15 As underlined by Bourboulon (2011), it is extremely significant that one of the most used formula employed in France to synthesize the logic of the new management is "Débrouillez-vous!"
16 For a definition of the commons of knowledge and a more detailed analysis of their dynamics in cognitive capitalism, see Vercellone (2015).
17 For a complete review of this approach, see Cardon and Casilli (2015).
18 For this concept, see Vercellone (2018).
19 For the analysis of these different aspects, see C. Marazzi (2006). It is noteworthy to point out that the centrality of cognitive labour led mainstream economists such as Rajan and Zingales (1998, 2000) to call back into question a conception of the firm based upon its property over material assets.
20 Here conceived in a broader sense than that employed by Kendrick, as the varied ensemble of immaterial assets owned by the firm, composed by human capital, organizational know-how, intellectual property (patents, brand and copyrights), reputation, position within the market, etc.
21 For a detailed analysis of this process in its various aspects, see Chapter 8.

References

Aglietta, A. (1976) *Régulation et crises du capitalisme*, Paris: Calmann Levy.

Arrow, K. J. (1962) *"Economic Welfare and the Allocation of Resources for Invention: The Rate and Direction of Inventive Activity: Economic and Social Factors,"* in National Bureau of Economic Research and R. R. Nelson (eds.), *The Rate and Direction of Inventive Activity: Economic and Social Factors*, Princeton, NJ: Princeton University Press, pp. 609–626.

Babbage, C. (1835) *On the Economy of Machinery and Manufactures*, 4th edn, London: Charles Knight.

Bellofiore, R. (2004) *La teoria marxiana del valore come teoria macroeconomica dello sfruttamento: una rassegna ragionata della letteratura*, Working paper 02/2004. Dipartimento di economia Cognetti de Martiis, Università di Torino, available at http://www.cesmep.unito.it/WP/2004/2_WP_Cesmep.pdf (accessed April 15, 2018).

Berle, A. A. and G. C. Means (1967) *The Modern Corporation and Private Property*, 2nd edn, New York: Harcourt, Brace & World.

Boltanski, L. and E. Chiappello (1999) *Le Nouvel Esprit du capitalisme*, Paris: Gallimard.

Bordiga, A. (1976) "Traiettoria e catastrofe della forma capitalistica nella classica monolitica costruzione teorica del marxismo," in A. Bordiga, *Economia marxista ed economia controrivoluzionaria*, Milan: Iskra, pp. 189–208.

Bourboulon, I. (2011) *Le Livre noir du management*, Montrouge: Bayard.

Boyer, R. (2014) *La Croissance, début de siècle*, Paris: Albin Michel.

Bradford DeLong, J. and L. H. Summers (2002) "The New Economy: Background, Questions, Speculations," *Economic Policies for the Information Age, Federal*

Reserve Bank of Kansas City, available at www.kansascityfed.org/PUBLICAT/SYMPOS/2001/papers/S02delo.pdf (accessed September 25, 2018).

Braudel, F. (1979) *Civilisation matérielle, économie et capitalisme, XVeme–XVIIIeme siècle*, 3 vols., Paris: Armand Colin.

Cardon, D. and A. Casilli (2015) *Qu'est-ce que le digital labor?*Bry-sur-Maene: INA Éditions.

Cardoza, K., J. Basara, L. Cooper, and R. Conroy (2006) "The Power of Intangible Assets: An Analysis of the S&P 500," *Les Nouvelles: The Journal of the Licensing Executives Society*, available at https://www.lesi.org/les-nouvelles/les-nouvelles-online/2006/march-2006/2011/08/08/the-power-of-intangible-assets-an-analysis-of-the-s-p-500 (accessed March 29, 2016).

Centre d'analyse stratégique (2008) "Évaluation et valorisation financière de la propriété intellectuelle: nouveaux enjeux, nouveaux mécanismes,"*La Note de la vieille*, 111: 1–8.

Chandler, A. (1977) *The Visible Hand: The Managerial Revolution in American Business*, Cambridge, Mass: Belknap Press of Harvard University Press.

David, A. and D. Foray (2002) "Une introduction à l'économie et à la société du savoir," *Revue Internationale des Sciences Sociales*, 1(171):13–28.

De Gaulejac, V. and A. Mercier (2012) *Manifeste pour sortir du mal-être au travail*, Paris: Desclé de Bouvier.

Dostaler, G. (1979) *Valeur et prix*, Paris: Maspero.

Engels, F. (1970) "Considerazioni supplementari," in K. Marx, *Il Capitale, libro terzo*, vol. I, Rome: Editori Riuniti, pp. 35–36.

Fumagalli, A. and C. Morini (2009) "La vita messa al lavoro: verso une teoria del valore-vita. Il caso del valore affetto," *Sociologia del lavoro*, 115: 94–115.

Fumagalli, A. and S. Lucarelli (2011) "A Financialized Monetary Economy of Production," *International Journal of Political Economy*, 40(1): 48–68.

Galbraith, J. K. (1974) *La Science économique et l'intérêt général*, Paris: Gallimard.

Gorz, A. (1988) *Métamorphoses du travail, quête du sens: critique de la raison économique*, Paris: Galilée.

Gorz, A. (2003) *L'Immatériel: connaissance, valeur et capital*, Paris: Galilée.

Gorz, A. (2004) "Économie de la connaissance et exploitation des savoirs: entretien avec Y. Moulier-Boutang and C. Vercellone," *Multitudes*, 15: 205–216.

Gramsci, A. (1975) *Quaderni dal carcere*, vol. I, Torino: Einaudi.

Hai HacTran (2003) *Relire "Le Capital,"* 2 vols., Lausanne: Éditions Page Deux.

Halary, I. (2004) "Ressources immatérielles et finance de marché: le sens d'une liaison," Working Paper, Séminaire Capitalisme Cognitif, MATISSE-ISYS, Paris.

Hardt, M. and A. Negri (2011) *Commonwealth*, Cambridge, Mass.: The Belknap Press of Harvard University Press.

Harribey, J. M. (2013) *La Richesse, la valeur et l'inestimable*, Paris: Les Liens qui Libérent.

Hodgskin, T. H. (1922) *Labour Defended against the Claims of Capital*, London: The Labour Publishing Company.

Kendrick, J. W. (1994) "Total Capital and Economic Growth," *Atlantic Economic Journal*, 22(1): 1–18.

Lundvall, B. A. and E. Lorenz (2009) "On the Role of Social Investment in the Learning Economy: A European Perspective," in N. Morel, B. Palier, and J. Palme (eds.), *What Future for Social Investment?*Stockholm: Institute for Futures Studies, pp. 79–97.

Marazzi, C. (2006) "L'Ammortissement du corps-machine," *Multitudes*, 27: 27–36.

Marx, K. (1969) *Theories of Surplus Value*, Moscow: Progress Publisher.

Marx, K. and F. Engels (2007) *Manifesto of the Communist Party*, Radford, VA: Wilder Publications.

Marx, K. (1988) *Economic and Philosophic Manuscripts of 1948 and the Communist Manifesto*, New York: Prometheus.

Marx, K. (1991) *Capital: A Critique of Political Economy*, vol. I, London: Penguin.

Marx, K. (1993a) *Capital: A Critique of Political Economy*, vol. III, London: Penguin.

Marx, K. (1993b) *Grundrisse: Foundations of the Critique of Political Economy*, London: Penguin.

Montalban, M. (2012) "De la place de la théorie de la valeur et de la monnaie dans la théorie de la régulation: critique et synthèse," *Revue de la Régulation*, 12 (autumn): 1–14. Available at http://regulation.revues.org/979 (accessed October 30, 2015).

Napoleoni, C. (1972) *Lezioni sul capitolo Sesto inedito di Marx*, Torino: Boringhieri.

Naville, P. (1963) *Vers l'automatisme social: problèmes du travail et de l'automation*, Paris: Gallimard.

Negri, A. (1979) *Marx oltre Marx*, Milan: Feltrinelli.

Negri, A. (1992) "Valeur-travail: crise et problèmes de reconstruction dans le post-moderne," *Futur Antérieur*, 10: 30–36.

Negri, A. and C. Vercellone (2008) "Le Rapport capital-travail dans le capitalisme cognitif," *Multitudes*, 32(1): 39–50.

Rajan, R. and L. Zingales (1998) "Power in a Theory of the Firm," *Quarterly Journal of Economics*, 113(2): 387–432.

Rajan, R. and L. Zingales (2000) "The Governance of the New Enterprise," in X. Vives (ed.), *Corporate Governance*, Cambridge: Cambridge University Press, pp. 201–232.

Ricardo, D. (1817) *On the Principles of Political Economy and Taxation*, London: John Murray.

Roubine, I. (1972) *Essays on Marx's Theory of Value*, Detroit, MI: Black & Red.

Serfati, C. (2011) "La Logique financiero-rentière des societés transnationale," *European Journal of Economic and Social Systems*, 24(1–2): 153–180.

Smith, A. (1976) *An Inquiry into the Nature and Causes of the Wealth of Nations*, 2 vols., Indianapolis, IN: Liberty Fund.

Sweezy, P. (1942) *Theory of Capitalist Development*, New York: Monthly Review Press.

Taylor, F. W. (1911) *The Principles of Scientific Management*, London and New York: Harper & Brothers.

Terranova, T. (2000) "Free Labor: Producing Culture for the Digital Economy,"*Social Text 63*, 18(2):33–57. Available at http://web.mit.edu/schock/www/docs/18.2terranova.pdf (accessed November 20, 2018).

Tiffon, G. (2013) *La Mise au travail des clients*, Paris: Economica.

Ure, A. (1835) *The Philosophy of Manufactures; or, An Exposition of the Scientific, Moral, and Commercial Economy of the Factory System of Great Britain*, London: C. Knight.

Veltz, P. (2000) *Le Nouveau Monde industriel*, Paris: Gallimard.

Vercellone, C. (2007) "From Formal Subsumption to General Intellect: Elements for a Marxist Reading of the Thesis of Cognitive Capitalism," *Historical Materialism*, 15(1): 16–36.

Vercellone, C. (2008a) "La Thèse du capitalisme cognitif: Une mise en perspective historique et théorique," in G. Colletis and P. Paulré (eds.), *Les Nouveaux Horizons du capitalisme*, Paris: Economica, pp. 71–95.

Vercellone, C. (2008b) The New Articulation of Wages, Rent and Profit in Cognitive Capitalism, Lecture Series, Queen Mary University School of Business and Management, available at www.generation-online.org/c/fc_rent2.htm (accessed October 12, 2018).

Vercellone, C. (ed.) (2015) "Managing the Commons in the Knowledge Economy," *Report D3.2, D-CENT (Decentralized Citizens ENgagement Technologies)*, available at http://dcentproject.eu/wp-content/uploads/2015/07/D3.2-complete-ENG-v2.pdf (accessed 12 January 2019).

Vercellone, C. (ed.) (2018) "Data-Driven Disruptive Commons-Based Models," *Report D2.4 DECODE (DEcentralised Citizens Owned Data Ecosystem)*, available at https://decodeproject.eu/publications/data-driven-disruptive-commons-based-models (accessed 14 January 2019).

Virno, P. (2008) "Forza Lavoro," in *Lessico Marxiano*, Rome: Manifestolibro, pp. 105–116.

Zarifian, P. (1995) *La Nouvelle Productivité*, Paris: L'Harmattan.

3 Twenty theses on contemporary capitalism (bio-cognitve capitalism)

Andrea Fumagalli

Introduction

In this chapter, our aim is twofold. On the one hand, it is an attempt at systematizing a series of reflections and concepts elaborated by a number of studies that appeared in the past decade. This research comes from scholars in different disciplines who identify, even in their internal differences, with a method of analysis rooted in the Italian workerist thought of the 1960s. For this reason, it is a work in progress and has no pretense of being exhaustive.[1] On the other hand, it ambitiously tries to communicate and clarify an issue that has provoked much debate in the past few years, especially in the field of heretic and heterodox thought, that is to say, the analysis of the salient characteristics of the current state of capitalism. From the very title, we formulate a thesis: the contemporary form of capitalism is defined in a univocal way as bio-*cognitive capitalism*. The twenty theses that follow are a means of justifying this definition.

In the past forty years, the current process of capitalist accumulation and valorization has assumed different names: the most common of these, *post-Fordism*, is also the oldest. The term *post-Fordism* became popular during the 1990s, especially through the French *école de la regulation.* [2] The term, however, is not without its ambiguities and diverse interpretations, as are all terms defined in a negative way. Our idea is that with the term *post-Fordism* we define the period, from the 1975 crisis to the early 1990s crisis, during which the process of accumulation and valorization is no longer based on the centrality of Fordist material production, the vertically integrated, large factory. At the same time, in this period, we do not yet possess an alternative paradigm. Unsurprisingly, in the prefix *post-* we express what is no longer there, without underlining what actually appears in the present. The post-Fordist phase is in fact characterized by the conjoined presence of more productive models: from the Japanese Toyotist model of the "just in time" derived from Taylorism[3] to the industrial district model of small enterprises[4] and the development of productive lines that tend to become international according to a hierarchy.[5] Among these models, it is still impossible to identify a hegemonic paradigm.

After the First Gulf War, innovations in the fields of transportation, language, and communication started to gather around a new single paradigm of accumulation and valorization. The new capitalist configuration tends to identify in "knowledge" and "space" (geographic and virtual) as commodities a new foundation for dynamic skills of accumulation. As a consequence, two new dynamic economies of scale are formed, which are the basis for the growth in productivity (or, the source of surplus value): learning economies and network economies. The first are connected to the process of generation and creation of new knowledge (based on new systems of communication and information technologies and today the manipulation and processing of increasing share of data); the second derive from the organizational modalities of each district (territorial networks or system areas), which are no longer used for production and distribution only but increasingly as a vehicle of diffusion (and control) of knowledge and technological progress, the "right" environment in which social cooperation and reproduction can be fostered. We can name this paradigm of accumulation *cognitive capitalism.* [6]

The term *capitalism* designates the permanence, though metamorphic, of the

> fundamental variables of the capitalistic system: the leading role of profit, and the wage system in particular, or more precisely, the different forms of employed labor from which surplus value is extracted. The attribute *cognitive* evidences the new nature of labor, of the sources of valorization and property structure, on which the process of accumulation is founded, and the contradictions that this mutation generates.
>
> (Lebert and Vercellone 2006: 36)

The centrality of learning and network economies, typical of cognitive capitalism, is put into question at the beginning of the new millennium, following the bursting of the Internet economy bubble and its speculations, in March 2000. The new cognitive paradigm alone is unable to protect the socio-economic system from the structural instability that characterizes it. It is also necessary for new liquidity to be directed into the financial markets. The ability of financial markets to generate "value" is tied to the development of "conventions" (speculative bubbles) which can create somewhat homogeneous expectations, thereby pushing the main financial operators to support certain types of financial activities (Orléan 2009). What the Internet economy did in the 1990s was followed in the 2000s by the great attraction to the development of Asian markets (China entered the World Trade Organization in December 2001) and real estate. Today, the focus is mostly on the performance of European welfare. Independently of the dominant convention, contemporary capitalism is always in search of new social and vital circles to absorb and commodify, involving more and more the bare vital faculties of human beings. It is for this reason that in the last few years we have been hearing about *bioeconomy* and *biocapitalism.* [7]

At this point, the reader should clearly understand how the term used in these pages is nothing but the contraction between cognitive capitalism and biocapitalism: *bio-cognitive capitalism* is the phrase that defines contemporary capitalism.

Thesis 1: In bio-cognitive capitalism, the financial markets, knowledge, and relations are the motor of accumulation.

Financial markets are the pulsating heart; knowledge is the brain; relational activities are the nervous system. Bio-cognitive capitalism is a single body, inside of which the "real" sphere cannot be separated from the "financial," nor can the productive sphere be separated from the unproductive, or work-time from life-time, or production from reproduction and consumption.

Thesis 2: In bio-cognitive capitalism, financial markets directly influence and condition the process of accumulation and valorization (Fumagalli and Mezzadra 2010: 237–239)

In a broader sense, financialization marks the definitive passage from *commodity money* to *sign money* (Amato and Fantacci 2009: 65–90). With the complete dematerialization of money (after the Bretton Woods crash in 1971, marking the end of the convertibility of the dollar to gold), financial markets define the social and hierarchic conventions that are able to secure short-term monetary value. At the same time, they leave open the relations of debit and credit, provided sufficient trust is generated in the operators. From this viewpoint, financial markets lubricate the process of accumulation. In the capitalistic system, in fact, there is no accumulation without debt. It is no coincidence that, from the 1990s onward, financial markets have taken care of financing accumulation activities: the liquidity drawn by financial markets rewards the restructuring of production aimed at exploiting knowledge and the control of spaces external to the enterprise. Second, in the presence of surplus value, financial markets have the same role in the current economic system that the Keynesian multiplier (activated by deficit spending) had in industrial-Fordist capitalism. However, unlike the classic Keynesian multiplier, the new financial multiplier leads to a distorted redistribution of revenues. For such multiplier to be operative (> 1), the financial basis (that is, the extension of financial markets) must be constantly growing, and the capital gain must be, on average, higher than the median salary loss. On the other hand, the polarization of revenues increases the risk of debt insolvency, which is the basis of the growth of the very financial foundation, and reduces the median salary.[8] Third, financial markets, forcibly channeling growing portions of work revenues (such as severance indemnity and social security, as well as earnings that, through the social state, turn into institutions for health and public education), substitute in this way the state as a social provider. From this point of view, financial markets represent the privatization of the reproductive sphere of life. Finally, financial markets are the place where today capitalistic valorization is established, that is, the place where the exploitation of social cooperation and of the general intellect is measured by way of the dynamic of stock-market values. As a consequence, profit transforms into rent (see Thesis 3), and financial markets become the place where labor value is determined and transformed into *finance value*. The latter is nothing other than the subjective expression of the expectation of future profits articulated by financial markets, which in this way secure a rent. Financial markets thus exercise biopower (Lucarelli 2010).

Thesis 3: In bio-cognitive capitalism, we register the becoming-rent of profit.[9]

Rent is the main capturing tool of both surplus value and the desocialization/privatization of what is common. The meaning and the key role of this becoming-rent of profit can be appreciated at two levels. On the one hand, this process is evident at the level of the social organization of production and of the distribution of revenues: the criteria underlying the traditional distinction between profit and rent become less and less pertinent. The confusion of the frontiers between rent and profit finds one of its expressions in the way in which financial power remodels the very criteria of company governance under the sole aim of creating value for the shareholder. In cognitive biocapitalism, not only do we witness the final decline of the Weberian entrepreneur (the figure combining the functions of ownership and direction of the firm, who had already partly disappeared in industrial-Fordist capitalism after the marginalist revolution of the 1930s). We also see the irreversible crisis of the Galbraithian techno-structure, legitimized in its role by the planning of innovation and the organization of labor. The new governance of today's companies is increasingly founded on a type of management whose principal competence is exercising financial and speculative functions while delegating to employed labor the real functions of the organization of production.

On the other hand, the competitiveness of a company is largely dependent not on internal economies but on external ones, that is to say on the ability to capture productive surpluses that come from the cognitive resources of a territory. Capital, then, does benefit freely from the collective knowledge of society, as if it were a "gift of nature." From this point of view, the becoming-rent of profit takes the form of a privatization of what is common,[10] gaining revenues from the creation of a scarcity of resources that is only artificial. It is the common that links together, in a single logic, the rent coming from real-estate speculation and financial rent, which, since the beginning of the 1980s, played a major role in fiscal crisis and the dismantling of welfare-state institutions, as a result of the privatization of currency and public debt. The becoming-rent of profit derives, then, from the attempt at privatizing knowledge and life (*bios*). This is achieved thanks to a politics promoting the reinforcement of intellectual property rights so that the cost of numerous commodities is kept artificially high, although their reproduction costs are extremely low or even close to zero.

Thesis 4: In bio-cognitive capitalism, value production is no longer founded on material production alone.

Productive activity is increasingly based on immaterial elements, that is to say, on intangible "raw materials," which are very hard to measure and quantify and which come directly from the utilization of the relational, sentimental, and cerebral faculties of human beings. The process of valorization loses, in this way, the measuring unit usually connected to material production. This measure used to be somewhat defined according to the necessary amount of labor needed for the production of commodities, measurable on the basis of the tangibility of production and the necessary time for production. With the advent of cognitive capitalism, valorization tends to graft itself onto different forms of labor, which go beyond the official work-time and coincide more and more with the whole lifetime. Today, the value of labor at the basis of biocapitalistic accumulation is also the value of knowledge, of affects and relationships; it is the value of the imaginary and the symbolic (cf. Thesis 15).

Thesis 5: In bio-cognitive capitalism, value production is no longer founded on a homogeneous, standardized scheme for the organization of labor, independently of the type of goods produced.

The activity of production is carried out with different organizational modes, which are characterized by a network structure, thanks to the development of technologies for linguistic communication and transportation. What follows is a disruption of the traditional and unilateral hierarchic form typical of the factory. This is substituted by hierarchic structures activated on the territory along sub-supply production chains and characterized by relations of cooperation and/or control.

Thesis 6: In bio-cognitive capitalism, the division of labor takes on itself cognitive characteristics and therefore is based on the differential success and use of different form of knowledge.

Knowledge can be divided into four levels: (1) *information*; (2) *codified knowledge*; (3) *tacit knowledge*; and (4) *culture* (or *systemic knowledge*), characterized by unilateral relations of dependence. *Information* is the basic level of knowledge that is more and more incorporated into the machine element. *Codified knowledge* is a specialized knowledge (a know-how) that derives from tacit knowledge but that is transmitted through standardized procedures, with machines as intermediary, as a consequence of which its bearer can be substituted at any moment, having no contractual power. *Tacit knowledge* can derive from personal learning processes, or from specific investments in R&D (thanks to intellectual property rights); furthermore, at least until codified, it can only be transmitted through a human being, thus possibly generating forms of *enclosures.* Those who possess tacit knowledge, which is relevant for the productive process, therefore have a high contractual power and define the hierarchical structure of labor and production. However, tacit knowledge, if relevant, is destined to transform into codified knowledge, sooner or later, and thus lose value. Lastly, *culture* is the set of knowledges that allows one to hold the *intellectual function*, that is to say, the ability to act critically and creatively, not immediately subsumed to the logic of biocapitalist valorization. As a consequence, culture is dangerous for the reproducibility of the socio-economic system, and it constitutes also a surplus that exceeds control.

Thesis 7: In cognitive biocapitalism, the condition of the labor force goes hand in hand with mobility and the predominance of individual contracting (precarity).

This derives from the fact that nomadic individualities are put to work, and the primacy of private rights over workers' rights brings about a transformation of the contribution of individualities, especially if characterized by cognitive, relational, and affective activities, into contractual individualism. Work relations based on precarious conditions, that is to say, the temporal limit and spatial mobility of labor, are the basic paradigm in which the relationship between capital and labor takes place. Precarity then becomes a structural, existential, and generalized condition.

Thesis 8: In bio-cognitive capitalism, the accumulation process is founded on the exploitation of two new types of scale economies: the dynamic learning processes and the dynamic network processes.

If knowledge is the basis of accumulation, it becomes unavoidable to analyze how its exchange and diffusion affect the dynamics of productivity. The peculiarity of bio-cognitive capitalism is its ability to enlarge both knowledge-learning processes and network economies. Learning economies depend on the degree of *cumulativeness, opportunity* and *appropriability* (Nelson and Winter 1982). Here, *opportunity* is defined as the expected rate of profit and, therefore, the higher the expected profit in adopting a new technology, the higher is the speed of its diffusion. *Cumulativeness* and *appropriability* represent the capacity of new knowledge to generate further innovation while avoiding the possibility of its imitation, thanks to the existence of intellectual property rights. Network economies depend on the level of income and positive externalities. When learning economies are constrained by intellectual property rights, we shall see that the consequence is that the greater the degree of *appropriability* of knowledge, the smaller becomes its capacity of diffusion—affecting, *de facto*, its ability to positively influence the associated productivity.[11] While it is during the learning process that the generation of knowledge occurs, network economies define the way in which the produced knowledge is diffused. In a social system geared around innovation and production, investment policies depend upon R&D and "learning by doing" strategies and processes. In cognitive biocapitalism, the impact of new information and communication technologies based on computer science, micro-electronics and the new organizational productive changes (e.g., just-in-time, zero stock) have sped up the "learning by doing" processes, spreading them well beyond the firm. At the same time, part of the R&D process unfolds within territories each having one or more specific competencies. Where to locate economic activities is determined mainly by the search on the part of the firm for advantages in the development of its competencies (Mouhoud 2006). Consequently, the productivity entailed by the exchange of knowledge cannot be assimilated to material productivity.

Thesis 9: An essential character of bio-cognitive capitalism is the dematerialization of fixed capital and the transfer of its productive and organizational functions to the living body of labor power.

This process lies at the origin of one of the paradoxes of new capitalism: the contradiction between the rise in importance of cognitive work as a lever for the production of wealth and, at the same time, the devaluation of that work as far as salary and the profession are concerned. This paradox is inherent in Marazzi's definition of "the anthropogenetic character of contemporary capitalistic production," underlined in one of his essays.[12] In bio-cognitive capitalism, the living being contains within itself the functions of both fixed and variable capital, that is, of both the material and machinery forms of labor belonging to the past and of the living labor of the present: *bios*.

Thesis 10: In bio-cognitive capitalism, the separation between abstract labor and concrete labor is not as clear as it was in industrial-Fordist capitalism.

First of all, what Marx used to call "concrete labor," or labor producing use value, can be renamed today *creative labor*.[13] This term allows us to better understand the cerebral contribution inherent in such activity, while the term "concrete labor," though being conceptually its synonym, refers more to the realm of "making" than to that of "thinking," with a closer allusion to craftsmanship proper.

Thesis 11: In bio-cognitive capitalism, we see more and more an interpenetration between place of production and productive networks.

Space, be it geographic or virtual, becomes a place of production no longer characterized by a unique and self-centered presence but rather by an ensemble of polycentric formal and informal networks. Production is the result of a flux structure, and such flux is always more immaterial or redesigned and directed by immaterial networks, especially when the commodities produced are material. A flux structure presupposes the centrality of linguistic networks of communication and the development of social cooperation. Such cooperation involves both the transmission of symbols and the logistical transportation of commodities and goods. Within this space, however, cooperation, which is far from being horizontal, develops along new trajectories of spatial partition of production, and cognitive division of labor. Reticular production—the network—is, in other words, a molecular space, and as such it is individualized, characterized by individual relations that most of the time produce cooperation in the end, but are not necessarily cooperative with one another.

Thesis 12: In bio-cognitive capitalism, commodities have new meanings.

The value of commodities is no longer definable only along the lines of necessary "work-time". To that value, which does not disappear, another value is added, which derives from the degree of social symbolicity [*simbolicità*] that the commodity contains. The symbolic value of commodities increases in direct relation to their level of immateriality. It is in this field that the relation between production and realization (consumption) of commodities is played out. Not only does consumption realize the value of commodities, but it valorizes them at the same time (Arvidsson 2005).

Thesis 13: In bio-cognitive capitalism, life itself becomes value.

The labor-value theory becomes a life theory of value (Fumagalli and Morini 2011). This happens through the valorization of the differences that individuals possess. These differences, in their uniqueness, make possible the relational activities that are the basis of the social cooperation producing *general intellect*. Beside the general differences based on race, gender, and so on, we need to add up differences *tout court*, which are valorized without any relation to the anthropological characteristics that define them. What is now starting to be segmented and divided are cerebral differences, that is to say, individualities. Spatial and biologic differences, gender and race in particular, can at most be instruments for the immediate disciplining of the social body. The preoccupying emerging tendency, however, is the constitution of a human subjectivity characterized by the contradictory conflict between creative actions and cerebral standardization: the creation of a sort of bionic being, capable of managing the anthropogenetic process of production. These elements suggest a world where individuality is erased but individualism is exalted. Bio-cognitive capitalism is bioeconomic production: it is *bioeconomy.*

Thesis 14: In bio-cognitive capitalism, differences become value (Morini 2013; see Thesis 13).

The traditional binary dichotomies inherited from industrial-Fordist capitalism are no longer topical. We are witnessing the overcoming of the *separation between life-time and work-time.* As soon as work activities use the vital faculties of individuals, it becomes impossible to define a temporal barrier between work time and non-work time. Even if this distinction can nominally continue to exist on a formal-juridical level, the difference between life and work no longer exists in reality, and this is also due to the new language and communication technologies. Life appears completely *subsumed* into work. We are also witnessing the overcoming of the *separation between workplace and life space.* The multiple forms of bio-labor are in fact *nomadic labor*, where mobility is a primary requisite. This phenomenon leads to the definition of *non-places of work*, as opposed to classic forms of *domestication.* In this case, indeed, we should not talk about a coincidence between workplace and life space but rather about the expropriation of the workplace, and of all possible consequences that this process might have on work identity. We are witnessing the overcoming of the *separation between production and reproduction.* This is the first consequence of life becoming work. When we talk about life, we do not only mean it as directly finalized to productive activity but also to the social reproduction of life itself—a clear example of which is the almost exclusively female caretaking work. But, not only: Social reproduction is going to have a preeminent role in the present valorization when it has to do with welfare, health, and education conditions (Morini 2013). Having said this, we can state that the erasure of this distinction implies the partial overcoming of the specific gender difference and poses the question of *differences tout court* (Morini 2013). In conclusion, we are witnessing the overcoming of the *separation between production, circulation, and consumption.* In bio-cognitive capitalism, the act of consumption is, at the same time, a participation of public opinion, an act of communication, and self-marketing. In this sense, it allows further valorization of the commodities (see Thesis 10).

Thesis 15: In bio-cognitive capitalism, value creation is based *pre-eminently* on the process of expropriation of the general intellect for private accumulation.

The *general intellect* is the outcome of basic social cooperation: it allows the passage from *tacit* knowledge to *codified* knowledge as social knowledge. This passage is regulated by the evolution of the juridical forms of intellectual property rights. Such a property is thereby added to that of the means of production, giving private property the control of the process of generation (intellectual property) and diffusion of knowledge (ownership of the means of production). Since the exploitation of the *general intellect* implies the valorization of the very existence of individuals, the process of value creation is no longer limited to the workday but extends to include the entire human existence. This means that the measure of exploitation is not really the time of the workday generating *surplus work* but rather that part of the life span that is necessary to generate tacit knowledge—and hence social knowledge—which is then expropriated by the process of accumulation. The effective and direct forms with which the expropriation of the *general intellect* creates value can be different. Among these, the valorization of commodities through the *branding* process is particularly significant. The value of commodities increases together with the increase of their symbolic meaning and of their ability to create an imaginary which is shared by consumers. Even in this case, surplus value originates from totally immaterial elements created by behavioral conventions and by shared relational activities, just as happens for the financial markets. If private ownership of the means of production implies partly stealing the workday and allowing for the generation of surplus work, private intellectual property is then the theft of social knowledge understood as *commonwealth* [*bene comune*]. In bio-cognitive capitalism, creation of value happens through the expropriation of the "common."[14]

Thesis 16: In bio-cognitive capitalism, value creation is based *pre-eminently* on the process of expropriation of the social (re)production for private accumulation.

One of the primary elements for the constitution of commonwealth, beyond the general intellect, is the social reproduction. It is the result of the (re)productive commonwealth, generated not only by the care work but by the same welfare, in a broader sense. After the dismantling of the public welfare system, as it was known after the Second World War period, today, welfare is becoming a "mode of production,"[15] that is, the source of a direct capitalistic valorization. Social reproduction at the same time is a paradigmatic representation of the potential power of the commonwealth and of its expropriation, through privatization and gender discrimination.

Thesis 17: In bio-cognitive capitalism, basic income is the remuneration for work.

The idea of basic income is centered on the concept of "remuneration" or "compensation" and not of support or assistance (subsidies, transfer payments, etc.). The logic that justifies its existence is then completely opposed to the doxastic interpretation of the current situation, that is, to measures which would guarantee a continuity of revenue in a temporary, conditioned way.[16] In the present context of bio-cognitive capitalism, wealth is divided between those whose life becomes value (all residents regardless of citizenship, etc.), on the one hand, and all those (much less) who create value from the private appropriation of common goods [*beni comuni*] (exploitation of intellectual property rights, of the territory, of financial flux, etc.), or who profit from productive and service activities. As a consequence, basic income is by definition *unconditioned* and *perpetual* (for the duration of one's life).In other words, basic income is nothing other, today, than the equivalent of salary in Fordist times (Fumagalli 2009).

Thesis 18: In bio-cognitive capitalism, the most adequate structure of welfare is the commonfare, or welfare of the common (General Intellect 2018).

The welfare of the common is based on two important concepts. On the one hand, the guarantee of a continuity of unconditioned revenue, disregarding working conditions, professional, or citizenship status. This is complementary to any other form of direct revenue, as compensation for the productive social cooperation that forms the basis of value creation, currently expropriated for private rent and profit. On the other hand, access to common material and immaterial goods that allows full participation in social life by way of the free fruition of common natural/environmental goods (water, air, environment) and immaterial common goods (knowledge, mobility, socialization, currency, primary social services).

Thesis 19: In bio-cognitive capitalism, the trade unions' keyword "right to work" should be changed into "right to choose work."

We are witnessing an ethical overturning of how we conceive of actual work activity. If in industrial-Fordist capitalism the right to work is the foundation of many national constitutions (the Italian first of all) as well as the first objective of union struggle as a pass to revenue stability and the enjoyment of civil rights, in cognitive biocapitalism, insofar as life itself is productive, the necessity of work has largely taken up a function of blackmailing and control of the actual work activity and is increasingly less relevant to accumulation. From this point of view, capital tends to reach "autonomy," even though it still depends on the social connections that are inherent in the relationship between labor and capital. In contrast, the right to choose one's work opens the path to autonomous work, and for this reason this objective is not compatible with the current capitalistic valorization or subsumed by it. In other words, if in industrial-Fordist capitalism the right to work was, on the one hand, functional to the process of accumulation, while, on the other, it represented the basic condition for the right to struggle, in bio-cognitive capitalism the right to choose one's work is uniquely the right of subversion.

Thesis 20: There is no space for an institutional politics of reform able to reduce the structural instability characterizing bio-cognitive capitalism.

No new *new deal* is possible. And this is increasingly true the more we seem to detect measures that favor a re-stabilizing of the process of accumulation. These measures promote a salary regulation based on the proposition of *basic income* and a productive ability founded on free circulation of knowledge. These proposals, from a purely theoretical and economic point of view, could have the effect of exploiting the economies of learning in a better way (a continuity of revenue increments the ability and intensity of learning). They could also better exploit network economies (the free circulation of knowledge augments their diffusion and valorisation). As a consequence, they could compensate for the structural instability deriving from the distorted effects of financialization on productive activity and revenue distribution. In any case, these measures would undermine the very nature of the capitalist system, that is to say, the necessity of work, the blackmailing allowed by differences in revenues as an instrument of domination of a class over another, and the principle of private ownership of the means of production (machines yesterday, knowledge today). In other words, we can conclude that in bio-cognitive capitalism a possible social Keynesian compromise, one adequate to the characteristics of the new process of accumulation, is possible only in theory, but could not be carried out politically *sic rebus stantibus*. A real reformist politics that can guarantee structural stability of the paradigm of bio-cognitive capitalism (which would tend to individuate a form of mediation between labor and capital that is satisfying for both, without paving the way to the overcoming of this very economic system) cannot exist. Let us clarify this point: a possible social compromise based on *basic income* and the free diffusion of knowledge and other common goods undermines the basis, the real foundations of the capitalistic economic system, that is, the necessity of work to live (hence its subaltern condition), and private property as a source of accumulation. Such compromise is not possible, unless it is imposed by force (Fumagalli and Negri 2008).

Acknowledgments

This chapter has been already published on *Angelaki: Journal of Theoretical Humanities*, vol. 16, 2011, pp. 7–17, under the title: “Twenty Theses on Contemporary Capitalism (Cognitive Biocapitalism).”

Notes

1 The twenty theses presented here are pre-eminently of a socio-economic nature, and as such they are incomplete. There is no explicit reference, for instance, to the evolution of the structure of ownership (juridical analysis) or the theme of the *common* as a way of overcoming the public–private dichotomy. The very aspect of international relations and the end of the economic hegemony of the United States,

with the consequent shift of the economic-financial center to the East (China and India, primarily) is not treated with due detail.

2 As M. Turchetto reminds us: "The origin of the notion of postfordism does not lie in orthodox Marxism or Workerism. These two currents of thought imported the term and its correspondent definition from France, adapting them to their conceptual apparatus. The copyright of postfordism belongs in fact to the French Ècole de la Régulation" (see Turchetto 1999: 5). One of the first authors to use the term "post- Fordism" was the English geographer A. Amin (1994). Within the Regulation School, see Jessop (1995); Lipietz (1997); Boyer and Durand (1998). As far as the Italian debate is concerned, the first text to use the term post-Fordism was Bologna and Fumagalli (1997). See also Rullani and Romano (1998) and the already quoted critical text by Turchetto.

3 See, among others, Ohno (1995); Bonazzi (1993); Revelli (1995); Coriat (1991).

4 See Priore and Sabel (1984); Brusco (1989); Becattini (2000). For a critical analysis, see Lazzarato et al. (1993), Fumagalli (1996, 1997).

5 See Palloix (1979, 1982); Bertin (1985).

6 This term originated in France in the early 2000s from the research of the Laboratoire Isys-Matisse, Maison des Sciences Économiques, Université de Paris I, La Sorbonne, under the direction of B. Paulré, and it is diffused by the journal *Multitudes* with very heterogeneous texts by Corsani, Lazzarato, Moulier-Boutang, Negri, Rullani, Vercellone, and others. On this topic, see also Paulré (2000); Azais, Corsani, and Dieuaide (2001); Moulier-Boutang (2002); Vercellone (2003); Corsani et al. (2004). For a more recent analysis, see Vercellone (2006); Fumagalli (2007); and Moulier-Boutang (2007). See also the monographic issue "Le Capitalisme cognitif: Apports et perspectives" of the *European Journal of Economic and Social Systems* 20 (1) (2007), edited by Fumagalli and Vercellone, with contributions by Arvidsson, Cassi, Corsani, Dieuaide, Lucarelli, Monnier, and Paulré, as well as by the editors.

7 The terms *bioeconomy* and *biocapitalism* are very recent. The concept of bioeconomy was introduced by Fumagalli (2004, 2005, 2007). For an interesting analysis of the concept of bioeconomy, see also Chicchi (2008); and Bazzicaluppo (2006). The term *biocapitalism* was coined by Codeluppi (2008). See also Morini (2010).

8 On these topics, for a deeper analysis, see Chapter 6 of this book.

9 See Negri and Vercellone (2007) and Chapter 2 in this book. See also Marazzi (2010), especially Chapter 3.

10 For a discussion of the concept of the "common," see Hardt and Negri (2009); Fumagalli (2017), Vercellone et al. (2017).

11 This argument can be presented in terms of tacit and codified knowledge; see Malerba and Orsenigo (2000).

12 See Marazzi (2005). Here is the complete quotation that defines the concept of anthropogenetic model of production: "A model of production of man through man, in which the possibility of cumulative and endogenous growth is due, above all, to the development of the education sector (investment in human capital), the health sector (demographic evolution, biotechnologies) and the cultural sector (innovation, communication, creativity)."

13 J. Halloway writes the following: "The center of class struggle is located here: it is a struggle between creative action and abstract labor. In the past, we always thought of class struggle as a struggle between labor and capital, thus understanding labor as abstract, wage-earning labor. As a consequence, the working class was defined as the class of wage-earners. This is wrong. Wage-earning labor and capital are mutually completing, the former being a stage of the latter. Doubtlessly, there is a conflict between wage-earning labor and capital, but it is rather superficial: a conflict on salary levels, on work conditions, on the length of the work day. All these things are important, but they presuppose the existence of

capital. The real threat to capital does not come from abstract labor, but from use-value labor or creative action, because it is the latter that is radically opposed to capital, that is, to its own abstraction. Creative action says 'No, we will not let capital control us; we need to do what we think is necessary or desirable'." See Halloway (2006).

14 I cannot develop here an in-depth analysis of the theme of the "common." On this topic, see Hardt and Negri (2000, 2007). See also Fumagalli (2017); Vercellone et al. (2017).

15 Vercellone et al.(2017).

16 Such as, for instance, the French RSA and analogous apparatuses (like the recent law on citizens' income in Italy), which simply function as social shock absorbers and promote the return to work.

References

Amato, M. and L. Fantacci (2009) *Fine della finanza*, Rome: Donzelli.

Amin, A. (1994) *Post-Fordism: A Reader*, Oxford: Blackwell.

Arvidsson, A. (2005) *Brands: Meaning and Value in Media Culture*, London and New York: Routledge.

Azaïs, C., A. Corsani, and P. Dieuaide (eds.) (2001) *Vers un capitalisme cognitive: entre mutations du travail et territoires*, Paris: L'Harmattan.

Bazzigaluppo, L. (2006) *Il governo delle vite: biopolitica ed economia*, Bari and Rome: La Terza.

Becattini, G. (2000) *Distretti industriali e sviluppo locale*, Turin: Bollati Boringhieri.

Bertin, G. (1985) *Multinationales et propriété industrielle:le contrôle de la tecnologie mondiale*, Paris: Presses Universitaires de France.

Bologna, S. and A. Fumagalli (1997) *Il lavoro autonomo di seconda generazione: Scenari del postfordismo in Italia*, Milan: Feltrinelli.

Bonazzi, G. (1993) *Il tubo di cristallo: Modello giapponese e fabbrica integrata alla Fiat*, Bologna: Il Mulino.

Boyer, R. and J.-P. Durand (1998) *L'Après-fordisme*, Paris: Syros.

Brusco, S. (1989) *Piccole imprese e distretti industriali*, Turin: Rosemberg.

Chicchi, F. (2008) "Bioeconomia: ambienti e forme della mercificazione del vivente," in A. Amendola, L. Bazzicaluppo, F. Chicchi, and A. Tucci (eds.), *Biopolitica, bioeconomia e processi di soggettivazione*, Macerata: Quodlibet, pp. 143–158.

Codeluppi, V. (2008) *Il biocapitalismo: Verso lo sfruttamento integrale di corpi, cervelli ed emozioni*, Turin: Bollati Boringhieri.

Coriat, B. (1991) *Penser a'l'invers*, Paris: Bourgois.

Corsani, A., P. Dieuaide, M. Lazzarato, J. M. Monnier, Y. Moulier-Boutang, B. Paulré, and C. Vercellone (2004) *Le Capitalisme cognitif comme sortie de la crise du capitalisme industriel:un programme de recherche*, Communication au Forum de la Régulation, Paris, Ronétypé, Isys-Matisse, URM 85-95 CNRS-Université de Paris 1, unpublished.

De Marchi, E., G. La Grassa, and M. Turchetto (1999) *Oltre il fordismo: Continuità e trasformazioni nel capitalismo contemporaneo*, Milan:Unicopli.

Fumagalli, A. (1996) "Lavoro e piccolo impresa nell'accumulazione flessibile in Italia," Part 1, *Altreragioni*, 5: 11–28.

Fumagalli, A. (1997) "Lavoro e piccolo impresa nell'accumulazione flessibile in Italia," Part 2, *Altreragioni*, 6: 127–148.

Fumagalli, A.(2004) "Conoscenza e bioeconomia,"*Filosofia e Questioni Pubbliche*, IX(1): 141–161.

Fumagalli, A. (2005) "Bioeconomics, Labour Flexibility and Cognitive Work: Why Not Basic Income?" in G. Standing (ed.), *Promoting Income Security as a Right: Europe and North America*, London: Anthem, pp. 337–350.

Fumagalli, A. (2007) *Bioeconomia e capitalismo cognitivo: Verso un nuovo paradigma di accumulazione*, Rome: Carocci.

Fumagalli, A. (2008) "Trasformazione del lavoro e trasformazioni del welfare: precarieta' e welfare del comune (commonfare) in Europa," in P. Leon and R. Realfonzo (eds.), *L'economia della precarieta'*, Rome: Manifestolibri, pp. 159–174.

Fumagalli, A. (2009) "Per una nuova interpretazione della teoria del basic income," in Basic Income Network (ed.), *Reddito per tutti. Un'utopia concreta per l'era globale*, Rome: Manifestolibri, pp. 125–140.

Fumagalli, A. (2017) *Economia politica del commune*, Rome: Derive Approdi.

Fumagalli, A., and C. Morini (2011) "Life Put to Work: Towards a Life Theory of Value," *Ephemera*, 1(3–4): 234–252.

Fumagalli, A., and C. Vercellone (eds.) (2007) "Le Capitalisme cognitif: apports et perspectives," *European Journal of Economic and Social Systems*, 20(1).

Fumagalli, A., and S. Mezzadra (eds.) (2010) *Crisis in the Global Economy: Financial Markets, Social Struggles and New Political Scenarios*, Cambridge, MA: Semiotext(e).

Fumagalli, A. and T. Negri (2008) "John Maynard Keynes, Capitalismo Cognitivo, Basic Income, No Copyright: e' possibile un nuovo 'New Deal'?" in *Quaderni di Ricerca del Dipartimento di Economia Politica e Metodi Quantitativi*, University di Pavia, no. 211.

General Intellect (2018) "Commonfare or the Welfare of the Commonwealth," in I. Gloerich, G. Lovink, and P. de Vries (eds.), *MoneyLabReader #2: Overcoming the Hype*, Amsterdam: Institute of Net Cultures, pp. 243–251.

Halloway, J. (2006) "Noi siamo la crisi del lavoro astratto," intervention at the UniNomade seminar, Bologna, May 11–12, manuscript.

Hardt, M. and T. Negri (2000) *Empire*, Cambridge, MA: Harvard University Press.

Hardt, M. and T. Negri (2009) *Commonwealth*, Cambridge, MA: Harvard University Press.

Jessop, B. (1995) "The Regulation Approach: Governance and Post-Fordism," *Economy and Society*, Oxford: Blackwell.

Lazzarato, M., Y. Moulier-Boutang, A. Negri, and G. Santilli (1993) *Des Enterprises pas comme les autres*, Paris: Publisud.

Lebert, D., and C. Vercellone (2006) "Il ruolo della conoscenza nella dinamica di lungo periodo del capitalismo: l'ipotesi del capitalismo cognitivo" in C. Vercellone (ed.), *Capitalismo cognitivo*, Rome: Manifestolibri, pp.13–36.

Lipietz, A. (1997) "The Post-Fordist World: Labor Relations, International Hierarchy and Global Ecology," *Review of International Political Economy*, 4(1): 1–41.

Lucarelli, S. (2010) "Financialization as Biopower," in A. Fumagalli and S. Mezzadra, (eds.), *Crisis in the Global Economy: Financial Markets, Social Struggles and New Political Scenarios*, Cambridge, MA: Semiotext(e), pp. 119–138.

Malerba, F. and L. Orsenigo (2000) "Knowledge, Innovative Activities and Industrial Evolution," *Industrial and Corporate Change*, 9(2): 289–314.

Marazzi, C. (2005) "Capitalismo digitale e modello antropogenetico del lavoro. L'ammortamento del corpo-macchina," in J. L. Laville, C. Marazzi, M. La Rosa, and F. Chicchi (eds.), *Reinventare il lavoro*, Rome: Sapere 2000, pp. 107–126.

Marazzi, C. (2010) *The Violence of Financial Capitalism*, Cambridge, MA: Semiotext(e).

Morini, C. (2010) *Per amore o per forza. Femminilizzazione del lavoro e biopolitiche del corpo*, Verona: Ombre Corte.

Morini, C. (2013) "Social Reproduction as a Paradigm of the Common: Reproduction Antagonism, Production Crisis," in O. Augustin and C. Ydesen (eds.), *Post-Crisis Perspectives*, Frankfurt and New York: Peter Lang, pp. 83–98.
Mouhoud, E. M. (2006) "Global Geography of Post-Fordism Knowledge and Polarisation," in B. Coriat, P. Petit, and G. Schméder (eds.), *The Hardship of Nations*, Cheltenham and Northampton: Elgar, pp. 75–92.
Moulier-Boutang, Y. (2002) *L'Eta' delcapitalismo cognitivo*, Verona: Ombre Corte.
Moulier-Boutang, Y. (2007) *Le Capitalisme cognitif: Comprendre la nouvelle grande transformation et ses enjeux*, Paris: Éditions Amsterdam.
Negri, A. and C. Vercellone (2007) "Il rapporto capitale/lavoro nel capitalismo cognitivo," *Posse*, November.
Nelson, R., and S. Winter (1982) *An Evolutionary Theory of Technical Change*, Cambridge, MA: The Belknap Press of Harvard University Press.
Ohno, T. (1995) *Toyota Production System: Beyond Large-Scale Production*, New York: Productivity.
Orléan, A. (2009) *Del'euphorie à la panique: Penser la crise financière*, Paris: Rue d'Ulm.
Palloix, C. (1979) *L'Economia mondiale e le multinazionali*, vol. I, Milan: Jaca Book.
Palloix, C. (1982) *L'Economia mondiale e le multinazionali*, vol. II, Milan: Jaca Book.
Paulré, B. (2000) "De la New Economy au capitalisme cognitif," *Multitudes*, 2 (May–June): 25–42.
Priore, M., and C. Sabel (1984) *The Second Industrial Divide: Possibilities for Prosperity*, New York: Basic Books.
Revelli, M. (1995) "Economia e modello sociale nel passaggio tra fordismo e toyotismo," in P. Ingrao and R. Rossanda (eds.), *Appuntamenti di fine secolo*, Rome: Manifestolibri, pp. 161–224.
Rullani, E., and L. Romano (1998) *Il Postfordismo: Idee per il capitalismo prossimo*, Milan: Etas Libri.
Turchetto, M. (1999) "Fordismo e post fordismo: Qualche dubbio su un'analisi un po' troppo consolidata," in \o "Edoardo De Marchi" E. De Marchi, G. La Grassa, and M. Turchetto (eds.), *Oltre il fordismo: Continuità e trasformazioni nel capitalismo contemporaneo*, Milan: Unicopli, pp. 6–41.
Vercellone, C. (ed.) (2003) *Sommes-nous sortis du capitalisme industriel?*Paris: La Dispute.
Vercellone, C. (ed.) (2006) *Capitalismo cognitivo*, Rome: Manifestolibri.
Vercellone, C., A. Giuliani, F. Brancaccio, and P. Vattimo (2017) *Il Comune come modo di produzione: Per una critica dell'economia politica dei beni comuni*, Verona: Ombre Corte.

4 New form of exploitation in bio-cognitive capitalism

Towards life subsumption

Andrea Fumagalli

The concept of subsumption beyond formal and real

With the crisis of the Fordist paradigm, that is the crisis of *the real subsumption* based on material production, a transition starts to the present day, where we see a shift from the production of money by means of commodities (M-C-M′) to the production of money by means of knowledge and relational activities (C[k]): (M-C[k]-M′), with structural effects on the mode of production and on the valorisation process (*bio-cognitive capitalism*).

We are entering a new phase of *subsumption* of labor to capital, where at the same time *formal subsumption* and *real subsumption* tend to merge and feed off one each other.

Today we can still talk of *formal subsumption* of labor to capital when labour activity refers to the ability and to relational learning processes that the individual worker holds on the basis of his experience of life. These are skills that are partially completed in a period prior to time of their use for the production of exchange value. The learning and the relationship, initially, arise as use values, such as tools and manual skills of the artisans of the first pre-Tayloristic stage of capitalist, are then "salarized,"*obtorto collo*, [1] and *formally subsumed* in the production of exchange value.

Mass education and the development of a diffuse intellectuality make the educational system a central site for the crisis of the Fordist wage relation. The key role attributed to the theme of the development of a "socialised and free" sector of education in the conflicts concerning the control of "intellectual powers of production" is, therefore, an essential element of Marx's elaboration of the notion of the general intellect. The establishment of a diffuse intellectuality is configured as the necessary historical condition, even if, in the *Grundrisse*, this reference is implicit and, in some cases, concealed by a dialectical approach to the evolution of the division of labour that privileges the analysis of structural changes instead of the institutions and the subjects which could have originated these transformations.[2]

Unlike Marx, the *general intellect* is not fixed in machinery, it is not just "growth of fixed capital" but today is more and more dependent on living labour, i.e. the variable capital.[3] As well argued by Marazzi, the *bio-cognitive capitalism* tends to be seen as an anthropogenetic model of production and accumulation:

> The metamorphosis toward the capitalist anthropogenetic model or, if you prefer, the "biopolitical turning point" of the economy, has a precise amount reflected in the evolution of employment of the labor force. Over the past decade the secular decline of the manufacturing sector compared to the service sector accelerates. This is not only a decrease in the number of industrial activity for increases in population (a phenomenon that has been going on since the beginning of the 1990s), it is a decline in absolute terms, since 1996, which in United States, England and Japan is equivalent to a reduction of one-fifth of jobs and, in Europe, at an average net loss of 5%. [...] The difficulties, which we encounter in analyzing these trends in the labour market, indirectly confirm that the emerging model is an anthropogenetic paradigm, a model in which growth factors are in fact directly attributable to human activity, to his communication, relational, creative and innovative skills.
>
> (Marazzi 2005:112)

The valorisation process works by exploiting the capabilities of learning, relationship, and social (re)production of human beings. It is in effect a kind of primitive accumulation, which is able to put to labour and to value those activities that in the Fordist-Taylorist paradigm were considered unproductive. The *formal subsumption* in biocapitalism, therefore, has the effect of broadening the basis of accumulation, including training, care, breeding, consumption, social, cultural, artistic, and leisure activities. The idea of the human productive act changes, the distinction between directly productive labour, the artistic and cultural work (*opus*), leisure activities (*otium* and *play*) fail and tend to converge into labour, a directly and indirectly productive (of surplus value) activity (Fumagalli 2015).

At the same time, in bio-cognitive capitalism, the *real subsumption* is modified with respect to Taylorism, but we believe that it still operates. Carlo Vercellone was right when he wrote, "From the moment in which knowledge and its diffusion is affirmed as the principal productive force, the relation of domination of dead labour over living labour enters into crisis" (2007: 26) and, quoting Marx, "Labour no longer appears so much to be included within the production process; rather, the human being comes to relate more as watchman and regulator to the production process itself" (Marx 1973: 704). But, in our opinion, the changing relation between dead and living labour leads to a redefinition of the two concepts, as well as for the concepts of abstract and concrete labour.

As already suggested, the *formal subsumption*, implicit in bio-cognitive capitalism, has to do with the redefinition of the relationship between productive and unproductive labour, by making productive what in the Fordist paradigm was unproductive.

Now the *real subsumption* has to do with dead to living labour ratio, as consequence of the transition from repetitive mechanical technologies to linguistic relational ones. Static technologies, at the basis of the growth of productivity and of intensity in labour performance (large-scale economies) switch to dynamic technologies able to exploit learning and network economies by simultaneously combining manual tasks and brain-relational activities. The result has been the increase of new, more flexible forms of labour, in which design and manufacturing stages (CAD-CAM [computer-aided design and computer-aided manufacturing) are no longer perfectly separable but more and more interdependent and complementary. Even the separation between manufacturing and service production becomes more difficult to grasp. They become inseparable within the *production filière*. As far as material production is concerned, the introduction of new computerized systems of production, such as CAD-CAM and CAE necessitate a professional skill and knowledge that make the relationship between humans and machines increasingly inseparable, to the point that now it is the *living labour* to dominate the *dead labour* of the machine, but inside new form of labour organization and of social governance. On the production side of services (financialisation, R&D, communication, brand, marketing), we are witnessing a predominance of the downstream valorisation of material production.

It should be noted that the reduction in industrial employment, however, does not correspond to an actual decrease of the share of manufacturing on total GDP, which in the United States and in all the developed countries, remains, since 1980, more or less unchanged.

In bio-cognitive capitalism, *real subsumption* and *formal subsumption* are two sides of the same coin and feed off one another. Together they create a new form of *subsumption*, which we can define *life subsumption*. We prefer this term to that of *subsumption of general intellect*, as proposed by Carlo Vercellone (2007), since we do not refer only to the sphere of knowledge and education but even to the sphere of human relations, broadly speaking. This new form of the modern capitalist accumulation highlights some aspects that are at the root of the crisis of industrial capitalism. This leads to the analysis of new sources of valorisation (and increasing returns) in bio-cognitive capitalism. They derive from the crisis of the model of social and technical labour division (generated by the first industrial revolution and taken to the extreme by Taylorism) and they are powered by "the role and the diffusion of knowledge which obeys a co-operative social rationality which escapes the restrictive conception of human capital" (Vercellone 2007: 31).

It follows that the certified and direct labour time cannot be considered the only productive time, with the effect that a problems of the unit of measure of value arises. The traditional theory of labour value needs to be revised towards a new theory of value, in which the concept of labour is increasingly characterized by "knowledge" and is permeated with human life and life time.

We can call this step as the transition to a *theory of life value*, [4] where the fixed capital is the human being "in whose brain resides the knowledge accumulated by the company" (Marx 1973: 725).

When life becomes labour force, working time is not measured in standard units of measurement (hours, days). The working day has no limits, if not the natural ones. We are in the presence of *formal subsumption* and extraction of absolute surplus value. When life becomes labor force because brain becomes machine, or "fixed capital and variable capital at the same time," the intensification of labour performance reaches its maximum: we are in the presence of *real subsumption* and extraction of relative surplus value.

This combination of the two forms of *subsumption*—precisely *life subsumption*—needs a new system of social regulation and governance policy, and it mainly manifests itself in four ways.

The forms of life subsumption

In bio-cognitive capitalism, the subsumption of labor by capital becomes a vital subsumption, going further and making the concepts of formal and real subsumption, singularly considered, non-exhaustive. Now it is a matter of analyzing in more detail how this life subsumption takes shape and becomes concrete.

Precisely because we speak of life subsumption and life is not univocally standardizable in terms of abstraction (as it is possible for the concept of abstract labor), we must necessarily consider the different ways in which life subsumption operates. They are mainly four: (1) dispossession, (2) extraction, (3) financial subsumption, and (4) imprinting. The first two actually refer to the idea of formal subsumption, albeit in a divergent way.

Their analysis is preliminary to define a life-value theory.

Dispossession: extractivism and extraction

The *accumulation by dispossession* was treated and initially actualized by David Harvey in the well-known essay "The 'New' Imperialism: Accumulation by Dispossession" (2004) to then be resumed and expanded in other writings. This term refers immediately to the concept of original accumulation and therefore to the idea of formal subsumption, although articulated in a different way from what Marx had described in the first stage of capitalism. In fact, the concept of dispossession does not immediately refer to the productive factor of labor (as for Marx) but rather to the processes of urban gentrification (and not only) that have accompanied the process of globalization. It has to do not so much with the Smithian division of labor but rather with its spatial dimension.

Harvey argues that capital is a flow that produces plus-value, a surplus, a flow that, as Marx had already noted, is based on the constant metamorphosis of money–commodity–production–commodity–money (monetary production economy), whose crucial moment is that of production, that is the exploitation of the labor force.

In this flow there are incomes—there is bourgeois consumption, but also that of workers—and the blockage of this constant flow, which for capitalism must be continuous, is precisely the crisis. It is in these moments of blocking that contradictions occur (crisis of realization). One of these contradictions, analyzed by Marx in the *Grundrisse* and in Books I and II of *Capital*, is that between production and realization of value. Marxist tradition has always been effective in analyzing the contradictions of value production, less in analyzing those of realization.

One of the effects of economic globalization has been precisely that of extending the base of production as a source of accumulation but also extending the networks of the process of realization. In this process, the fundamental point is that value is produced in one place and realized in another, now produced in China but realized elsewhere. To account for the complex geography of this relationship, Harvey sets the example of Walmart in the United States. If we begin to look at the practices of appropriation of value, we see that extra-economic methods (violence, exercise of power, etc.) come into play that Marx analyzed in the first book of *Capital* talking about the original accumulation (Chapter 24). The Marxian analysis of the original accumulation is that of the birth of the salaried labor force, but today the analysis should focus more on the way in which capitalism regains value in the flow circulation.

By dispossession, Harvey does not refer only to the processes of traditional colonization and to the processes of original accumulation through *land-grabbing*[5] or similar forms, but also to the typical sectors of contemporary valorisation of bio-cognitive capitalism: the *gentrificatio*n of space and finance, or real estate and financial speculation activities.

> Accumulation by dispossession is a structural character of capitalism, not specific to our age. However, as happens also to other concepts, such as that of financialization, that of accumulation by dispossession is more important at certain times and less in others. In the last thirty-five years he has played an absolutely central role in the development of capitalism. The reason why I am a little reluctant to associate accumulation by dispossession with colonialism is that it is no longer limited solely to colonial territories, but intervenes in the very heart of the West [...]. There is a question we must ask ourselves about who and how extraction works. For example, copper in Zambia is a very coveted target for the mining practices of the two major corporations that are disputing it, one Chinese and one Indian. Much of Latin America has been transformed into a large soybean cultivation, naturally oriented towards China. It is not happening that China does today what England has done to India: it would be wrong to think so. Some of the most hateful labor exploitation practices today can be traced back to Korean and Taiwanese corporations. There is

> a continuous shift in the geography of the extraction so we must always ask ourselves who is extracting what.
>
> (Harvey 2014)

In this statement by David Harvey we can see how the accumulation for dispossession is represented as a form of accumulation of extractive capitalism but generates confusion between extractivism and extraction. In this regard, following Harvey, it seems to us that the term *extractivism* seems more congenial, unlike the concept of extraction. In fact, the concept of extraction must be read in a broader perspective than Harvey does. This is in fact the reading matrix of a component of neo-operaist thought, which starts from the assumption of cognitive capitalism as a new phase that would have modified in a structural way the process of valorization of Taylor-Fordist derivation (Vercellone 2013;Mezzadra 2009). The reading given by Carlo Vercellone and Antonio Negri (2008), in particular, but also by Sandro Mezzadra, means by extraction (differently from extractivism) the ability on the part of capital to externally capture the self-valorisation capacity of social cooperation and thus transform it into a source accumulation.[6]

> It is essential to analyze the ways in which financial capital touches the ground, both from the spatial point of view and from the point of view of the changes that occur in the relations between capital and labor. It seems to me [...] that an extensive extraction concept can be used in this regard to define the way in which financial capital relates to the different forms of social cooperation (and competition). The difference compared to industrial capital is particularly important here: while the worker, once through the factory gates, is inside a cooperation system organized by the owner, the black woman alone (to use a stereotypical figure) who contracts a subprime mortgage must pay the debt monthly by entering a series of relations of cooperation, dependence and exploitation that are essentially indifferent to financial capital, which is limited to "extract" a share of value produced from within those relationships.
>
> (Mezzadra 2014)

In this framework, social cooperation is understood as a potential autonomous capacity for the production of use value (therefore an expression of concrete work), or the municipality (in the singular), the result of the transformation of the indistinct value produced in society by the same concrete work in immediately social value.

In this perspective, extraction also contains the logic of dispossession: the practice of direct expropriation is therefore one of the possible components of extractivism. Extractivism thus becomes one of the modalities of the extraction process.[7]

In this context, the whole problem of the measurement and the dichotomy extractivism/extraction emerges. And we advance the hypothesis, very intriguing, that it is the financial measure that transforms the concrete work of social cooperation (Hardt and Negri 2017: 159–177), and the general intellect into abstract labor and that "The metropolis is today for the multitude what the factory was for the working class" (Negri 2014).

And together with the theme of identifying a unit of measure capable of defining the value of the common there is also the question of defining a political composition of the work appropriate to the one that is outlined (with the terms *multitude* and *extraction*) being the new technical composition of work in bio-cognitive capitalism.

These are questions that still require answers and which also open new questions. What is the role of the production unit, that is the firm?

> [S]tarting from the supposed externality between the common and multitude, on the one hand, and financialized accumulation on the other, the moment of the enterprise disappears, or rather, the enterprise is essentially the corruption of the cooperation already given, it is not seen as a moment still central to the accumulation, even if reconfigured, which still today organizes the extraction of value from the inside.
>
> (Sciortino 2016: 119)[8]

Here the difference between extraction and extractivism comes out again. In this regard, to mark the differences, the concept of extraction has an ancient root but its term is very recent. As we have already stressed, its root lies in extractivism. Its use is in fact linked to the political history of the last decade in South America and especially to the post-crisis period 2007, in the aftermath of the financial crisis (Gago and Mezzadra 2015).

When Antonio Negri and Carlo Vercellone affirm that today the surplus value originates from the exploitation of the "immaterial" labour (Negri) and the expropriation of the general intellect (Vercellone) and which tends to become fixed in financial income ("the becoming rent of the profit," according to the happy expression of Carlo Vercellone), they refer to the return of formal subsumption.[9]

The term *extractivism* was rarely used and, if it was, it was referred to the countries of the southern hemisphere regarding their rapid industrialization process and the new international division of labor that was developing. It was most often linked to the theme of original accumulation (Sacchetto and Tomba 2008; Perelman 2001; Mezzadra 2008; Van der Linden 2010).

We know that the global economic crisis of 2007 has accentuated predatory policies, already existing, from the imposition of monocultures, to the exploitation of natural resources, to land-grabbing. Such policies of extraction, or more properly, of dispossession, have changed the structure of geographical boundaries, as evidenced by the studies of Sandro Mezzadra and Brett Nielsen (Mezzadra and Nielsen 2013).

In this context, the relationship between financial capital and extractivism seems to be lacking and the political management of the territory and of the urban space, within a dialectic relationship with the constituent power (especially with reference to the progressive governments of South America) assumes a new centrality (Negri 2012). And it is in this context that extractivism turns into extraction.

In conclusion, extractivism and its extraction declension defines the internal exploitation of human social cooperation: instead, dispossession refers more to the external exploitation of natural resources and social and organizational networks (logistics) which today is the basis of accumulation.

In this sense, the studies by Melinda Cooper and Catherine Waldby (Cooper and Waldby 2014) show how the bioeconomy developed from the biological capabilities inherent in the bodies themselves, and particularly in the bodies of women. In fact, the productive sectors driven by the life sciences are today the most flourishing ones of capitalism. Reproductive and regenerative medicine have opened new global markets, whose source of surplus value coincides directly with the generative potential of women's bodies, but not only. If today bio-cognitive capitalism makes the appropriation of life a new frontier of colonization behind the thrust of new technologies, how does this vital expropriation manifest itself?

Are the concepts of extraction and dispossession adequate to grasp the processes of exploitation that unfold directly on the biological bodies of individuals and not only on the environment in which they live? (Rossi 2012).

Trying to answer these questions obliges us to go beyond the simple formal subsumption, albeit within an extension of the primitive accumulation base of capital. The link "formal subsumption–original accumulation" is no longer able today to grasp the complexity of contemporary exploitation.

Financial subsumption

The start of the financial crisis and the outbreak of the crisis of the so-called "sovereign debt" clearly highlighted the role of the financial markets and of the debt instrument as an integral part of the process of subsumption of labor to capital. In this context, the link between the financial and real sphere becomes indissoluble (Fumagalli and Mezzadra 2011). It follows that the financial markets enter directly into the biopolitical sphere of individuals (Lucarelli 2010). Riccardo Bellofiore grasps this aspect speaking of "real subsumption of labor to finance": "it deals with the subaltern integration of the working class households, as well as of the middle class, into the financial markets, and of their slipping into a growing bank debt" (Bellofiore 2012a: 191). And more:

> The two pillars at the basis of the reaction of capital to the workers' struggles and to the crisis of the seventies have been the labor fragmentation and financialization. Both had new characters. Labor fragmentation, in fact, has been significantly the other side of a new "centralization

> without concentration." Financialization, in turn, was embodied in an authentic "real subsumption of labor to finance and debt": an inclusion of households and consumers—hence of the world of labor—within the financial universe. The real subsumption of labor to finance led to the deepening of centralization without concentration, and more generally a further crackdown of the exploitation of labor.
>
> (Bellofiore 2011: 49)

The very moment when, in the aftermath of the Taylorist–Fordist–Keynesian paradigm crisis, the "new" capitalism manifests itself,[10] it is based on the nexus between finance and precariousness, within a new productive organization for supply chains, which Bellofiore calls "centralization without concentration" (2012: 16). Finance "has real effects on the management of production" (Bellofiore 2012: 17) and not only on investments or output. This is why Bellofiore talks about financial subsumption as an "aid that is no longer just formal, it is now also real" (2012: 18).

This form of real subsumption is therefore not new compared to that of the past, acted in the Fordist period where the real subsumption reaches its apogee: it presents itself with different forms and modalities, mediated by the necessity of income causing increasing indebtedness: "it pushes the workers, close into the poincer 'rent/indebtedness' to work harder and harder. Extraction of absolute and relative surplus labor is inextricably interwoven, while the center-periphery dichotomy is generalized to every area and nation" (Bellofiore 2012b: 18).

Let us remember that, for Marx, "the real submission of labor to capital operates in all the forms able to relative surplus value, not absolute surplus value" (1976: 69). It is essential, however, to underline that for Marx "real submission is accompanied by a complete revolution that continues and is constantly repeated in the same mode of production, in the productivity of labor and in the relationship between capitalists and workers" (Marx 1976: 69).

The extraction of relative plus-labor involves direct control of the organization of work and labor performance. This control is certainly inherent to the process of precariousness, even if the "real submission of labor to capital" takes different forms from those described by Marx, more indirect than direct. Is it also inherent to the process of financialization, as Bellofiore claims? We doubt it. From this point of view, financial valorization appears more like a form of formal subsumption, as claimed by the extraction theorists.

Real and formal subsumption tend therefore to mix, but, according to Bellofiore, without however giving life to ways of exploitation that deviate from those already experienced in the past. From this point of view, the fight against exploitation takes the form of the wage battle and the reduction of working time certified as productive of surplus labor. In fact, in the transition from Fordist capitalism to *money-manager capitalism*, there is no significant change in the accumulation process, while, as regards valorization, it is increasingly induced by both individual (micro-) and macro-level indebtedness (double indebtedness, for example the United States: the domestic one—

public debt—and the external one—trade balance deficit) managed by financial markets on a global scale.

Imprinting

Quite different is the analysis conducted by Federico Chicchi, Emanuele Leonardi, and Stefano Lucarelli who, in a recent publication (Chicchi et al. 2016) present a theory of exploitation that goes beyond the concept of subsumption of Marxian memory. The starting point, according to the authors, is the dissolution of the wage ratio. "It is in fact the explosion of wage dynamics as the driving force of value creation that leads us to question ourselves about the ways of contemporary exploitation and the logics that inform them by problematizing and forcing the heuristic potential of the Marxian categories of analysis" (Chicchi et al. 2016: 16).

Furthermore, capitalism presents itself as an "axiomatic" system. Recalling Deleuze and Guattari (2005), in fact, it is argued that the axiomatics of capital is defined by a set of "common characters" that define basic principles. As Sandro Mezzadra rightly recalls, the axiomatic capitalism of Deleuze and Guattari "surely corresponds to an'isomorphism', but not to a 'homogeneity'. On the contrary, axiomatic not only tolerates but constantly promotes the generation of social, temporal and spatial 'heterogeneity'" (Mezzadra 2014). This is why capitalism is an organism in constant transformation, able to continuously shift its operating limits, assuming the crisis as an opportunity.

Faced with the crisis of the wage society, based on the increase in the centrality of wages as a measure of exploitation, there are two elements of novelty that must be grasped:

1. Formal subsumption, in its Marxian meaning, that is the process of salarization, is no longer able to explain the new original accumulation that the transition from Fordist to bio-cognitive capitalism has generated: the extension of the basis of accumulation not only in terms of lengthening of working hours but also in terms of the productive production of surplus value of previously unproductive activities.
2. Any idea of real subsumption based on the figure of the wage earner loses its effectiveness.

Just starting from the inadequacy of the concept of subsumption in the dual form of formal and real, Chicchi, Leonardi and Lucarelli do not investigate the possible existence of a new form of subsumption but tend to exclude it *a priori*. The authors do, in fact, a reading of Marx that indissolubly links the concept of subsumption to the salary relationship. It is well known that in the unpublished Chapter 6 of *Capital*, Marx clearly states that:

> Material wealth is transformed into capital only because the worker, to be able to live, sells his work capacity; only through the wage labor

> relationship, the things that are the objective conditions of work, that is, the means of production, and the things that are the objective conditions of the maintenance of the worker, that is, the means of subsistence, become *capital.*
>
> (Marx 1976: 36)

Hence, "Wage labor, or wage worker, is therefore a necessary social form for capitalist production" (Marx 1976: 36). In these as in other statements, Marx does not refer to the existence of a direct relationship between the process of labor subsumption and the wage relationship. He claims that wage labor is a necessary social form of capitalist command, not *the* social form. The capitalist mode of production that Marx analyzes in the nineteenth century sees the wage ratio as the main and constituent process of the subsumption of labor to capital, in its dual form, formal and real. But nothing prevents us from thinking that, in its "axiomatic" developments, capitalism can prefigure others.

It is necessary to consider, as well as Chicchi et al. in part allude, that the wage ratio implies the existence of a clear and clean separation between human activity and machine. And it is this separation that is reunited in the process of material production (aspect on which Marx, in the above quotations—not by chance—particularly dwells) thanks to the salary ratio. But if this separation is no longer necessary to define the exploitation of labor, then the salary ratio may also fail, without however the process of subsumption (and exploitation) fails. A confirmation is given by the dissemination of free and unpaid labor in recent years.

Contemporary capitalism can then be represented as a social axiomatic that constantly shifts beyond its operating limits; therefore it has an "elastic delimitation" able to include different and non-traditional areas, "the shoreline," "the threshold," "the escape lines." Its great adaptive capacity, which oscillates between "de-territorialization of flows and contemporary continuous re-territorialization," exploits the "crises" to reinvent itself. The axiomatic machine is also the product of an algorithm, a process of machine automation that does not necessarily need a salary ratio.

As Cristina Morini writes:

> This means that the subsumption logic of the exploitation of the industrial phase, is no longer, does not explain enough, what is a theme in a continuous sway between freedom and dependence, a pressure-impressing mechanism that puts you in shape: a little you're there, a little undergo the intimidation, the fear of an ambush and whose exclusion is no longer social but individual.
>
> (Morini 2016)

Here it derives "the paradigm shift imposes by *de-salarization* on the analysis of exploitation" (Chicchi et al. 2016: 30), represented by the concept of imprinting. Always referring to Cristina Morini:

> The word imprinting refers to the studies of Konrad Lorenz on animal learning systems but also the impression on a photographic film, to focus the biopolitical device that marks the subject with a latent image or the limit beyond which everything is granted: everything is aimed at the selection of potentially functional trajectories (from the point of view of capitalist valorization). In the Marxian subsumption "the subordinate/salaried labor relationship is central and indeed necessary." In the imprinting process "labor and valorization process do not coincide on the level of wages but they find different conditions of realization." Here is the point, the architrave of the discourse: to derive surplus value from subjectivity without necessarily passing through wage convention. The passage from the real subsumption to the logic of imprinting takes place "through the progressive loss of the cogency of the wage ratio," in the amplification of the subjective condition and of the adhesion; "Diffusion of a more humiliated and less salaried working condition," not to mention the situations in which "the expropriation of surplus-value takes place completely outside the wage relationship and the employment contract": data profiling on the web, clinical work, forms of voluntary and civic participation, financial conventions, exploitation of the common goods of nature.
>
> (Morini 2016)

The concept of imprinting as the new frontier of capitalist exploitation highlights a new component of contemporary bio-cognitive capitalism, the one that refers to the prefix *bios*-. Increasingly, the component of subjectivity and continuous self-subjectivation defines the ambiguous and problematic ridge of forms of liberation and subsumption at the same time. At the moment when this condition becomes central, upstream for the development of that social cooperation or general intellect from which the process of accumulation of capital draws and downstream for its expropriation and capture, not only the category of wage labor but also that of capital must be rethought and redefined.

If, in fact, the category of wage labor falls (understood as a mere condition of dependent work), what happens to the capital category? Mario Tronti, in *Operai and Capitale*, breaks with traditional Marxism, based on the old and traditional Hegelian dialectic.

> I wrote somewhere that there is no class without the class struggle, because the class is not a pure sociological aggregation: the classes are potentially political. This had already been identified by Marx. The classes need each other, they never stand *in themselves*. They become classes, Marx said, when they become *for themselves*. When they become class for the class that stands against itself. And so we must elevate, Marx argued, to class consciousness. Lenin said that they must be organized. And in this struggle between the classes, the Hegelian dialectic of recognition is triggered, and the consequent reciprocal relationship, in the sense that a

> class, finding itself in front of its class adversary, recognizes also itself, acquires awareness of itself. This was the dialectic, which we did not call in this way, because we were critical of it; but it is the old Hegelian dialectic of the servant-lord, in which each one needs the other, and one does not know who the servant and the lord is because as one hand—depending on the balance of power—one becomes a servant and the other lord.
>
> (Tronti 2007)

For the workerist approach, it is the unilateral point of view that allows us to have the general point of view: it is that of worker subjectivity. If the worker can exist without capital, capital cannot work without the worker. In other words, constant capital cannot exist without variable capital.

We ask ourselves: does variable capital always take the form of paid work? If so, even constant capital would have no reason to exist, nor the Marxian notion of organic composition of capital and the concept of subsumption would no longer make sense.

In the monumental analysis that analyzes the passage from slavery to the wage relationship (Moulier Boutang 1998), Yann Moulier Boutang critically discusses the idea that leads "to consider the affirmation of capitalism and that of the wage system" (Maltese 2013: 27) as consubstantial. The wage form is not the prototype of the subsumed labor because of its high compatibility. According to Moulier Boutang, it is more relevant, in the constitution of capitalism, the exodus (exit) from dependent labor. This fact "would determine the dynamics of capitalist competition to the extent that the prism of defection would illuminate the tortuous path of the legal construction of labor control" (Moulier Butang 1998: 23–24).

Even if the disappearance of wage labor as a medium- to long-term trend is assumed (since, in any case, the wage ratio is still strongly present today, even if to a lesser extent in the cognitive-relational labour segments, segments that increasingly mark a growing trend to the detriment of wage labor, especially in countries with older industrialization), does this mean that the notion of subsumption of labor to capital also disappears, that is to say its subordination and its being exploited?

We doubt it. Chicchi et al. define the notion of subsumption in a very limited way. As is known—and as mentioned by the authors themselves—the concept of subsumption arises in the logic of Aristotelian derivation as "assumption of the minor premise of the syllogism as coherent with the major one" (Battaglia 2002: 17.816); it is later used in the *Critique of Judgment* by Immanuel Kant (*die Subsumtion*) with the meaning of classification in a classification.

We have already mentioned the Marxian use of the term, with the distinction between formal and real subsumption. In the unpublished sixth chapter of *Capital*, Marx uses the notion outside the sphere of logic for which it was conceived, reformulating it in order to frame the social and non-logical terms of capital and labor. Marx refers above all to the historical context of the capitalist phase that he could observe, in which the diffusion of the wage ratio represented the constituent characteristic. But this does not mean that the wage relationship is the constitutive element of the process of subsumption, as also Moulier Boutang reminds us. It is more plausible that the wage ratio is *one* of the forms in which the subsumption of labor to capital manifests itself.

We agree with Massimo Bontempelli, when he writes:

> The conceptual operation that I have long proposed for its possible interpretive fertility is to reformulate, to transpose it as an illuminating category in a broader context, the Marxian notion of subsumption, in the same way that Marx has reformulated the Kantian notion of subsumption to refer to the relationship between capital and labor. It is a matter of thinking of the distinction between formal subsumption and real subsumption no longer only of labor to capital, but of human life itself to capital.
>
> (Bontempelli 2008)

From this point of view, *imprinting* can be understood as one of the forms that defines the current subsumption process. A *life subsumption*.

Conclusion

Our thesis is that in a context of bio-cognitive valorization, where finance defines the scope of the same valorization, the forms of subsumption and therefore the forms of exploitation multiply. The heterogeneity of these forms derives from the lack of the clear separation between the human element and the mechanical element. This hybridization highlights new modes of conflict and at the same time possible self-organization processes. Hierarchy and cooperation are constantly intermingled and "dividing" differences represent the primary step of accumulation.

Notes

1 "In the absence of other means of access to money and/or to non-marketable appropriation of the means of subsistence" as C. Vercellone writes (2007, p. 22). See Chapter 2 by C. Vercellone and S. Dughera in this book: "Metamorphosis of the Theory of Value and Becoming-Rent of Profit: An Attempt to Clarify the Terms of a Debate."
2 Vercellone (2007).
3 On this point there are different interpretations about Marx thought. From one side, Paolo Virno identifies the general intellect with fixed capital *in toto* (see P. Virno 1992); from the other, Carlo Vercellone underlines that the same general intellect presents itself as living labour and, hence, cannot be considered solely as fixed capital. This discussion is still open.
4 See Fumagalli and Morini (2011). Carlo Vercellone introduces the concept of theory of knowledge-value, when he discusses "the concomitant passage from a theory of time-value of labour to a theory of knowledge-value where the principal

fixed capital is man 'in whose brain exists the accumulated knowledge of society'" (Vercellone 2007:31, quoting Marx 1973: 711).

5 The term "land-grabbing" identifies a controversial economic and geopolitical issue coming to the fore in the first decade of the twenty-first century, concerning the effects of large-scale occupation of agricultural land in developing countries, through rent or purchase of large agricultural extensions by transnational companies, foreign governments, and private individuals. Although the use of such practices has been widely disseminated throughout human history, the phenomenon has assumed a particular connotation since the years 2007–2008, when land grabbing has been stimulated and driven by the consequences of the agricultural price crisis of those years and the consequent willingness on the part of some countries to secure their food reserves in order to protect national interests of food sovereignty and security.

6 In particular, it is useful to underline the following passage: "the measure of capital and the foundation of its power over society depends less and less on past labor and knowledge embedded in constant capital and are now based mainly on a social convention that finds its main spring in the power of finance." In line with this reading is also Christian Marazzi (2010, 2011). See, also Hardt and Negri (2004, 2009).

7 This is the reading that I recognize from the intervention of Sandro Mezzadra at the seminar of Euronomade: *Le piattaforme del capitale*, March 3–4, 2017, Macao, Milan.

8 In their latest book, Michael Hardt and Antonio Negri partly resume the idea of the centrality of the firm as agent of production, in which a principle of exploitation can already emerge. See Hardt and Negri (2017: 107–124).

9 See Chapter 2 of this book.

10 Bellofiore defines this "new" capitalism by resuming the term *money manager capitalism*, coined by Hyman P. Minsky in the 1980s. This term will then be successfully reused, once the subprime crisis has begun, by L. Randall Wray (Randall Wray 2009, 2011). Charles Whalen writes: "*Money manager capitalism* is the name that Hyman P. Minsky (1919–1996) has assigned to the current economic period in his historical analysis of the capitalist development of the United States. It had emerged in 1980 when "institutional investors"—holders of the largest share of corporate and bond stocks at the end of the decade—began to exert their influence on financial markets and businesses. The study of Money manager capitalism has been the focus of Minsky's attention during the last decade of his life" (Whalen 2012:254). Bellofiore, further, adds to the central role of finance the aspect of precariousness: "this 'new' capitalism—new compared to the capitalism of the twentieth century, even if in some ways it raises some aspects of nineteenth-century capitalism—moves along the axis finance-precarity" (2012b: 16).

References

Battaglia, S. (2002) *Grande dizionario della lingua italiana*, 21 vols., Turin: Utet.

Bellofiore, R. (2011) *La Crisi capitalistica: La barbaria che avanza*, Trieste: Asterios.

Bellofiore, R. (2012a) "L'ascesa e la crisi del money manager capitalism," in A. Simoncini (ed.), *Una rivoluzione dall'alto: A partire dalla crisi globale*, Milan: Mimesis, pp. 185–204.

Bellofiore, R. (2012b) *La Crisi globale:l'Europa, l'Euro, la Sinistra*, Trieste: Asterios Editore.

Bontempelli, M. (2008) "Capitalismo, sussunzione, nuove forme della personalità," available at www.ariannaeditrice.it/articolo.php?id_articolo=17114 (accessed March 25, 2019).

Chicchi, F., E. Leonardi, and S. Lucarelli (2016) *Logiche dello sfruttamento*, Verona: Ombre Corte.
Cooper, M., and C. Waldby (2014) *Clinical Labor: Tissue Donors and Research Subjects in the Global Bioeconomy*, Durham, NC: Duke University Press.
Deleuze, G., and F. Guattari (2005) *A Thousand Plateaus: Capitalism and Schizophrenia*, Minneapolis, MN: University of Minnesota Press.
Fumagalli, A. (2015) *La Vie mise au travail: Nouvelle formes du capitalisme cognitive*, Paris: Eterothopia.
Fumagalli, A. and S. Mezzadra (eds.) (2010) *Crisis in the Global Economy: Financial Markets, Social Struggles, and New Political Scenarios*, Los Angeles, Calif.: Semiotext(e).
Fumagalli, A., and C. Morini (2011) "Life Putto Work: Towards a Theory of Life-Value," *Ephemera*, 10 (3–4): 234–252.
Gago, V., and S. Mezzadra (2015), "Para una crítica de las operaciones extractivas del capital. Patrón de acumulación y luchas sociales en el tiempo de la financiarización,"*Nueva sociedad*, 255: 38–52.
Hardt, M. and A. Negri (2017) *Assembly*, Oxford: Oxford University Press.
Hardt, M. and A. Negri (2004) *Multitude: War and Democracy in the Age of Empire*, London: Penguin.
Hardt, M. and A. Negri (2009) *Commonwealth*, Cambridge, MA:Harvard University Press.
Harvey, D. (2004) "The New Imperialism: The Accumulation by Dispossession," *Socialist Register*, m. 40.
Harvey, D. (2014) "Capitalism by Dispossession (or Accumulation by Expropriation)," at the Yearly Seminar organized by EuroNomade at Passignano, Italy, September 18, available at http://gabriellagiudici.it/david-harvey-a-passignano-perugia/ (accessed March 25, 2019).
Lucarelli, S. (2010) "Financialization as Biopower," in A. Fumagalli and S. Mezzadra (eds.), *Crisis in the Global Economy: Financial Markets, Social Struggles, and New Political Scenarios*, Los Angeles, CA: Semiotext(e), pp. 119–138.
Maltese, P. (2013) "Lavoro imbrigliato e lavoro flessibile. Appunti su una teoria politico-pedagogica dell'esodo," in *Bollettino della Fondazione Nazionale Vito-Fazio Allmayer*, 1, p. 2. Available at www.academia.edu/3800145 (accessed March 25, 2019).
Marazzi, C. (2005) "Capitalismo digitale e modello antropogenetico del lavoro. L'ammortamento del corpo macchina," in J. L. Laville, C. Marazzi, M. La Rosa, and F. Chicchi (eds.), *Reinventare il lavoro*, Rome: Sapere 2000, pp. 107–126.
Marazzi, C. (2010) *Il comunismo del capitale*, Verona: Ombre Corte.
Marazzi, C. (2011) *The Violence of Financial Capitalism*, Los Angeles, CA: Semiotext(e).
Marx, C. (1973) *Grundrisse*, London:Penguin Books.
Marx, C. (1976) *Capital: A Critique of Political Economy*, London:Penguin.
Mezzadra, S. (2009) "La 'cosiddetta' accumulazione originaria" in LUM (Libera Università Metropolitana) (a cura di)., *Lessico Marxiano*, Rome: Manifestolibri, pp. 17–40. Available at www.lumproject.org/wp-content/uploads/2013/01/lessico-marxiano.pdf (accessed March 25, 2019).
Mezzadra, S. (2014) "Le Geografie della crisi e dello sviluppo capitalistico: Appunti preliminari e ipotesi di ricerca", available at www.euronomade.info/?p=465 (accessed March 25, 2019).
Mezzadra, S., and B. Nielsen (2013) *Border as Method; or, The Multiplication of Labor*, Durham, NC: Duke University Press.

Morini, C. (2016) "Le Pillole azzurre del capitale: recensione a Federico Chicchi, Emanuele Leonardi, Stefano Lucarelli, Logiche dello sfruttamento—Oltre la dissoluzione del rapporto salariale," available at http://effimera.org/le-pillole-azzurre-del-capitale-cristina-morini (accessed March 25, 2019).

Moulier Boutang, Y. (1998) *De l'esclavage au salariat: Economie historique du salariat bridé*, Paris: Presses Universitaires de France.

Negri, A. (2004) *Il Comune della cooperazione sociale: intervista sulla metropoli* (by Federico Tomasello), available at www.euronomade.info/?p=2185 (accessed March 25, 2019).

Negri, A. (2012) "Perché Toni Negri?" Interview by Veronica Gago and Diego Sztulwark, November 13, available at www.euronomade.info/?p=831 (accessed March 25, 2019).

Negri, A. and C. Vercellone (2008) "Le Rapport capital-travail dans le capitalisme cognitif," *Multitudes*, 32(mars): 39–50.

Perelman, M. (2001) *The Invention of Capitalism: Classical Political Economy and the Secret History of Primitive Accumulation*, Durham, NC: Duke University Press.

Randall Wray, L. (2009) "The Rise and Fall of Money Manager Capitalism: A Minskian Approach," *Cambridge Journal of Economics*, 33: 807–828.

Randall Wray, L. (2011) "Minsky's Money Manager Capitalism and the Global Financial Crisis," Working Paper No. 661, Levy Economics Institute of Bard College.

Rossi, U. (2012) "On the Varying Ontologies of Capitalism: Embeddedness, Dispossession, Subsumption," *Progress in Human Geography*, 37(3), 348–365.

Sacchetto, D. and M. Tomba (eds.) (2008) *La lunga accumulazione originaria*, Verona: Ombre Corte.

Sciortino, R. (2016) "Tutto un programma di ricerca," in E. Armano and A. Murgia (eds.), *Le Reti del lavoro gratuito: Spazi urbani e nuove soggettività*, Verona: Ombre Corte.

Tronti, M. (2007) "Intervention," in G. Roggero (ed.), *Rileggere Operai e capitale Lo stile operaista alla prova del presente*, Faculty of Political Science, University of Rome, "La Sapienza,"January 31, p.4. Available at www.academia.edu/5135508/Rileggere_Operai_e_capitale (accessed March 25, 2019).

Van der Linden, M. (2010) *Workers of the World: Essays toward a Global Labor History*, London:Brill.

Vercellone, C. (2007) "From Formal Subsumption to General Intellect: Elements for a Marxist Reading of the Thesis of Cognitive Capitalism," *Historical Materialism*, 15.

Vercellone, C. (2013) "The Becoming Rent of Profit? The New Articulation of Wage, Rent and Profit," *Knowledge Cultures*, 1(2): 194–207.

Virno, P. (1992) "Quelques notes à propos du general intellect," *Futur Antérieur*, 10: 45–53.

Whalen, C. J. (2012) "Money Manager Capitalism," in J. Toporowsky and J. Michell (eds.), *Handbook of Critical Issues in Finance*, London: Edward Elgar, pp. 254–262.

5 A financialized monetary economy of production

Andrea Fumagalli and Stefano Lucarelli

Introduction

In a short 1933 article titled "A Monetary Theory of Production," which was a contribution to the *Festschrift für Arthur Spiethoff*, J. M. Keynes argued that "the main reason why the problem of crises is unsolved, or at any rate why this theory is so unsatisfactory, is to be found in the lack of what might be termed a monetary theory of production." And he explained what "a Monetary Theory of Production" is:

> The distinction which is normally made between a barter economy and a monetary economy depends upon the employment of money as a convenient means of effecting exchanges as an instrument of great convenience, but transitory and neutral in its effect … Money, that is to say, is employed, but it is treated as being in some sense neutral. That, however, is not the distinction which I have in mind when I say that we lack "a Monetary Theory of Production." An economy, which uses money but uses it merely as a neutral link between transactions in real things and real assets and does not allow it to enter motives or decisions, might be called—for want of a better name—a real-exchange economy. The theory which I desiderate would deal, in contradistinction to this, with an economy in which money plays a part of its own and affects motives and decisions and is, in short, one of the operative factors in the situation, so that the course of events cannot be predicted, either in the long period or in the short, without a knowledge of the behavior of money between the first state and the last.
>
> (Keynes 1978: 408–411)

Among the economic theories that serve as a description of economic reality in order to formulate analytical rules concerning its functioning, an important role is played by the so-called theory of the monetary circuit. The monetary circuit, as a social macroeconomic analysis, considers the modern economy as a monetary *production* economy, and, thereby, it involves a completely different mechanism from that of a barter economy. A monetary economy entails that all exchanges are settled in money, and this raises immediately the problem of how money is created and introduced into the system. In modern economies, money is created by the interaction between the banking and enterprise sectors, and it is then made available for the latter through the granting of bank credit. Because just those who have money can enter the market, the decisions made by banks as regards to whom to grant credit and also how much credit they wish to grant become crucial elements in the discussion over the various stages of the economic process. The capital advanced by industrial capitalists amounts to the money needed to pay for workers' wages only. Through their hierarchical access to credit, firms decide the amounts of consumer goods and investment goods in such an economy.[1] Once production has occurred, then the price of consumer goods is determined. Given the equilibrium value of the profit rate prevailing in the whole economic system, it can then be used in order to derive the price of investment goods compatible with profit uniformity. Once prices are fixed, the distribution of income is clearly also fixed.[2] Creating money contributes thus to determine the quantity produced as well as the distribution of national income. The result is that money is never neutral: "[to] the social group being admitted to bank credit, money is, at the economic level, a source of profits and, at the social level, a source of power" (Graziani 2003: 26). The systemic approach to any economic activity comprised in a monetary circuit approach can be represented, as in Figure 5.1.

In the traditional version of the monetary circuit scheme, there are three classes (bankers, capitalists, and workers) and two sectors (producing consumption and investment goods). Capitalist production is described as a process characterized by sequential phases, the first one being the creation of money by banks. Credit money enters the economic process on the basis of entrepreneurial demand (Step 1). When firms increase the flow of investment, they demand a new amount of money. The credit money demanded from the banking sector may be satisfied through *ex novo* money creation. The amount of money used to fund productive activity and pay wages (Step 2) is endogenous since it varies according to the changes in the investment plans of business enterprises. But banks are not passive players in the circuit: the supply of credit is not automatic. It depends on the selecting and rationing criteria in force in the banking sector.[3]

Firms set the amount of both the consumption and investment goods to be produced. Production plans chosen by entrepreneurs can be affected by both the availability of liquid assets in order to fund new investments and the expectations concerning the placement of products on the market aimed at the valorisation of production. Thus, it would seem that the only actual constraint for productive activity to take place is given by monetary conditions established by the banking sector. Wage earners allocate their income either for consumption or saving (Step 3).

For the closure of the monetary circuit to take place, firms have to be able to pay off not just the loan granted to them at the beginning of the

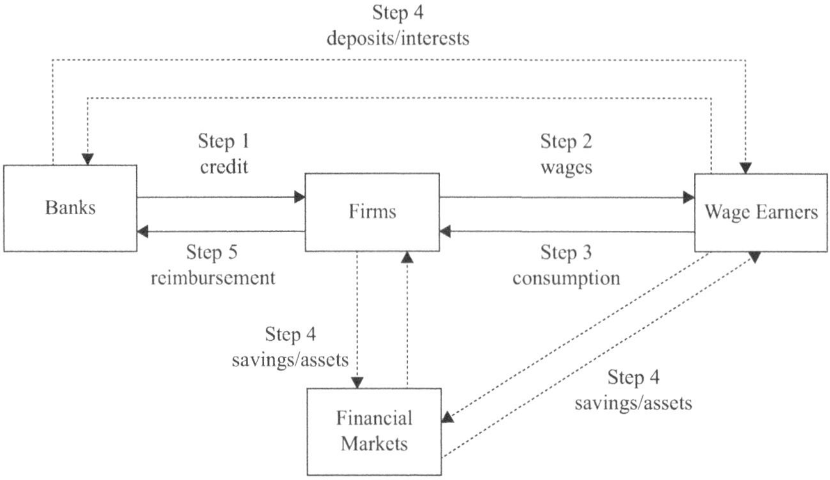

Figure 5.1 The traditional framework of a monetary economy of production

production process by the banks but also the interest accrued over the same period of time. In this traditional framework, financial markets are logically relevant at the end of the economic process. Financial operators play the role of recuperating the liquidity not collected through the sale of goods: when wage earners receive their monetary income and choose to divide it between consumption and saving, they may decide to use part of their savings to purchase assets in the financial market (Step 4). In other words, "'final' finance to repay firms' total initial financing of production comes both from sales in the consumption goods market and from new securities issues in the financial market" (Bellofiore and Seccareccia 1999: 755). Once goods and shares have been sold, firms repay the banks (Step 5, i.e. closure of the circuit). This traditional framework of a monetary economy of production well describes the so-called Fordist regime of accumulation (Aglietta 1979), where firms' decisions relating to both the level of production and employment are essentially determined by the expected level of aggregate demand (Realfonzo 2006).

The new monetary economy of production: a brief critical survey

By the late 1960s, as Aglietta (1979) argued, the growth of productivity decelerated and the Fordist labor process, based upon the extraction of ever greater amounts of surplus value through the intensification of labor, was reaching its limits. Consequently, real wages could not continue to grow, and the institutional conditions for the Fordist growth model (i.e. high productivity increases potential, stable capital/labor compromise, limited international openness) were radically modified.

The structural changes that occurred in the past thirty years have substantially modified the interaction between banks, firms, wage earners, and financial markets. As we argue elsewhere (Fumagalli and Lucarelli 2010), the main changes within the new capitalism concern mainly two spheres: the dominant technological paradigm (especially the role played by the knowledge–power relation in the development of the division of labor within it) and the importance of finance.[4] Boyer introduces the concept of "finance-led growth" to describe the potentially new accumulation regime that combines "labor-market flexibility, price stability, developing high-tech sectors, as well as booming stock market and credit to sustain the rapid growth of consumption" (2000: 116).

Financialization changed the capitalist economy dramatically and represented a systemic transformation of production and finance. Accumulation, the operation whereby wealth is reinvested by increasing the total quantity of capital, has become increasingly subordinate to finance. Especially in the American economic system, the structure and operation of financial markets, particularly regarding credit availability, deeply changed.

Modern financial systems contain a lot of amplifiers that multiply the impact of both losses and gains: (1) the use of derivatives to create exposures to assets without actually having to own them; (2) the application of fair-value accounting, which requires many institutions to mark the value of assets to current market prices; (3) counterparty risk, the effect of a given institution getting into trouble vis-à-vis those it deals with; (4) the excessive leverage. As *The Economist* wrote in May 2008, many banks and other financial institutions loaded up on debt in order to increase their returns on equity when the asset process was rising. Financial institutions were exposed to product leverage via instruments which needed only a slight deterioration in the value of underlying assets for losses to escalate rapidly. Finally, *The Economist* stressed the fact that financial operators overindulged in liquidity leverage, using structured investment vehicles or relying too much on wholesale markets to exploit the difference between borrowing cheap short-term money and investing in higher-yielding long-term assets (The Economist 2008: 4). In a finance-led capitalism, where monetary policy is driven by financial markets and motives, the role of banks is modified, and, consequently, the traditional monetary circuit framework has to change.

The 2007–2009 financial crisis is stimulating new interesting perspectives within the framework of the monetary theory of production. Using a monetary circuit approach, Seccareccia (2011) represents a first attempt to highlight some of the important transformations in the strategic role played by the banks during the financialization era (the "Money Manager Capitalism," in Hyman Minsky's words). He particularly affirmed that "the dynamics of credit creation has been sustained not by business indebtedness but by household indebtedness" and "the traditional link between firms and banks has been largely severed [...] and it is the dynamics of the bank/financial markets axis [...] which has taken center stage" (Seccareccia 2011: 6). Rochon and Rossi (2010) wrote that the rise of a finance-led capitalism resulted in very profound changes to the way domestic economies operates. In particular, as Pilkington (2009) argued, many financial services supplied by commercial banks today do not fit into the categories of monetary and financial intermediation as defined by the theory of money emissions. Circuitist literature has to consider the theoretical distinction between banks and non-banking financial institutions (insurance companies, venture-capital firms, securitization firms, mutual funds, etc.).[5] Stellian (2010) focused on American home-equity extraction that has given support to consumption during the past decade. This argument is closely related to Forges Davanzati and Tortorella (2010) that suggested that the crisis ultimately depends on neo-liberal policy prescription, particularly labor market deregulation that stimulates workers' indebtedness.

Following Seccareccia's suggestions, Passarella (2011) considered that the principal novelty of new capitalism is the creation of credit money increasingly sustained by household indebtedness. He proposed, within a "Money Manager Capitalism" monetary circuit, the following sequence which leads to the 2007–2009 economic and financial crisis:

> (1) households try to keep a given "desired" level of consumption, in spite of the tendential decrease in the wage-bill, and resort to bank loans (on the basis of their stock of assets); (2) non-financial firms use their extra-profits (arising from the decrease in the wage level, in spite of a quite constant flow of consumption) in order to purchase financial assets (either equities or bank bonds, in our simplified model); (3) the inflow of new capitals makes financial markets grow, but, at the macroeconomic level, firms' share buyback reduces the "soundness" of the business sector, because it increases the leverage ratio on investments; (4) at the same time, the increase in the price of (financial) assets can lead the central bank to increase the target rate of interest (in order to "cool" the asset price level); (5) finally, in the medium-run, the reduction in the households' stock of assets and the increase in the bank interest rate affects consumption and investment, giving rise to the crisis.
>
> (Passarella 2011: 14–15)

The previous contributions highlight the important transformations in the role played by the banking sector in the economy. They also put at the center of financial capitalism both the reduction in the profitability of firms' investment in the production process and the workers' indebtedness. But there is still work to do to describe the new role played by the bank–financial markets interactions. In his guide to the coming real-estate collapse, Hudson (2006) represented the new way of American financing in a schematic overview very close to the logic of the circuitists and clearly described the so-called FIRE sector (short for Finance, Insurance and Real Estate):

> These industries are so symbiotic that the Commerce Department reports their earnings as a composite. (Banks require mortgage holders to insure their properties even as the banks reach out to absorb insurance companies. Meanwhile, real-estate companies are organizing themselves as stock companies in the form of real-estate investment trusts, or REITs—which in turn are underwritten by investment bankers.) The main product of these industries is credit. The FIRE sector pumps credit into the economy even as it withdraws interest and other charges. The FIRE sector has two significant advantages over the production/consumption and government sectors. The first is that interest wealth grows exponentially. [...] The FIRE sector's other advantage is that interest payments can quickly be recycled into more debt. The more interest paid, the more banks lend. And those new loans in turn can further drive up demand for real estate—thereby allowing homeowners to take out even more loans in anticipation of future capital gains. Some call this perpetual-motion machine a "post-industrial economy," but it might more accurately be called a rentier economy. [...] The miracle of compound interest will allow every one of us to be a rentier, feasting on interest, dividends, and capital gains.
>
> (Hudson 2006: 43–44)

The FIRE sector is composed of a traditional banking part and a new financial part. Funds originate in the banking part of the FIRE sector and either circulate in the real economy, or they return to the FIRE sector as financial investments or in payment of debt service and financial fees. But when and why did this role of FIRE commence?

Our thesis is that the vital roots of the bubble that burst in 2007 are to be found in the euphoria of the 1990s. The crisis stems from the overinvestment in new information technologies and communication, and the exhaustion of the profit opportunities offered by new technologies. The financialisation of the monetary economy of production is explainable if we understand the shift towards a new technological paradigm, as general *outlook* on the productive problems faced by firms, where the relevance of the so-called "immaterial" production increases. In order to describe this dynamic we need to develop two different frameworks of a monetary economy of production: the first one represents the New Economy *scenario*, while the second one represents the (financialized) monetary circuit during the real-estate bubble.

Towards a financialised monetary economy of production

Linking the subprime crisis with the crisis of the dot.com, from the point of view of a monetary production economy, requires the adoption of what we call a Schumpeterian perspective. A monetary economy of production should be designed by taking into account the technological dynamics that characterize it. Each technological paradigm shift may be accompanied by speculative pressures that have significant consequences on the way business enterprises finance their own productive activity.

Following a Schumpeterian perspective, each new industrial technology favours its own sort of financing: joint-stock companies abounded when businessmen needed to finance the railways in the nineteenth century:

> As regards financing, we must distinguish the task of creating the conditions of profitableness of the enterprise from the task of providing the money for construction. [...] Previous profits or domestic savings being inadequate, railroad construction was, therefore, mainly financed by credit creation. From the standpoint of the United States, foreign buying of American railroad bonds amounted to this—even if the bonds were paid for out of, say, English savings—as did European credit extended in anticipation of bond issue or simply as overdraft. [...] Domestic credit creation was even more freely resorted to. We do not know its amount, but we can, in most cases, trace it in one or more of the following forms: direct lending by banks to companies against their notes or on bonds to be sold later to the public [...]; and financing speculation—there is a significant coincidence between the increase of railroad stock prices and of deposit in 1852.
>
> (Schumpeter 1989: 215–218)

In much the same way, the internet revolution did spill over into the rest of the business sector and finance. The synergy between financial instruments and technological innovations is the factor explaining the rapid expansion of the so-called New Economy in the early 1990s. In the second half of the 1990s, the idea of a digitalized society, with liberating effects on the world of work and life, became a convention.[6] Whether true or false, there is no doubt that this convention pulled the real transformation processes of the world ahead (Orléan 1999). The new technological paradigm, as general *outlook* on the productive problems faced by firms, implies a new way to finance investment activity, a new form of money regulation and a new form of capitalistic valorization.

The dynamism of the US economy during the 1990s in the areas of information and communication technologies (ICT) and biotechnology is complementary to the spread of new types of financial markets specializing in the commodification of intellectual property rights (IPR). In 1984, the National Association of Security Dealers regulation introduced the possibility of evaluating the intangibles (consisting mainly of IPR) as an asset in the balance sheet of enterprises. This regulation permitted the promotion of such firms (in deficit but holding a stock of IPR) no longer on the over-the-counter market but on the NASDAQ National Market. Finally, the law on pension funds was modified so as to authorize them to invest part of their holdings in risky securities and stocks. "In this way, part of the enormous liquidities concentrated in the pension funds expanding rapidly during this period allowed the financial markets to promote hundreds of new firms which were in deficit but deemed 'high potential' in view of their intangible assets" (Orsi and Coriat 2003: 3). The complementarity between financial markets and IPR was at the heart of the New Economy: the formation of a new intellectual property law regime coexisting and coevolving together with the introduction on the market of non-profitable firms whose assets were composed of IPR. This *institutional complementarity* permitted the launching of very special kind of companies following unprecedented business models. The New Economy was not only an opportunity for these new innovative firms; it produced pervasive effects on traditional sectors of the economy. At the same time, it favored a process of accumulation that was mainly based upon the globalization of financial markets, utilized by the investors both for financing economic activity and for stimulating investment via the increased financialization of the productive activities.

As shown in Figure 5.2, within the past quarter century, the market value of the S&P 500 companies has deviated greatly from their book value. This "value gap" indicates that physical and financial accountable assets reflected on a company's balance sheet now comprises less than 20 percent of the true value of the average firm. A significant portion of this intangible value is represented by patented technology.

But, as Orsi and Coriat (2003: 5) asked, "How do we determine the 'value' of a firm whose assets are composed of a patent on a gene? Or, in the case of firms on the Internet, one that has a 'virtual' number of customers?" The value of a corporation's patents is a unique, forward-looking indicator of corporate value. What is important to stress is that patent value reflects itself in stock price and can be used to create investment and, starting in the 1990s, to get finance by the banking system in order to improve the technological position thanks to mergers and acquisitions strategy.[7]

The most innovative companies—companies with the strongest patent portfolios—outperform their peers as a result of the federal government granting exclusionary rights on the production of the patented product or service, their proprietary market position, their related economies of scale, premium pricing associated with unique features, and their lower cost due to protected methods of manufacturing.

Figure 5.2 data show how patents, or more generally, IPR have become exploitable as the US economy matures in its progression from a manufacturing foundation to an innovation base, in other words, towards a cognitive capitalism paradigm. Starting in the 1990s, the US economy is now dominated by innovation value creation. This is substantiated by a 2005 report by economists Kevin Hassett and Robert Shapiro estimating US intellectual property to be worth some $5–5.5 trillion, which is more than the gross domestic product of most countries (Shapiro and Hassett 2005).

The increasing role of intangible assets is not only a property of the big corporations on the S&P 500 Index, but it is pervasive in the whole economy and it cannot be exclusively explained by patents and IPR. Figure 5.3 shows

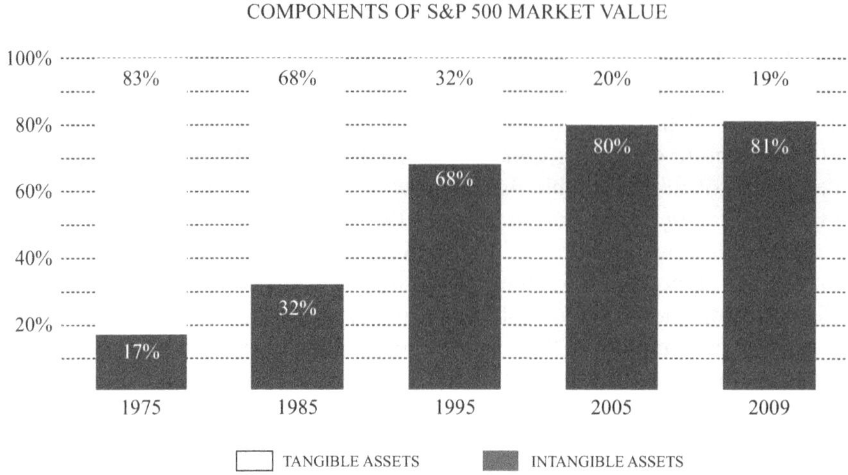

Figure 5.2 Share of intangible and tangible assets of S&P 500 market value
Note: Intangible book value is calculated by subtracting the tangible book value from the market capitalization of a given company or index. In practice, companies report tangible book value per share, number of shares outstanding, and market capitalization. Therefore, intangible book value can be calculated by subtracting the market capitalization from the tangible book value per share multiplied by the number of shares outstanding.
Source: Ocean Tomo: www.oceantomo.com/media/newsreleases/Intangible-Asset-Market-Value-Study

that intangible assets (measured by the gap between total and tangible assets) starts to increase exponentially, especially in the period after 1990, during the net-economy boom. After a period of stagnation in the first years of 2000, the process restarts until the beginning of the present economic-financial crisis. In this second period, patents and IPR play, of course, a role but differently from the 1990s. They are accompanied by an increasing share on assets value due to the brand strategy. It is in the past decade that the brand value reaches its maximum level, especially in the years of crisis (Interbrand 2010). In December 2010, the share of intangible assets is about 58.9 per cent of the total, after reaching a peak in the fourth quarter of 2007 (60.1 per cent). In 1980, it was about 39 per cent. This dynamics is the result of investment activity in the US economy from 1990 to 2010. Figure 5.3 shows an increasing role played by investment in ICT equipment.

The dynamics of private investment (as a share of GDP) shows that, between 1992 and 2000, it increased gradually before falling between 2002 and 2003 and then rising once again until 2007, before the financial crisis (Paulré 2008: 198). During the first decade of the new millennium, investment dynamics is more unstable. Until the first quarter of 2007, the level of gross investment remains more or less on the level of the previous years, with a pro-cyclical dynamics. What is astonishing is the sharp decline of US investment after 2007, which marks the strong impact of the crisis. But what is perhaps

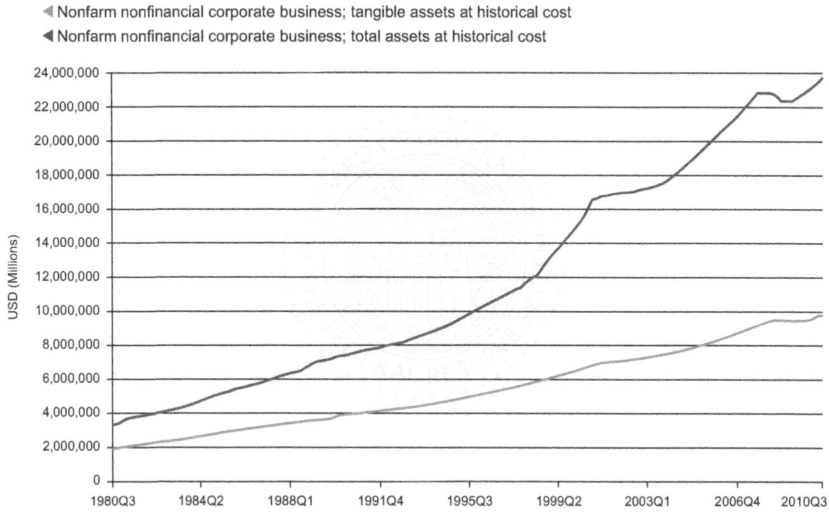

Figure 5.3 Total and tangible assets in the nonfarm, nonfinancial business corporations, 1980–2010

more relevant is the fact that net investment starts to decline in the first quarter of 2005, two years before the beginning of the financial crisis (see Figure 5.4). In the past two decades, the gap between net investment and inventories, on the one hand, and gross investment, on the other, constantly increased, at least until the financial crisis. From 1980 to 2005, the level of inventories is normally positive, but near the zero level. This would mean that the increasing gap between gross and net investment is partly due to the US investment abroad and to investment in not physical investment (brands, patents, etc.).

With an unstable dynamics, foreign investment by US corporations is particularly active after 2003, particularly following the entry of China in the World Trade Organization. But it is not sufficient to explain the relatively higher performance of gross investment in the presence of the contemporary sharp decline of physical investment and inventories. Our hypothesis is that the main reason for these changes lies in the increasing share of intangible investment, as the data displayed in Figures 5.2 and 5.3 corroborate.

The ICT revolution was largely financed by private-equity funds, especially venture-capital funds. Venture capitalism can be considered as a fundamental step towards the creation of a knowledge market (Antonelli and Teubal 2008: 167). During the 1990s, the goal of new company founders and of venture capitalists was principally the new knowledge-intensive firm listing on a dedicated stock market and its eventual acquisition by another company. Venture-capital funds generate a shift from intermediate to market financing that redistributed risk-taking from banks to institutional investors. As Aglietta (2008) pointed out, there was also a dramatic change in the norm of

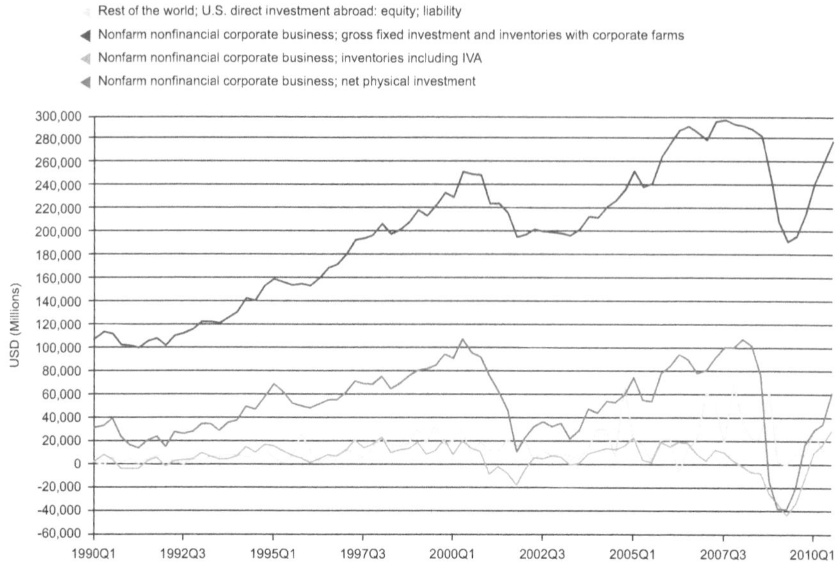

Figure 5.4 Gross and physical investment, investment abroad and inventories in the US economy, 1990–2010

profitability: market-value accounting has replaced reproduction-cost accounting as the yardstick of corporate performance.

> Combined with the long ascending wave in the stock market, the imperative of shareholder value gave rise to a much higher required rate of return than in the heyday of post-war growth. Most business strategies—downsizing, spin-offs and the like, but also external growth via mergers and acquisitions and share buybacks—were driven by the lucrative adjustment of corporate executives to the principle of shareholder value.
>
> (Aglietta 2008: 69)

The evolution of new commitments to venture-capital funds in the United States (Figure 5.5) is the proof of the relevance—especially during the 1990s—of this kind of funding in innovative investments. The decrease in the period 2000–2009 reflects the contraction of the venture-capital industry that began after the burst of the technology bubble in 2000.

In the 1990s, the financing of takeovers (to acquire the income, assets, and competences of others) via share-exchange offers grew in importance. In this accumulation system, various forms of remuneration tied to the whole of business yield developed: not only stock options for managers but also the retirement or investment funds mostly held by wage laborers. In the 1990s, the ICT sectors, in which production of goods by means of knowledge was able to create more value added per employee, and in which the financial activities

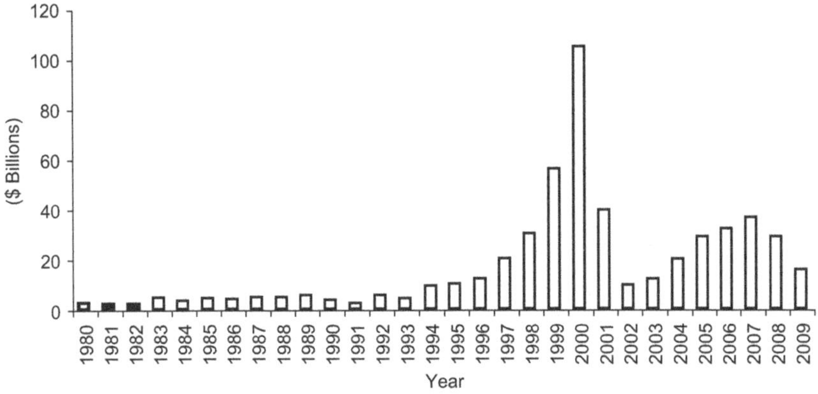

Figure 5.5 Capital commitments to USA venture funds ($ billions), 1980–2009
Source: National Venture Capital Association 2010.

has gone to excess, dragging the rest of the economy to the speculative bubble, were the areas where the appropriation of wealth by managers and workers was stronger. The costs of high-tech managers and workers, when considering stock options as wage costs, accounted for 73 percent of pre-tax profits (in June 2000, compared with 20 percent of the same costs for the 325 largest listed companies).[8] These forms of remuneration made financial-market liquidity grow, but, in the absence of an adequate redistribution rule, inside a capitalism in which the rule is to command living labor in any case, this also compressed wages, leading to systemic instability.

A (financialized) monetary circuit framework in the *New Economy* scenario is depicted in Figure 5.6. Credit money enters the economic process under entrepreneurial demand (Step 1). Firms use also private-equity funds (especially venture-capital funds) to increase the flow of investments. In a context of effervescence of financial markets (and monetary easing), such strategy leads to an increase in common stock, allowing to earn capital gains (Step 2) able to pay off the debts previously contracted from the banking system (Step 5a) and possibly to accrue profits to be returned or to be used as self-funding. The amount of money used to fund productive activity and pay wages (Step 3a) derives from both traditional credit money and financial returns, i.e. a sort of financialized money. Wage earners allocate their income either for consumption or saving (Step 4a, 4b). Consumption and the demand regime are directly affected by financialization. In order to avoid a crisis of effective demand, wage de-regulation (and the privatization of the welfare state) is compensated by the wealth effect reflected in the overall financial returns (Step 4c). The capital gains of financial markets function as a kind of multiplier for the real economy just like the deficit spending did during Fordism and the Keynesian era. If control of the financial activities is distributed in a

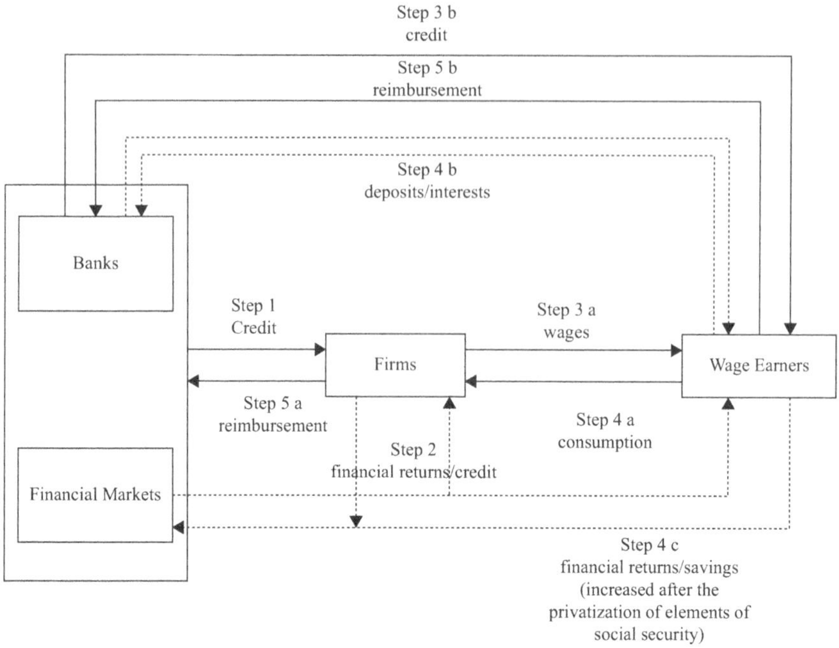

Figure 5.6 Framework of a financialised monetary economy of production (new economy)

distorted way, unlike the redistributive effects of the welfare state, the result is an increase in income polarization.

The stability condition of the economic system depends on the propensity to invest and on the wealth effect, both produced by capital-gains allocation. But when financial gains misrepresent the real effects of investment on productivity, then financial bubbles may emerge. If the wealth effects generated by the capital gains fail, the facilitated access to credit is used to sustain consumption (Step 3b) and guarantee, even if provisionally, the closure of the circuit. Necessarily, the final result is an ever-growing debt affecting more and more families that leads to an increase in the risk of debt insolvency.

On financialised money

Following the crisis of Fordism and the fall of the Bretton Woods system, money has increased its power of control. Throughout the 1980s, the general increase in economic uncertainty, that began with the adoption of flexible exchange-rate regimes, the downward rigidity of interest rates and the reduction of the referential time horizon (with activities becoming increasingly short term), has facilitated the rise of financial tools (the so-called derivative products, such as options and futures) aiming at insuring economic agents against risk and pre-dating the deadlines for trading and thus at predetermining the value of the exchange itself. Such operations allow to obtain liquidity ("cash") from financial debt and credit operations mainly concerning on government bonds or foreign-exchange market. Thereby, it's possible to meet an increasingly inescapable need of modern post-Fordist economies, which is to promote the realization of monetary exchange for some market activity, and thus insure against the risk of insolvency or unsold.

Since the 1990s, with the development of the "internet convention," financial markets start to play a key role in creating virtual money, by now completely dematerialized and, therefore, subjected to the evolution of conventional and trust mechanisms that are created within the financial markets themselves. Monetary policy becomes more and more dependent on the dynamics of financial markets, with its first goal being to support the creation of positive capital gains as engines of economic growth, in an otherwise low inflation environment. The institutional channel for money creation becomes less and less important. Public creation of money through deficit spending on social programs is strongly reduced. Public-sector deficits play a subordinate role within the dynamics of stock-exchange prices in an increasingly procyclical perspective. Hence, after the credit channel (previously discussed and identified in Figures 5.1 and 5.6) and the public-sector channel and the balance-of-payments channels (not analyzed in Figures 5.1 and 5.6 so as to simplify our earlier analysis), we now have a fourth channel of money creation: the financial-market channel of money creation.

> Certainly shares are not money. Their liquidity in only partial in the sense that they are not accepted as universal instrument of exchange. Nevertheless, their sphere of circulation is already extremely vast. Not only as reserve assets, but also as means of exchange for certain acquires another with the help of its own shares, or even better when a manager accepts to be paid in stock options. For this reason, then, we can consider shares as constituting an embryonic form of currency even if they still can't be used to purchase consumer goods. The question of whether or not this form will arrive at maturity, whether it will become currency in the full sense of the term, is in a certain sense, the challenge of our analysis because such a turn of events would constitute a radical change in the principle of sovereignty.
> (Orléan 1999: 242, translated in Marazzi 2008: 62)

The increasing financial liquidity actually means a *displacement* of money creation from the central bank to the financial markets. The money supply grew in response to the increase in demand from investors, both business enterprises and households and, in the United States, the Federal Reserve (Fed) *monetized* this demand for liquidity (Marazzi 2008: 63). One should not, however, conclude that the financial markets create their own specific currency, different from the one created by the central bank. Rather, in order to create money and assure the circulations of values, the central bank necessarily accommodates the movements of financial markets.

Towards the big crash

The 2007–2009 crisis stems from the overinvestment in new technologies. Thanks to credit easing, and also by means of securitization, speculative attitudes pass from one asset to another, and the economy jumps from one bubble to the next. Financial markets move in waves dominated by conventional behavior that is able to produce movements of public opinion through institutional financial operators.

The double taxation of profits during the 1990s led companies to borrow heavily to deduct their interest payments from pre-tax profits and then buy back their shares (buyback strategy) and to distribute stock options to managers and employees. With the mergers and acquisitions strategy between companies in order to keep up the speculative activity, the result was a great distortion in the price of securities in relation to their underlying economic value.[9]

After the 2000 crisis, investors began to switch from the equity market to the bond market and were especially fond of Freddie Mac and Fannie Mae bonds. The stock-exchange market was able to recover after the internet convention crisis and to provide liquidity in support of speculative excesses, fueled in part by the increased indebtedness of households in the United States and elsewhere in the Western world, in order to keep up with the living standard of the previous decade. At the same time, Chinese surpluses started to "finance" the US internal and external deficits.

In the two-year period following the March 2000 crisis (2001–2002), the US Fed funds rate was drastically lowered from 6.5 per cent in December 2000 to 1 per cent by June 2003. Also fiscal policy changed: the US Congress passed the Jobs and Growth Tax Relief Reconciliation Act of 2003, which George W. Bush signed into law on May 28, 2003. Under the new law, qualified dividends are now taxed at the same rate as long-term capital gains, that is, 15 per cent for most individual taxpayers (before the new law, the rate was 20 per cent). Moreover, qualified dividends received by individuals in the 10 per cent and 15 per cent income tax brackets were taxed at 5 per cent from 2003 to 2007 (before the new law, the rate was 10 per cent).

The new institutional context pushed economic agents to the edge of the precipice by going into unreasonable debt in order to benefit from the discrepancy between their own capital yield and the interest rate. This incentive to accumulate debt means that the wealth effect was articulated in different ways with respect to the roaring years of the New Economy: prices in the real-estate markets rose, and the Fed's monetary policy supported the buying power of American consumers. American households could thus obtain practically unlimited credit from the banking system, by putting up real estate with increasing value as collateral. The expected earnings came back high, sustained by a negative real interest rate. As Shiller affirmed in an interview in June 2005:

> Once stocks fell, real estate became the primary outlet for the speculative frenzy that the stock market had unleashed. Where else could plungers apply their newly acquired trading talents? The materialistic display of the big house also has become a salve to bruised egos of disappointed stock investors. These days, the only thing that comes close to real estate as a national obsession is poker.
>
> (Shiller 2005)

Favored by low interest rates, financial innovations (new types of derivatives), and increase in house prices, credit–debt relationship in the housing market (the "real-estate convention") developed with a positive impact on the financial markets. When house prices increase, a great wealth is produced, thereby strongly favoring the position of both borrowers and lenders. The dynamics of credit creation is sustained by household indebtedness. "The financial system has become a kind of four-layer cake: high-leverage banks have financed high-leverage investments, which invested in high-leverage securities (as Abs or Cdo) to significantly increase the households' degree of leverage" (Onado 2009: 58).

The real-estate convention lasted until September 2007, after the first shock in the mortgage market, due to the stop in the increase of house prices, on the one hand, and to the rise in interest rates on the other. As it is well known, the combination of these two phenomena made it more difficult for banks to expand the market for home mortgages in the face of an increase in defaults on homeowners' mortgage payments. The results were the collapse of the securitization castle and the impossibility to give a value to the linked derivatives. The instability of financial markets is definitely confirmed as an endogenous process by recent experience.

Credit default swaps are financial instruments used as a hedge and protection for debt holders, namely mortgage backed security investors from the risk of default.

> As its name suggests, the payoff on a credit default swap (CDS) depends on the default of a specific borrower, such as a corporation, or of a specific security, such as a bond. The value of these instruments is especially sensitive to the state of the overall economy. If the economy moves toward a recession, for example, the likelihood of defaults increases and the expected payoff on credit default swaps can rise quickly.
>
> (Squam Lake Working Group on Financial Regulation 2009: 2)

In other words, the risk–reward asymmetry works in the opposite way to stocks: "People buy them not because they expect an eventual default but because they expect the CDS to appreciate in case of adverse developments"

(Soros 2009: 166). CDSs were invented only in 1997 by J. P. Morgan, but the market increased tremendously starting in 2003. The International Swaps and Derivatives Association (ISDA) estimates the total notional amount of outstanding CDSs to be around $ 62.2 trillion, making these contracts the most widely traded credit derivative product as of December 2007 (see Figure 5.7).

The evolution of CDSs seems to describe the principal novelty that, after the 2000 crisis, characterizes the financialized monetary economy of production, i.e. a new channel of money creation in which financial markets are directly involved. This process occurs through the close link between banks and financial institutions, following the role played by the CDS, a real bridge between the traditional way of money creation via credit and the new creation of *near money*, via capital gains, on the CDS market (Step 1 in Figure 5.8).

As far as the other steps are concerned, in this framework, we do not present other novelties. The dynamics of credit creation is sustained by increasing household indebtedness; in other words, Step 3b and Step 5b describe a more abundant flow than the same steps in Figure 5.6. The most important aspect to underline is that the direct role played by financial activities and derivatives in the money-creation process poses some theoretical problems. In the previous scheme (Figure 5.6), in fact, capital gains played the role of redistributive mechanisms—via the financial multiplier—and facilitated access to bank loans by developing strategies for technology acquisition and the financing of investment in innovative activities. For instance, venture capital was a

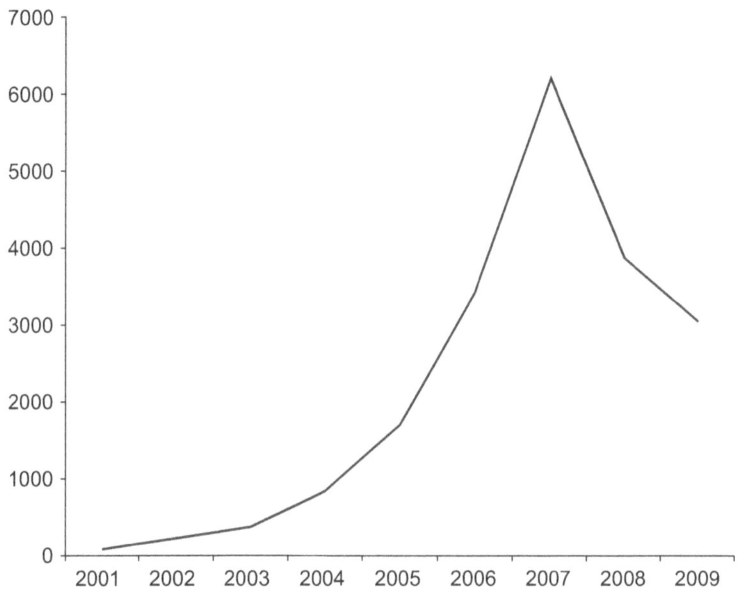

Figure 5.7 Total credit default swap outstanding
Source: ISDA Market Survey

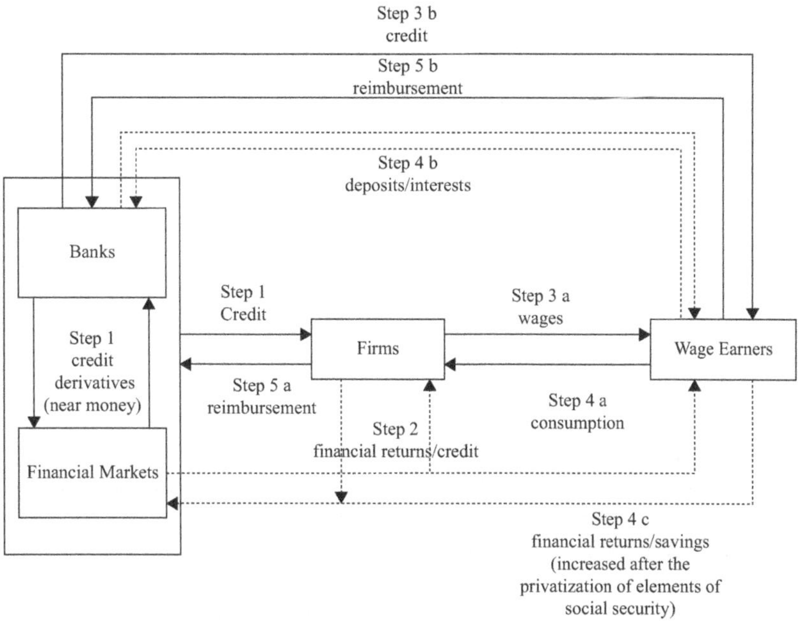

Figure 5.8 A framework of the financialized monetary economy of production (real-estate bubble)

strategy that disclosed the role of financial markets in being directly involved in investment activities. In the latter framework (Figure 5.8), financial markets are able to create *near money* with the effect of increasing the liquidity of the system according to the growth of the real-estate bubble.

Conclusion

The causes of the ongoing crisis are endogenous to the regime of accumulation that characterized especially American capitalism after the crisis of Fordism (Aglietta 2008). The new capitalism has emerged after 1971 largely as a result of President Nixon's decision to cancel unilaterally the direct convertibility of the US dollar to gold, which essentially ended the Bretton Woods system of international financial exchange. It had been accelerated by Paul Volker's policy that imposed monetary austerity (1979–1986). In the new disinflationary environment, markets became very flexible, and restructuring operations and cost-cutting programs became very frequent. Consequently, there ensued a lack of pressure on wages as a result of changes in the behavior of employees who became more "docile."

Financial markets are today the pulsing heart of a restructured capitalism. Wage moderation helps corporate profitability and increases the value of financial stocks. Wage earners, especially in the 1990s (the era of the so-called

New Economy), have been increasingly pushed by governments, by trade unions, and by the media, to entrust money to financial operators, both directly and indirectly. Pension funds, investment funds, insurances and, in certain cases, part of the transfers to workers depends on financial returns. In the American growth model, especially during the past two decades, financial and real variables are deeply intertwined: corporate profits, and also household consumption, are increasingly governed by Wall Street. Supporting the financial performance became managers' imperative and the hope of many households was to become increasingly indebted.

Interpreting the 2007 crisis as the result of a malfunctioning of financial markets is wrong: as André Orléan wrote, it is not due to the fact that the financial rules were circumvented, but by the fact that they were followed (Orléan 2009). Securitization can be interpreted as the last stage of profound transformation of financial systems began in the late 1970s, and it is connected with the shift of US monetary policy in October 1979. The low level of wages, and the consequent under-consumption, is not the unique cause of the crisis. Financialization is not only limited in changing behavior of consumer-savers; the investments have also changed. Particularly during the 1990s, as the new industrial technology favored its own sort of financing.

This trend, *mutatis mutandis*, seems to reflect the same dynamics studied by Joseph Alois Schumpeter about railroadization in the nineteenth century in his *Business Cycles* (1989: 215–231). As affirmed by Antonelli (2009), the big crisis began when interest rates reported relative to their normal levels did not allow the survival of marginal activities. The over-financed leverage may be better understood starting from the 1990s technological paradigm. After the so-called internet bubble burst, something remained (for example, new large companies as Microsoft and Apple). The stock-market crash of 2000–2002 did not really stop American growth and was not interpreted as a proof of financial fragility. The financial bubble was delayed and contained mainly by Fed monetary policy.

The monetary theory of production offers a systemic approach to avert systemic crises; but it needs to be modified. Faced with post-Fordist capitalism, scholars are seeking to address this challenge. In accordance with the Schumpeterian perspective, we propose to emphasize within the circuitist approach both the monetary nature and the qualitative change of the capitalist system, in order to explore the profound transformation of the antagonistic relation of capital to labor related to the development of an economy founded on knowledge as its driving force.

Notes

1 We refer to Graziani (1984), where the author describes three classes (bankers, capitalists, and workers) and two sectors (consumption and investment goods). Lunghini and Bianchi (2004) interpret Graziani's scheme as a reproduction scheme, where the condition of profit equalization determines the value of relative prices but leaves absolute prices ad income distribution undetermined. Consequently, the monetary circuit scheme remains an open scheme.

2 Lunghini and Bianchi (2004) consider Graziani's (1984) scheme unsatisfactory because "the two conditions of profit equalization and given supplies are mutually inconsistent and one must be relaxed in order to provide an appropriate description of the working of the economic system and avoid logical and analytical faults. In a short-run perspective, when supplies are given, the condition of profit equalization must be dropped. [...] Profit equalization requires, even in the presence of given demands, free mobility of capital and output between sectors. In this perspective supplies cannot be given and prices will be determined by costs" (Lunghini and Bianchi 2004: 157). To be coherent, Graziani's scheme may be interpreted as an open-ended system.

3 Graziani (1984) does not consider this possibility that is considered in many contributions by Italian circuitists. See Realfonzo (2006: 110–111).

4 In our previous work (2010), and in agreement with Vercellone (2003, 2007), Paulré (2008) and Marazzi (2010), we propose the notion of "cognitive capitalism" by taking account of the way in which the crisis of Fordism has corresponded to a superior level of "great crisis," entailing the profound transformation of the antagonistic relation of capital to labor related to the development of an economy founded on the driving role of knowledge. The thesis of financial capitalism is often opposed to the thesis of a cognitive capitalism, but, as Paurlé (2008) argued, financialisation finds a development opportunity in the context of cognitive capitalism. To complete the analysis of the knowledge/power relation in the development of the division of labor, we need to consider together the new form of production and financialization. See also the essays collected in Fumagalli and Mezzadra (2010).

5 In order to perform the conceptual integration of the financialization of modern economies in monetary circuit theory, Pilkington proposes an extended version of the Lavoie–Godley stock/flow framework including a finance sector defined as a broad accounting category that is constantly interacting with the other institutional sectors of the economic system.

6 Conventions are market trends originated within the investment community according to a logic of self-referential rationality (Orléan 1999). The irrationality that supports the 1990s financial boom gathers in itself the desire of an *anthropogenetic* model in which the productive power of diffused intellectuality is recognized outside of the logic of exploitation. "Beyond information technology lies the knowledge economy, a concept which international agencies, such as OECD and World Bank, are only now beginning to take seriously. This, however, is merely part of a much wider development involving 'the production of humans by humans'" (Boyer 2004: xv).

7 See *The Economist* (2004).

8 Data source from Plender (2003).

9 As *The Economist* wrote in February 2004, "After a long hibernation, company bosses are beginning to rediscover their animal spirits. The $145 billion-worth of global mergers and acquisitions announced in January was the highest for any month since October 2000, and the figure for February seems likely to beat that."

References

Aglietta, M. (1979) *A Theory of Capitalist Regulation: The US Experience*, London and New York: Verso.

Aglietta, M. (2008) "Into a New Growth Regime," *New Left Review*, 54 (November–December): 61–74.

Antonelli, C. (2009) "Appunti per una lettura schumpeteriana della crisi e implicazioni di politica economica," Dipartimento di Economia "S. Cognetti de Martiis." Working Paper, no. 14.

Antonelli, C. and M. Teubal (2008) "Knowledge-Intensive Property Rights and the Evolution of Venture Capitalism," *Journal of Institutional Economics*, 4(2): 163–182.

Bellofiore, R. and M. Seccareccia (1999) "Monetary Circuit," in P. A. O'Hara (ed.), *Encyclopedia of Political Economy*, London and New York: Routledge, pp. 753–756.

Boyer, R. (2000) "Is a Finance-led Growth Regime a Viable Alternative to Fordism? A Preliminary Analysis,"*Economy and Society*, 29(1): 111–145.

Boyer, R. (2004) *The Future of Economic Growth: As New Becomes Old*, Cheltenham: Edward Elgar.

The Economist (2004) "A Special Report on Mergers and Acquisitions," February 19.

The Economist (2008) "A Special Report on the Future of Banking," May 17–23.

Forges Davanzati, G. and G. Tortorella (2010) "Low Wages, Private Indebtedness, and Crisis: A Monetary-Theory-of-Production Approach," *European Journal of Economic and Social Systems*, 23(1): 25–44.

Fumagalli, A. and S. Lucarelli (2010) "Cognitive Capitalism as a Financial Economy of Production," in V. Cvijanović, A. Fumagalli, and C. Vercellone (eds.), *Cognitive Capitalism and Its Reflections in South-Eastern Europe*, Frankfurt: Peter Lang, pp. 9–40.

Fumagalli, A. and S. Mezzadra (eds.) (2010) *Crisis in the Global Economy: Financial Markets, Social Struggles, and New Political Scenarios*, Los Angeles, CA:Semiotext(e).

Graziani, A. (1984) "Moneta senza crisi," *Studi Economici*, 39(24): 3–37.

Graziani, A. (2003) *The Monetary Theory of Production*, Cambridge: Cambridge University Press.

Hudson, M. (2006) "The Road to Serfdom: An Illustrated Guide to the Coming Real Estate Collapse," *Harper's Magazine*, May: 39–46.

Interbrand (2010) "Best Global Brands 2010," available at www.bestglobalbrands.com (accessed January 2011).

Keynes, J. M. (1978) "Contibution to a Festschrift for Professor A. Spiethoff," in *Collected Writings*, London: Macmillan, vol. XIII, pp. 408–411.

Lunghini, G. and C. Bianchi (2004) "The Monetary Circuit and Income Distribution: Bankers as Landlords?" in R. Arena and N. Salvadori (eds.), *Money, Credit and the Role of the State: Essays in Honour of Augusto Graziani*, Burlington: Ashgate, pp. 152–174.

Marazzi, C. (2008) *Capital and Language: From the New Economy to the War Economy*, Los Angeles, CA:Semiotext(e).

Marazzi, C. (2010) "The Violence of Financial Capitalism," in A. Fumagalli and S. Mezzadra (eds.), *Crisis in the Global Economy: Financial Markets, Social Struggles, and New Political Scenarios*, Los Angeles, CA:Semiotext(e), pp. 17–59.

National Venture Capital Association (2010) "Yearbook 2010," available at https://nvca.org/research/research-resources/ (accessed January 2011).

Olréan, A. (1999) *Le Pouvoir de la finance*, Paris: Odile Jacob.

Onado, M. (2009) *I nodi al pettine:la crisi finanziaria e le regole non scritte*, Rome: Laterza.

Orléan, A. (2009) *De l'euphorie à la panique: penser la crise*, Paris: ENS rue d'Ulm.

Orsi, F. and B. Coriat (2003) "Intellectual Property Rights, Financial Markets and Innovation A Sustainable Configuration?," *Issues in Regulation Theory*, 45 (July): 1–5.

Passarella, M. (2011) "Systemic Financial Fragility and the Monetary Circuit: A Stock-Flow Consistent Approach," MPRA Paper, no. 28498. Available at https://mpra.ub.uni-muenchen.de/28498 (accessed March 25, 2019).

Paulré, B. (2008) "Capitalisme cognitif et financiarisation des économiès," in G. Colletis and B. Paulré (eds.), *Les Nouveaux Horizons du capitalisme*, Paris: Economica, pp. 173–209.

Pilkington, M. (2009) "The Financialization of Modern Economies in Monetary Circuit Theory," in S. Rossi and J. F. Ponsot (eds.), *The Political Economy of Monetary Circuits: Tradition and Change in Post-Keynesian Economics*, Basingstoke: Palgrave Macmillan, pp. 188–216.

Plender, J. (2003) *From Going Off the Rails: Global Capital and the Crisis of Legitimacy*, Chichester: John Wiley & Sons.

Realfonzo, R. (2006) "The Italian Circuitist Approach," in P. Arestis and M. Sawyer (eds.), *A Handbook of Alternative Monetary Economics*, Cheltenham: Edward Elgar, pp. 105–120.

Rochon, L. P. and S. Rossi (2010) "The 2007–2009 Economic and Financial Crisis: An Analysis in Terms of Monetary Circuits," *European Journal of Economic and Social Systems*, 23(1): 7–23.

Schumpeter, J. A. (1989) *Business Cycle: A Theoretical, Historical and Statistical Analysis of the Capitalist Process*, Philadelphia, PA: Porcupine Press.

Seccareccia, M. (2011) "Financialization and the Transformation of Commercial Banking: Understanding the Recent Canadian Experience before and during the International Financial Crisis," *Journal of Post Keynesian Economics*, 35(2): 277–300.

Shapiro, R. and K. Hassett (2005) *The Economic Value of Intellectual Property*, USA for Innovation (October), available at www.sonecon.com/docs/.../IntellectualPropertyReport-October2005.pdf (accessed January 2011).

Shiller, R. (2005) "The Bubble's New Home: Interview by Jonathan R. Laing,"*Barron's*, Monday, June 20, available at https://www.wsj.com/articles/SB111905372884363176 (accessed March 25, 2019).

Soros, G. (2009) *The Crash of 2008 and What It Means*, New York: Public Affairs.

Squam Lake Working Group on Financial Regulation (2009) "Credit Default Swaps, Clearing House, and Exchanges," Council of Foreign Relations Working Paper (July).

Stellian, R. (2010) "Home Equity Extraction, Growth, and the Subprime Crisis within the Theory of the Monetary Circuit," *European Journal of Economic and Social Systems*, 23(1): 45–62.

Vercellone, C. (2007) "From Formal Subsumption to General Intellect: Elements for a Marxist Reading of the Thesis of Cognitive Capitalism,"*Historical Materialism*, 15(1): 13–36.

Vercellone, C. (ed.) (2003) *Sommes-nous sortis du capitalisme industrielle?*Paris: La Dispute.

6 Cognitive capitalism, an empirical and theoretical analysis

Andrea Fumagalli and Stefano Lucarelli

Introduction

The purpose of this chapter is to provide a theoretical framework of cognitive capitalism and to discuss the conditions of stability and instability of the model. In the first part of the chapter we present a panel data analysis to support the hypothesis that welfare-state systems, by increasing knowledge, is positively correlated with the increasing value of immaterial capital. In other words, the generation of knowledge and its spatial diffusion are the basic features of cognitive capitalism. However, the capitalist system is inherently an unstable system, subject to indecision and crises, in which transformations along time imply to renew its theoretical analysis. Cognitive capitalism defines a form of accumulation without a viable mode of regulation among social classes. Particularly knowledge exploitation and capital-gains allocation are deregulated. As we argue in the second part of the chapter, on the demand side the increasing polarization of income distribution penalize effective demand not only by reducing the level of consumption but also by negatively affecting the investment. Indeed, knowledge-learning process and network economies have to be supported. A too-high rate of precariousness can negatively affect productivity, with the risk to worsen financial gains, notwithstanding a pragmatic monetary policy.

The role of knowledge in the transition from Fordism to cognitive capitalism: some empirical evidence

The starting point for the formation of cognitive capitalism is the process of diffusion of knowledge generated by the development of mass schooling and the rise of the average level of education. As shown in the previous chapters, the scholars that proposed the cognitive capitalism thesis (first of all Carlo Vercellone [2015]) affirm that, starting from the 1970s, the increase of immaterial capital, already described by Kendrick (1976, 1994) for the United States, does not mainly depend on R&D investments but on the positive effects of the social policies promoted by welfare-state systems.[1]

An empirical confirm of this thought may be presented by considering the following European countries for the period 1995–2014: Finland, France,

Germany, Greece, Italy, Spain and the UK. We present a panel data to estimate the correlation between the value of immaterial capital and the following dependent variables:

- Public expenditures in the healthcare system (Health), from OECD health statistics;
- Public expenditures in education (EDU), from the World Bank education statistics;
- General expenditure in R&D (GERD), from Eurostat;
- GDP, from Eurostat.

In order to describe the long-term effects of the welfare state's social policies, we built other lagged variables for Health and EDU:

- Health(−5): that describes the five years lagged public expenditures in the healthcare system;
- EDU(−5): that describes the five years lagged public expenditures in education;
- EDU(−17): that describes the seventeen years lagged public expenditures in the healthcare system.

We also consider various time dummies and especially a dummy that measures the presence of the European crisis since 2008 to 2014 (named simply "Crisis"). To measure the dependent variable (immaterial capital), we use the data provided by Corrado et al. (2012). These authors identified all the relevant *intangible asset types*, that are:

- computerised information: software and databases;
- innovative property: R&D, design, product development in financial services, mineral exploration and spending on the production of artistic originals;
- economic competencies: market research, advertising, training, organisational capital (own account and purchased).

The data elaborated by Corrado et al. (2012) cover the period 1995–2010. We use a simple statistical forecasting model based on the moving average method to complete the historical series until the 2014 (see Table 6.1).

The data show a notorious dichotomy that characterises European countries: the core European countries presents the higher values. Our results are presented in Table 6.2 where we compare six different models: the first two by using the Pooled OLS empirical methodology, the second four by using the Fixed Effects methodology. As known, Fixed Effects is a feasible generalised least squares technique which is asymptotically more efficient than Pooled OLS when time constant attributes are present.

Table 6.1 Intangible assets (in millions of national currency)

	Finland	*France*	*Germany*	*Greece*	*Italy*	*Spain*	*United Kingdom*
1995	7,343	96,571	149,018	1,350	36,651	15,324	58,190
1996	7,631	100,067	143,651	1,522	43,220	16,814	62,376
1997	7,429	90,332	129,405	1,592	42,151	15,643	71,668
1998	8,175	100,220	134,427	1,815	42,801	17,095	83,673
1999	8,778	99,704	137,814	1,849	45,555	18,710	87,619
2000	8,450	88,373	126,847	1,733	45,455	17,600	87,154
2001	8,682	91,158	124,743	1,732	41,756	18,463	85,363
2002	9,078	97,366	127,434	2,164	47,634	20,934	92,745
2003	11,455	122,824	149,964	2,781	54,933	27,584	105,939
2004	12,744	141,389	159,592	3,466	67,533	33,464	123,848
2005	13,864	145,670	155,984	3,767	70,941	37,781	134,003
2006	14,504	161,287	160,876	3,929	71,002	41,495	144,442
2007	17,392	179,814	180,402	5,139	80,468	50,245	173,652
2008	19,689	198,377	195,860	5,596	86,441	57,752	167,617
2009	17,319	176,366	181,289	4,912	74,413	48,855	137,353
2010	16,629	176,652	174,406	4,429	71,922	46,843	141,218
2011	17,363	192,827	184,735	4,360	75,301	47,980	145,817
2012	16,201	190,150	175,372	3,720	70,002	43,134	140,487
2013	16,965	207,570	187,713	3,388	73,072	43,793	137,441
2014	17,067	212,536	190,631	3,092	73,575	43,234	144,256

Source: Our computations on dataset www.INTAN-Invest.net. Accessed September 2017.

Notes: New intangibles and national account intangibles; gross fixed capital formation, current prices, millions of national currency.

All the models we tested clearly show that the magnitude of the single coefficients related to healthcare and education public expenditures are higher, in absolute value, than the magnitude of the coefficient related to R&D (GERD).

The most relevant variable seems EDU(−5), that is statistically significant with a positive coefficient, in model 1, 2, 3, 5 and 6. Model 5 and 6 show that time dummies are meaningful and positively correlated with "Intangibles." Their presence does not affect the relevance of EDU(−5), which remains positively correlated with the dependent variable. It also contributes to show the importance of Health and Health(−5), which have a high positive coefficient.

Models 2 and 6 show a negative correlation between the dependent variable and the dummy variable that describes the recent European economic crisis.

The empirical analysis is coherent with the idea that past generation of knowledge promoted by a society based on public education and healthcare represents the engine for the actual value if the immaterial capital (measured by today's intangible assets). Differently from the Fordist phase, the present

Table 6.2 Panel estimations: intangible assets determinants in Europe

	OLS Pooled		*Fixed Effects*			
	Mod. 1	Mod. 2	Mod. 3	Mod. 4	Mod. 5	Mod. 6
k	3752.65 **	−1777.61	11049.1 ***	−21742 ***	−157286 ***	−144231 ***
Health	4.17481 ***	6.67667 ***	6.92664 **	−2.73036	27.4229 ***	18.5784 ***
Health (−5)	−9.94387 ***	−7.94971 ***	−6.87112 *	2.97717	32.1815 ***	39.5071 ***
EDU	1.80729 ***	2.48179 ***	0.0822032	−1.28445 **	−2.62284 ***	−3.58837 ***
EDU (-5)	3.10691 ***	3.7216 ***	5.43777 ***	0.611536	6.59946 ***	1.60878 *
EDU (-17)	3.43362 ***	3.46148 ***	0.428684	−0.740576	0.0387744	−1.32126 **
GERD	0.0555959 **	0.043494 *	−0.046984 **	−0.063922 ***	−0.0548515 **	−0.0747174 ***
GDP		−0.014777 **		0.0970828 ***		0.0977854 ***
Crisis (2008–14)		−7335.45 ***		−1333.59		−47330 ***
Time dummies					Yes + dt9 and dt25 ** dt10 to dt24 ***	Yes + dt20 ** d9 to dt26 ***

Table 6.2 (cont.)

	OLS Pooled		*Fixed Effects*			
Adj. R^2	0.966521	0.965332	0.976731	0.984633	0.979499	0.987300
DW			0.305845	0.235778	0.428400	0.493994
Wald test for joint significance of time dummies					Asymptotic test statistic: Chi^2 (19) = 36.1498 p-value = 0.0101172	Asymptotic test statistic: $Chi^2(18)$ = 44.2539 p-value = 0.000530596

Notes: 140 observations: 7 cross-sectional units; time-series length = 20
p-value <0.01***, p-value<0.05**, p-value<0.1*

diffusion of knowledge no longer depends upon technological transfers of machineries alone, but rather upon relational *flows* generated by immaterial process.

Knowledge-learning process and network economies

If knowledge is the basis of accumulation, it becomes unavoidable to analyze how its exchange and diffusion affect the dynamics of productivity. The peculiarities of cognitive capitalism are its ability to enlarge both knowledge-learning process (λ) and network economies (k). The variable λ depends on the degree of *cumulativeness, opportunity* and *appropriability* (Nelson and Winter 1982). Here, *opportunity* is defined as the expected rate of profit (P^e) and, therefore, the higher the expected profit in adopting a new technology, the higher is the speed of its diffusion. *Cumulativeness* and *appropriability* represent the capacity of new knowledge to generate further innovation while avoiding the possibility of its imitation, thanks to the existence of intellectual property rights (IPR). The variable k depends on the level of income (Y) and positive externalities (E). When λ is constrained by IPR, we shall see that the consequence is that the greater is the degree of *appropriability* of knowledge, the smaller becomes its capacity of diffusion—affecting, *de facto*, its ability to positively influencing the associated productivity.[2] While it is during the learning process that the generation of knowledge occurs, network economies define the way in which the produced knowledge is diffuse. To a higher level of knowledge corresponds, in terms of its generation (λ) and diffusion (k), more innovative technologies. From a systemic perspective, an innovation is a change in the economic process occurred as a result of the investment activity. Whether the investment is devoted to the already existing technology or to new technologies will establish the amount of innovation. The crisis of Fordism led to a new investment activity based on new sources of growth (electronic marketing, informational goods, encoding software, control over the quality of information, branding, control over the lifestyles, etc.). In a social system geared around innovation and production, investment policies depend upon R&D and "learning by doing" strategies and process. In cognitive capitalism, the impact of new ICT based on computer science, microelectronics and the new organizational productive changes (just-in-time, zero stock) have speed up the "learning by doing" processes, spreading them well beyond the firm (Venturini 2006). At the same time, part of the R&D process unfolds itself within territories each having one or more specific competencies. Where to locate economic activities is mainly determined by the search on the part of the firm of advantages in the development of its competencies (Mouhoud 2006: 300). Consequently, the productivity entailed by the exchange of knowledge cannot be assimilated to material productivity.

Some notes about financial markets and production

The realization of production is compensated by financial markets acting as a *multiplier* of aggregate demand and by the processes of globalization (delocalization, outsourcing, lower labour costs). The efficiency of the system is assured by both the growth of financial markets—primary source of surplus distribution—and by massive processes of outsourcing and delocalization characterizing advanced countries (which are by definition the places where the accumulation of knowledge occurs more intensely). In this context, the capital–labour compromise, based on the connection between productivity gains and real wage dynamics, is declining, with subsequent effects on polarization of income distribution.

Second, an income distribution that penalizes workers, negatively affects learning and network economies, because these last ones require higher remunerations in order to be better exploited. Consequently, the loss of productivity gains reduces the efficiency of the system. The high degree of precariousness on the one hand represents the necessary precondition for perpetrating a situation of exploitation and command within the relationship between capital and labour; and, on the other, it represents an obstacle to the development of knowledge. In such a context, a new form of the capitalistic exploitation is the production of political lines in order to improve the financialization of social production. In this respect, exploitation in cognitive capitalism has been defined as "the seizure, the centralization, and the expropriation of the form and the product of social co-operation," "the political sign of domination above and against the human valorisation of the historical/natural world," the "command above and against productive social cooperation" (Negri 1997).

In the above framework, aggregate demand is influenced both by the dynamic of the financial markets and by the capital gains deriving from the internationalization of production. With the weakening of the wage–productivity nexus, these dynamics had a greater impact on consumption and the investment activity. In a finance-led economy in order to avoid a demand crisis, the wage regulation ought to be based upon the distribution of capital gains. However, the shortcomings intrinsic to this approach are, first, that given the widespread uncertainty generated by working precariousness, knowledge loses its generative capacity, and, second, as there is no guarantee that the overall produced wealth will be re-invested into the financial market or elsewhere, a finance-led growth is always at risk of instability.

As far as the supply side is concerned, changes in the ability to generate new knowledge, as a basic condition for the spread of new technologies, depend on the characteristics of the environment in which R&D activities are organized. This environment is positively affected by the income level and by a set of variables, such as education, an overall macroeconomic and political stability, a fair wealth redistribution, a balance between material and immaterial activities, and the existence of a good system of infrastructures, which we define as positive externalities.

The power of finance capital resides in its ability to impose the criteria of financial returns. Companies, in order to obtain liquidity for *mergers and acquisitions* (M&A) run into debts. Through the M&A strategy the company control technologies, skills, and know-how of other potential competitors. Thus, business expectations should increase, managers should sustain the positive dynamics of shareholder values on one hand, and pay the debts to the banks, on the other hand. More importantly, indebtedness is not directed to capital expenditures, but it is a powerful means of satisfying the financial criteria of shareholder value. Such a process requires specific monetary policies by a massive injection of liquidity and lowering of interest rates to prevent the emergence of financial bubbles.[3]

Monetary policy may sustain the financial boom of a knowledge-based economy. But each financial boom has a double result: from one side, the positive dynamics of shareholder values favours the increase in aggregate consumption, from the other, because of its unequal allocation, leads to a distorted income distribution.

The model

Building upon the French regulation theory (see Boyer 2004a, 2004b), our formalization[4] will highlight first the dynamic function of productivity as key variable of the supply side and, second the dynamic function of aggregate demand, composed of private consumption, increase in investment, and public expenditure as autonomous variable. Although the generation of knowledge, its spatial diffusion, and financialization affect open economies, including third-world economies, *we have chosen to deal only with the pure case of the closed economy in which knowledge-learning process, network economies and financial dynamics develop entirely in the domestic arena.* In such a context, we will clarify under which conditions productivity and aggregate demand dynamics can provide a stable rate of growth. The model is described by a linear differential equations system in Figure 6.1.

Equations from (1) to (4) describe supply-side dynamics, based on productivity. It is supposed, as already showed, that this latter mainly depends on dynamic scale economies (Equation 1):

- network economies ($\dot{k}$) are positively correlated to the level of production as proxy of the value of the spatial diffusion of economic activities, and to externalities E, supposed to be exogenous (Equation 2);
- learning economies ($\dot{\lambda}$) are a positive function of investment activity and a negative function of exogenous IPR (that may also comprehend the innovative tools used in contemporary digital platforms, like Facebook, to accumulate users' private information) (Equation 3).

Productivity changes are also related to changes in volume of output ($\dot{Y}$): as the so-called Verdoorn Law affirms, in the short run an increase in output can determine a more efficient use of labour, realizing static scale

SUPPLY SIDE

$\dot{\pi} = a\dot{k} + b\dot{\lambda} + cI + d\dot{Y}$ [1]

$\dot{k} = e\dot{Y} + E$ [2]

$\dot{\lambda} = hI - IPR$ [3]

$I = I_K + I_\lambda$ [4]

$I_K = \sigma\dot{Y}$ [4a]

$I_\lambda = \gamma\,\dot{CG}$ [4b]

$\dot{CG} = \beta\dot{\pi} + \mu$ [4c]

DEMAND SIDE

$\dot{D} = \dot{C}_n + I + G$ [5]

$\dot{C}_n = \alpha\dot{W}$ [6]

$\dot{W} = w\dot{N} - t\dot{Y} + (1-\gamma)\dot{\pi}$ [7]

$\dot{N} = \dot{Y} - \dot{\pi}$ [8]

EQUILIBRIUM

$Y = D \quad \dot{Y} = \dot{D}$ [9]

$\dot{\pi}$ = rate of growth of productivity
$\dot{k}$ = dynamic network economies
$\dot{\lambda}$ = dynamic learning economies
I = investment activity
IPR = intellectual property rights
$\dot{Y}$ = rate of growth of output
σ = given parameter which defines the propensity to invest based on demand expectations and on realized profit level in the previous period.
γ = given parameter which defines the propensity to invest based on financial capital gains.
β = given parameter which defines the effect of productivity trend on firms' valorisation (capital gains)
$(1-\gamma)$ = share of capital gains which is distributed to shareholders and to high-skilled workers, according to individual bargain.
E = externalities (given and constant in the short run)
$\dot{CG}$ = capital gains dynamics
μ = monetary policy
$\dot{D}$ = demand dynamics
$\dot{C}_n$ = consumption dynamics
G = parameter which denotes a constant dynamics of public expenditure
$\dot{W}$ = rate of growth of labour income
$\dot{N}$ = rate of growth of employment
w = wage rate
t = flat rate taxation

Figure 6.1 The equation system

economies. Our productivity equation is similar to the Sylos Labini's one $\dot{\pi} = +b\dot{Y} + c\frac{\dot{w}}{Pma(t-n)} + dI_{t-n} - eI$, where the w/P_{ma} ratio represents the incentive to save labour either absolutely or by introducing labour-saving machines (Ricardo's effect), I_{t-n} is the long-run effect and I the short-run effect of investment.

The most relevant difference is that in order to describe productivity in cognitive capitalism, we divide the Smith's effect ($b\dot{Y}$ in Sylos' equation) separating static economies ($d\dot{Y}$) from dynamic economies ($a\dot{k} + b\dot{\lambda}$).[5]

Investment is composed both by routine investment (I_k) and investment in innovation and knowledge (learning and human capital) (I_λ) [4]. Routine investment. traditionally depends on demand expectations and on realized production level in the previous period ($\sigma\dot{Y}$) (Equation 4a). Investment in innovation and knowledge is characterized by very high potential returns and, at the same time, by possible catastrophic losses, since we suppose that this type of investment is strictly correlated to capital-gains dynamics ($\dot{CG}$), through the parameter γ (Equation 4b). Capital gains are supposed obtained by the dynamics of systemic productivity gains ($\dot{\pi}$),[6] through the parameter β; given the numerous sources of uncertainty intervening in financial markets, capital-gains dynamics need to be sustained by monetary policy (μ) (Equation 4c). Indeed, especially in the past two decades, the most relevant macro-economic changes depend on monetary policy: particularly the USA Fed has played a decisive role, averting deflation by bringing the interest-rate curve to very low levels over the 2001–2008 period. The result has been a massive transfer of corporate risk onto households, which thus saved company profitability (Aglietta and Rebérioux 2005: 4). It is worth noticing that σ, γ, and β are strategic parameters that denote firms' behaviour in terms of investments and allocation of capital gains. On the contrary, all the other parameters, a, b, c, d, e, and h, represent the characteristics of existing technology.

The second part of the model—from (5) to (8)—describes the demand side. In a very traditional Keynesian way, the aggregate demand is composed by consumption (C_n), investment (I) and exogenous public expenditures (G). Consumption (C_n) is supposed to be dependent on the total labour income. Total labour income is not only intended as the overall amount of wage but even as the earnings from financial activities. In cognitive capitalism a share of capital gains is, in fact, distributed to some categories of workers (especially high-skilled).[7] The effect is to induce a sort of "financial income multiplier." It operates through the expected capital gains by sustaining effective demand.

Equilibrium is defined by the equality between the rate of growth of output and the rate of growth of demand (9). By simplifying and substituting where necessary, the system can be reduced to two linear differential equation models, (10) and (11) (see Figure 6.2).

Productivity dynamics (10) is positively correlated to network and learning economies; moreover, the impact on productivity depends upon the $1/\beta^*$, according to the level of the propensity to invest based on financial capital gains (β) and to the effects of the learning economies on productivity itself (bh).

$\dot{\pi} = A + B\dot{Y}$ [10] $\dot{Y} = C + D\dot{\pi}$ [11] where: $A = \frac{aE - bIPR + \gamma\mu(bh+c)}{\beta^*}$ $B = \frac{[(bh+c)\sigma + ae + d]}{\beta^*}$ $C = \frac{G + \mu\gamma}{\alpha^*}$ $D = \frac{\gamma\beta + \alpha(1-\gamma) - \alpha w}{\alpha^*}$	A = incidence of network economies and IPR on productivity B = effects on productivity both of dynamic economies (network & learning economies) and of static economies C = public expenditure weighted by α* D = trade-off effect on demand by investment on innovations & technological unemployment $\frac{1}{\alpha^*} = \frac{1}{[1-\alpha(w-t)-\sigma]} =$ incomemultiplier $\frac{1}{\beta^*} = \frac{1}{1-\beta\gamma(c+bh)} =$ financial productivity multiplier

Figure 6.2 The equilibrium condition

Financial markets fix the norm of profitability. Positive expectations on financial activities partially depend on the efficiency of knowledge generation and diffusion (tacit and codified knowledge), according to the exploitation of learning and network economies (exploited codified knowledge). Therefore, the impact of "financial multiplier" ($1/\beta^*$) on productivity is as much stronger as greater are the impact of investment on learning economies (h) and the impact of the learning economies on productivity (b).

$1/\beta^*$ can be indirectly influenced by monetary policy through the parameter μ. Nevertheless, it should be considered that the impact of monetary policy on capital gains is not able alone to strictly determine its dynamics, since it is intermediated by the parameter γ.

If we assume that $\beta^*>0$, then the angular coefficient (B) of productivity line (10) is always positive.

If we assume $\mu = 0$, then the intercept of productivity line (A) is positive only if $aE > bIPR$.

Result 1a

The higher the negative impact of IPR on knowledge diffusion, the lower the positive effect of network economies on productivity. As a result, the generation of knowledge and its spatial diffusion through the learning process are the basic features of cognitive accumulation.

If we consider the role of expansionary monetary policy, $\mu > 0$, then the intercept of productivity line (A) is positive only if $aE + \gamma\mu(bh+c) > bIPR$.

Result 1b

The lower the positive effect of network economies on productivity, the more incisive should be the monetary policy to sustain the impact of investment on productivity. As a result, the monetary policy pragmatism may preserve the generation of knowledge and its spatial diffusion only if the monetary push is used to sustain the investment in innovations and knowledge. From 2000 until 2010, money supply has been targeted to sustain more financial liquidity than the traditional credit system, in order to provide capital-gains stability.

Considering equation (11), there is a positive correlation between demand and productivity if and only if $\gamma\beta+\alpha(1 - \gamma) > \alpha w$. In order to discuss this condition, consider that:

- γ defines the propensity to invest based on financial capital gains;
- $\alpha(1 - \gamma)$ is the consumption level only based on share of capital gains which is distributed to shareholders and to high-skilled workers, according to individual bargain;
- αw is the traditional Keynesian demand of consumption goods based on wage rate.

Result 2

Output growth increases if the sum of investment and consumption deriving from capital-gains allocation is greater than consumption deriving from wage bargaining. We should emphasize that wage rate becomes the variable of adjustment to preserve the wealth effect by finance-led growth regime.

At last, by analysing the intercept of output line (C), it is easy to note that it is always positive and increasing according to the level of public expenditure (G) and the income multiplier ($1/\alpha^*$).

A discussion of the model's solutions

The equilibrium level of output and employment are calculated in the following equations:

$$\dot{Y}^* = \frac{C + DA}{1 - DB} \qquad [12]$$

$$\dot{N}^* = \frac{C(1 - B) + A(D - 1)}{1 - DB} \qquad [13]$$

According to Boyer (2004a: 81), the condition of stable equilibrium for the economic system is first of all defined by a smooth increase in employment: $N^* > 0$. (see Fig. 6.3).

By means of easy algebra, it is possible to verify that condition (14) can be reworded as follows:

$$\alpha w + \alpha^* < \gamma\beta + \alpha(1 - \gamma) < \alpha w + \frac{\alpha^* \beta^*}{(bh + c)\sigma + ae + d} \qquad [14^*]$$

Result 3

The stability condition of the economic system depends on the propensity to invest and the wealth effect both produced by capital-*gains allocation*. It follows that the allocation of capital gains (subtracting wage rate) should be regulated:

1 It should be higher than the inverse of income multiplier (α^*).
2 It should be lower than the positive combination of $\alpha^*\beta^*$, weighted by the sum of the impacts of investment ($[bh+c]\sigma$), externalities (ae), and static scale economies (d) on productivity.

$$\dot{N}^* > 0$$

i.e.: $$\frac{C(1-B)+A(D-1)}{1-DB} > 0 \qquad [14]$$

Figure 6.3 The stability condition

Consequently, consumption and the demand regime are directly affected by financialization.

In order to avoid a demand crisis, the wage de-regulation ought to be compensated upon the wealth effect stimulating by capital gains. On the other hand, knowledge effects on productivity must be preserved, and financial norms should not have negative impact on financial productivity multiplier. When financial gains misrepresent the real effects of investment, dynamic scale economies and static scale economies on productivity, then financial bubbles emerge.

Without a mode of regulation that guarantees that the overall produced wealth will be re-invested into the dynamic learning and network economies and without a policy that controls financial bubbles, a finance-led growth is always at risk of instability.

Concluding remarks

In cognitive capitalism, capital becomes productive of value by the private appropriation of the "commons," like tacit and codified knowledge. Capital is valorised by controlling the life-cycle of knowledge. In the long run, the exploitation of learning economies and network economies, and the central role of precariousness and subalternity, which prevents a new form of wages regulation, push the system into a zone of structural instability. As particularly shown in the recent debate about social platforms, exploitation is therefore realised by an armoury of instruments aimed at controlling the time of social cooperation.

Social productivity depends upon two factors which are inversely correlated:

1 On the one hand, the diffusion of different innovative tools (i.e. social platforms' ads) and norms (i.e. various forms of IPR) guarantee the appropriation of knowledge. The effect of this is that of limiting the diffusion of knowledge, making it artificially scarce resource.
2 On the other hand, there is the need of capital to create a "virtuous circle" so as to create the optimal condition for the circulation of knowledge and information and to increase their diffusion in order to accelerate the generation of new innovations and the codification of tacit knowledge.

The trade-off is currently unsolvable at the level of simple market exchange. A high degree of IPR leads to a deterioration of network economies and learning processes. Consequently the rate of growth of productivity will decrease.

On the demand side, a relevant role is played by the allocation procedure of capital gains generated in the financial markets. As is shown in the model above, the role of financial markets should be regulated. Specifically, the regulation has to consider the dynamics of capital gains that should be confined in a specific path: it must be higher than a first limit by allowing a positive effect on aggregate demand but lower than the general impact on productivity generated by investment activity propensity.

A distribution of the productivity gains that penalizes workers negatively affects learning and network economies. The absence of a fair social compromise determines also the instability of the finance-driven growth, even if monetary policy sustains the financial boom.

We may conclude that the unsolved political problems in cognitive capitalism resides in the fact that the unfair income distribution undermines the ability to generate knowledge and the excessive *appropriability* of technologies leads to a lower diffusion of knowledge and learning processes. In the long run, the absence of a viable social compromise based upon a fair distribution of productivity gains and the prevalence of individual bargain do not allow a valorisation of learning and network economies.

Notes

1 Following Kendrick, increases in non-tangible capital (mainly education, training, health, and R&D) largely explain the growth in total tangible factor (capital) productivity in the whole economy.
2 This argument can be presented in terms of *tacit* and *codified knowledge*, see Malerba and Orsenigo (2000).
3 The term "bubble" describes a situation on which current stock market prices are no longer justified by future dividends.
4 See Fumagalli and Lucarelli (2007).
5 Sylos Labini introduced his productivity equation for the first time in Sylos Labini (1983: 174).
6 In such a contest, *social productivity* represents the stock of cognitive resources activated by the cooperation, which are spread along the territory in a row. Changes in financing of investment activity—for instance the venture-capital boom—can be explained by the increasing relevance of social productivity (Marazzi 2005).
7 We could also consider the segmentation of labour market between stable and precarious work activity by breaking down into two parts the equation (8).

References

Aglietta and A. Rebérioux (2005) "Regulating Finance-Driven Capitalism," *Issues in Regulation Theory*, 51: 1–5.

Boyer, R. (2004a) *Théorie de la Regulation*, vol. I: *Les Fondamentaux*, Paris: La Découverte.

Boyer, R. (2004b) *The Future of Economic Growth*, Northampton: Edward Elgar.

Corrado, C., J. Haskel, C. Jona-Lasinio, and M. Iommi (2012) "Intangible Capital and Growth in Advanced Economies: Measurement Methods and Comparative Results," Working Paper, available at http://repec.iza.org/dp6733.pdf (accessed March 25, 2019).

Fumagalli, A. and S. Lucarelli (2007) "A Model of Cognitive Capitalism: A Preliminary Analysis," *European Journal of Economic and Social Systems*, 20(1): 117–133.

Kendrick, J. (1976) *The Formation and Stocks of Total Capital*, National Bureau of Economic Research, New York: Columbia University Press.

Kendrick, J. (1994) "Total Capital and Economic Growth," *Atlantic Economic Journal*, 22(1): 1–18.

Malerba, F. and L. Orsenigo (2000) "Knowledge, Innovative Activities and Industrial Evolution," *Industrial and Corporate Change*, 9(2): 289–314.

Marazzi, C. (2005) *Ricerca e finanza*, seminar paper, Laboratoire Isys-Matisse, Paris, May 27, available at http://seminarie.samizdat.net/spip.php?article87 (accessed December 2015).

Mouhoud, E. M. (2006) "Global Geography of Post-Fordism Knowledge and Polarisation," in B. Coriat, P. Petit and G. Schméder, *The Hardship of Nations*, Cheltenham: Edward Elgar, pp. 293–307.

Negri, A. (1997) "Vingt thèses sur Marx," in M. Vakaloulis and J.-M. Vincent (eds.), *Marx après les Marxismes*, Paris: L'Harmattan, vol. II, pp. 333–372.

Nelson, R. R. and S. G. Winter (1982) *An Evolutionary Theory of Economic Change*, Cambridge, MA: The Belknap Press of Harvard University Press.

Sylos Labini, P. (1983) "Factors Affecting Changes in Productivity," *Journal of Post Keynesian Economics*, 6(2): 161–179.

Venturini, F. (2006) "How Much Does Consumption Matter for Growth? Evidence from National Accounts," in A. Malgarini and G. Piga (eds.), *Capital Accumulation, Productivity and Growth*, Basingstoke: Palgrave Macmillan, pp. 81–133.

Vercellone, C. (2015) "From the Crisis to the 'Welfare of the Common' as a New Mode of Production," *Theory Culture & Society*, 32(7–8): 85–99.

7 Common and commons in the contradictory dynamics between knowledge-based economy and cognitive capitalism

Carlo Vercellone and Alfonso Giuliani

Introduction

Until the end of the 1980s, public and private, state and market still appeared as the two undisputed poles of economic and social organization and forms of property. Both in the debate on economic policies and systemic alternatives, beyond these two poles there seemed to be nothing. This dichotomic vision is increasingly questioned by the recent rediscovery of the theme of the *Common*, commons and common goods, both in the academic field and by social movements.

This powerful return of the commons takes concrete form in the emergence of alternative forms of self-government of production and resources that bring conflict on the very ground of the conception of the development of productive forces and the relationship between man and nature. In this context, the thesis defended in this chapter is that the Common and commons are far from being a new enclave that would simply complement the traditional representation of the economy based on the public–private dyad, contrary to what Ostromian neo-institutionalist approaches seem to suggest (Ostrom 1990; Coriat 2015a).

The ontological, historically determined ontological basis of the Common's actuality is not found, in fact, mainly in the intrinsic nature and particular characteristics of certain goods. It lies instead in the capacity of self-organization of work, a capacity that in contemporary capitalism rests on the potential autonomy of cooperation in cognitive work and the development of collective intelligence. In this sense, the Common is always a social and political construction, whether it is its way of organization, as in the choice of criteria that elect or not certain resources, goods or services to the statute of common goods. The Common may therefore in principle concern the management of any type of goods or resource (whether rival or non-rival, excludable or non-excludable, material or immaterial).

According to our approach, the Common must be thought, in Marxian terms, as a real "mode of production" emerging. It is the bearer of an alternative to both the hegemony of the bureaucratic-administrative logic of the state and the capitalist market economy, as a principle of coordination of production and trade in the Marxian sense of the term, an increasingly acute tension between two key elements: (1) the nature of relationships of production, ownership, and appropriation of the increasingly parasitic value of cognitive capitalism, on the one hand; and (2) the living productive forces of a knowledge-based economy and *production of humans for and by humans* on the other hand, economy that contains within it the possibility of overcoming the capitalist order.

To illustrate these theses, this chapter will be structured in three main stages. The first stage will be dedicated to the key role that the development *production of humans for and by humans of the welfare of humans* have played, through an eminently conflicting process, both in the training of the productive forces of a knowledge-based economy (KBE) and in the emergence of institutions of the Common. In this context, the strategic reasons that push capital to try to submit welfare institutions to the principles of private management and the extension of the commodification process will also be highlighted.

The second stage will be more specifically devoted to the extension of the commons of information and knowledge. As we will show, they are the result of a dual impulse. On the one hand, they stem from the endogenous dynamic linked to the encounter between collective intelligence and the informational revolution that favours forms of production of knowledge and innovation, based on pooling and free access to resources. On the other hand, they present themselves as a reaction to the movement that, in the opposite direction, pushes capital to unleash the forces of a new and disruptive process of primitive accumulation. The new enclosures of knowledge and living are the main evidence of this.

The result is an increasingly strong tension between the new ethic of knowledge, at the basis of what we will call the "spirit of the common," and the proprietary logic of cognitive capitalism which, in order to make survive the kingdom of the commodities, through the rarefaction of supply and the construction of annuities of position and monopoly.

In this context, we will return to the debate in economic theory on the justification of intellectual property rights (IPR), and we will analyse the real causes of the speculative bubble of patents that has been produced since the 1980s. This new form of conflict between capital and labour, between the new forms of development of the productive forces of the Common and the relations of capitalist production, does not, however, eliminate another possibility, that which certain theorists qualify as corruption of the Common (Hardt and Negri 2012).

The development of commons would become in this framework the support of a regeneration of the dynamics of cognitive capitalism that would subalternatively incorporate the forms of production of the so-called sharing economy. This is a logic in which the commons of knowledge would be reabsorbed within a new dynamic of so-called open innovation governed by the strategies of the great corporations of cognitive capitalism. This scenario, as we will see in the third part, can leverage a series of limits that affect the autonomy and development strength of commons. However, it faces both structural contradictions within the accumulation of capital and the continuing vitality of the Common.

The game is still open, defining the terms of a true historical forking at the heart of the current crisis of capitalism. It is also in this perspective that in the conclusions we will indicate three main axes of an economic and social development model that can guarantee the sustainability of commons and the affirmation of the principles of the Common as a mode of production.

From a welfare state system towards a commonfare system

The institutions of the welfare state present themselves as key pieces at stake in the development of a KBE and the contradictory relationship that the public, private, and common spheres maintain in this framework. In order to illustrate this concept, we shall start from the interpretation of a stylised fact which is often used by economic theory to characterise the emergence of the KBE. We are referring to the historical dynamic by which, in the United States, starting from the mid-1970s, the so-called intangible part of capital (R&D and, above all, education, training, and health) would have surpassed material capital in the global stock of capital (Kendrick 1994) and would have become the most decisive factor of development and competitiveness.

Intangible capital and knowledge economy: the driving role of welfare institutions

The interpretation of this stylised fact has many important and interrelated meanings which, however, are systematically concealed by mainstream economists. These meanings are nonetheless essential to understanding the role of welfare institutions and the profound and often misrepresented objective of the policies which aim at dismantling and privatising them.

The first meaning, on a conceptual level, is the following: in reality, that which we call intangible and intellectual capital is fundamentally incorporated in humans. It corresponds to the intellectual and creative faculties of the labour power, that which is often also called, using a controversial expression, the so-called human capital. Prolonging this reasoning it could be affirmed that the notion of intangible capital in reality merely expresses the way in which in contemporary capitalism the "living knowledge" incorporated in and mobilised by labour now perform, in the social organisation of production, a predominant role compared to dead "knowledge" incorporated in the steady capital and in the managerial organisation of businesses. The second meaning is that the increase in the part of capital called intangible is closely linked to the development of the institutions and collective services of welfare. In particular, it should in fact be emphasised how is actually the expansion of the collective welfare services that has allowed the development of mass education, carrying out a key role in the formation of what we can call collective intelligence or widespread intellectuality: it is in fact the latter, widespread intellectuality that explains the most significant part of the increase in the capital referred to as intangible which, as is emphasised, today represents the essential element of a territory's potential growth and competitiveness. The third meaning refers to the way in which expansion of the socialised salary (pensions, unemployment benefit, etc.) allows a freeing-up of time mitigating dependency on wage relationships.

From the point of view of the development of a KBE, this freeing-up of time occurs, to use the words of the thesis of general intellect, as an immediate productive force. The socialised salary thus favours access to voluntary mobility between different forms of activities, training, self-improvement, and labour, which create wealth. Even though it is stigmatised today as an unproductive cost and brought back into discussion by workfare policies, it has made an indisputable contribution to the development of the quality of the labour power and the social networks of KBE. It should be noted that even from this point of view Friot (2010, 2012), one of the major French theorists of the *sécurité sociale* (social-security system), is right to defend the principles of the allotment pension system, founded on the mutualisation of resources, in the terms of a Common institution.[1] Considering the active role of a large number of pensioners engaged in the third sector and in knowledge commons, he goes so far as to state that, after all, it is their free and voluntary work that pays a large proportion of their pensions.

The fourth meaning is defined in the fact that, contrary to a widespread idea, the social conditions and key institutions of a KBE are not reducible to only the private R&D laboratories of large companies. These social conditions also and above all correspond to the collective *production of humans for and by humans* traditionally guaranteed by the institutions of the welfare state, following a logic that essentially, at least in Europe, still escapes from the trade and financial circulation of capital. Furthermore, it is necessary to underline that this appreciation of the role of the welfare system is also confirmed by a comparative analysis on an international scale. Comparison at an international level in fact highlights a strong positive correlation between levels of development of non-commercial services and welfare institutions, on one side, and, on the other, that of the principal indicators of the economic and social effectiveness of a KBE (Vercellone 2010, 2014; Lucarelli and Vercellone 2011). A corollary of this observation is also that a weak level of social inequality, of income and of what is guaranteed by the welfare system goes hand in hand with a much more significant spread of the most advanced forms of organisation of labour, based on the centrality of cognitive labour These forms of organisation of labour, in fact, slip from the grasp of competition based on costs and guarantee lower vulnerability to the international competition from emerging countries (Lorenz and Lundvall 2009).

In conclusion, the main factors of long-term growth and competitiveness of a territory depend more and more, as emphasised by Aglietta (1997), on collective factors of productivity (general level of education and training of the labour power, the interactions of it within a territory, the quality of the infrastructures and research, and so on).

In particular, these are the factors that permit the circulation of knowledge in a territory, generating for the same businesses externalities of networks and dynamic learning economies, the essential foundations for technical progress and endogenous growth. On a macro-economic level, this also means that the conditions of training and reproduction of the labour power are by now directly or indirectly productive. To paraphrase Adam Smith, but reaching the opposite conclusion, the origin of "wealth of nations" rests ever more today on productive cooperation situated in society, outside companies, that is to say on social and institutional mechanisms that permit the circulation and pooling of knowledge, and with this a cumulative trend of innovation (Vercellone 2011). The development of the knowledge commons, like the attempt by enterprise to promote "open innovation platforms" in order to capture knowledge produced outside it, are one of the key manifestations of this. Despite their importance, teachings drawn from these stylised facts are generally ignored by academic output on the knowledge economy and by reports that contribute to the definition of guidelines of economic policies and structural reform in Europe. This forgetfulness is all the more serious in a context where the policies of austerity and privatisation risk profoundly destabilising, together with the welfare institutions, the very conditions for the development of a KBE and thus of potential long-run growth. The risk is thus to witness—notwithstanding the fact that it is happening for an opposite cause to that suggested by Garret Hardin's well-known article (1968)—what we can call a new "tragedy of the commons" caused by the dynamics of cognitive and financialised capitalism, a tragedy of the Commons that, it must not be forgotten, goes step by step with that of the anti-commons linked to the excessive privatisation of knowledge. Numerous researches have in fact made it possible to highlight the short-sightedness of the neoliberalist policies conducted in Europe today.[2]

Apart from the theoretical weight of the precepts of neo-liberalism, one of the explanations for the persistence of these policies (privatisation strategies) can probably be found in the stakes, represented for the large multinational companies by the control and commercial colonisation of the welfare institutions, and this is due to two main structural reasons. The first reason is that health, public research, education, training, and culture do not only form lifestyles and subjectivity but also constitute the pillars of regulation and orientation of a KBE. The second reason is that the *production of humans for and by humans* also represent a growing part of production and social demand, demand which up to now, at least in Europe, has mainly been satisfied outside the logic of the market. In the face of ever more pronounced stagnational trends, since before the outbreak of the crisis, the commodification of the welfare institutions thus constitutes one of the last frontiers for the expansion of the logic of the market and the financialisation of the economy (for example through the transformation to a capitalisation pension scheme).

On this point, we note that, contrary to the dominating ideological talk that censures costs and the supposed unproductiveness of welfare institutions, the objective of the neo-liberalist policies is thus not the reduction of the absolute amount of these expenses but rather that of their reintegration into private-sector commercial and financial circulation. To be sure, the expansion of the privatistic logic in these sectors is theoretically possible. Let us remember nevertheless that health, education, research, etc., correspond to activities that cannot be subordinated to the economic rationality of the private sector, unless at the cost of rationing of resources, profound social inequalities and, all in all, a drastic lowering of the social effectiveness of these productions. The result would be an unavoidable drop of the very quantity and quality of the so-called intangible capital that, as we have seen, by now constitutes in contemporary capitalism the key factor in the development of the productive forces and potential growth.

Three principal arguments support these theses regarding the counter-productive character and the perverse effects of subjugation of the collective *production of humans for and by humans* to the economic rationality of the private sector.

The first argument is linked to the intrinsically cognitive, interactive, and emotional character of these activities, in which the work does not consist of acting on inanimate matter but on humankind itself in a relationship of co-production of services. As a matter of fact, on the level of criteria of effectiveness, these activities escape from the economic rationality suited to capitalism, which is founded on an essentially quantitative concept of productivity that can be summarised through a concise formula: to produce more and more with a smaller quantity of labour and capital so as to reduce costs and increase profits. This type of rationality has without doubt given proof of some efficiency in the productions of standardised material commodities destined for private family consumption. In this way, it enabled, during the Fordist growth, a growing load of commodities to be produced with less and less work, thus also with decreasing costs and prices, in this way satisfying a significant volume of needs; it matters little whether they be authentic, driven or superfluous. Nonetheless, the *production of humans for and by humans* respond to a completely different productive rationality and this is for three main reasons:

1 Due to their intrinsically cognitive and relational nature, neither the activities of work, not the production can really be standardised.
2 In these activities, effectiveness in terms of result depends on a whole series of qualitative variables tied to communication, density of human relationships, uninterested care and thus to the availability of time for others, which the rationality of companies, or New Public Management, would be unable to integrate unless as costs and unproductive downtimes.
3 Lastly, as Boyer (2004) notes, in these activities, particularly in the health sector, technological progress that permits improvement in the qualitative

effectiveness of production is translated almost systematically in a cost increase and a decrease in overall productivity of factors that sets off the increase in the well-being of populations. All in all, the attempt to raise profitability and productivity of these activities therefore cannot be carried out except to the detriment to their quality and so to their social effectiveness. We could even argue that in these activities today, the problem regarding the improvement of effectiveness and quality does not require an increase in productivity but rather a reduction of it (Gadrey 2010). Here we have a first series of factors connected to their means of production which explain why these collective services are unlikely to be compatible with the logic of production and profitability of the private sector, and, on the other hand, they appear as a terrain with a predilection for practices of co-production and mutualisation of the resources themselves to the logic of common.

The second argument is tied to the profound distortions that application of the principle of solvent demand would introduce in the allocation of resources and the right of access to these common goods. By definition the productions of Common are based on universal rights. Financing them cannot therefore be ensured except through the collective price represented by social contributions, taxation or other forms of mutualisation of resources.

The third argument is tied to the way in which in the *production of humans for and by humans* the mythical figure of a perfectly informed consumer does not exist in reality, he/she who would make their own choices on the basis of rational calculation of the costs/benefits dictated by research into the maximum efficiency of the investment in their own human capital. This is certainly not the main criterion that stimulates a student in their search for knowledge. It is even less that of a sick person who, in the majority of cases, is imprisoned by a state of anguish that makes them incapable of making a rational choice and predisposes them instead to all the traps of a commercial logic in which selling hopes and illusions is a means of making a profit.

From this point of view. it is interesting to note how the neo-liberalist policies of financial responsibilisation of the consumer in the field of health which also make them bear a growing part of the expenses of social protection, seem to take up, almost passage for passage, Hardin's old argumentation on welfare as an example of the tragedy of the commons. As Boutifilier (2014) demonstrates, these policies nonetheless not only do not lead to a decrease in expenses (quite the opposite) but appear to have profoundly perverse effects on treatments and therefore on the effectiveness itself of the human capital. In conclusion, all these reasons tied both to their means of production, consumption, and finance explain the economic and social tensions provoked by the continuation of a policy of transformation of the *production of humans for and by humans* into private goods. This would risk dismantling the structure of the most essential conditions at the base of the reproduction of a KBE. Experimentation of a model of commonfare finds here one of its principal justifications and could constitute, in the age of the KBE, a fresh form of re-socialisation of the economy, in the manner of Polanyi (1944).

The knowledge-based and digital economy between the dynamics of commons and the new enclosures

In cognitive capitalism, the dynamics of the knowledge and digital commons is the other side of the coin, the reciprocal antagonist, of what is called the tragedy of the anticommons, tied to excessive privatisation of knowledge. Besides, the entire history of the development of a KBE and the information evolution itself is an illustration of this crucial aspect. From the conception of the first software up to that of the web protocols released by Tim Berners-Lee into the public domain, not forgetting the legal innovation of copyleft, the open nature of information technologies and the standards of the net is largely the product of a social construction of the commons. A construction in permanent conflict both with the state logic and with that of ownership generated by the great oligopolies of the internet and high-tech industries.

This evolution enters the in-depth debate which has started again of the regime of knowledge and innovation inherited from industrial capitalism and founded on the public–private pairing.

Knowledge as a public good and product of a specialized sector: the Fordist paradigm

In order to better comprehend the sense of this process on a theoretical and historical level, it is useful to start again from the dominant concept of knowledge theorized in the Fordist era by the founding fathers of the economic theory of knowledge and sociology of the science, that is respectively by Kenneth J. Arrow and Robert K. Merton.

The basic model of the economic theory of knowledge and market failures

Arrow's article, "Economic Welfare and the Allocation of Resource for Invention"(1962), is considered to be the founding essay on the KBE. The author's approach rests on two principal arguments. The first concerns the agents and the methods of knowledge production. According to Arrow, the essentials of scientific and technological knowledge are created by an elite of researchers who act and reflect in separate places from the rest of society and situated at a distance from production, in R&D laboratories and in highly intense technological industries. The activity of innovation is thus represented as the result of a sector specialized in the production of knowledge on the basis of a function of production that combines highly qualified labour and capital.[3] The second argument concerns the nature of knowledge or information as an "economic good."[4] In continuity with the neo-classical typology of goods, knowledge (or information), according to Arrow presents three main characteristics that make it an imperfect public good: its non-rivalrous, difficultly excludable, and cumulative nature. Unlike material goods, consumption of knowledge does not destroy it. On the contrary, it is enriched when it circulates freely among individuals. Every new item of knowledge generates another item of knowledge following a virtuous (not vicious) circle that permits each creator, as Newton reminded us, to be "like dwarves perched on the shoulders of giants." For these reasons, knowledge is a good which is difficult to control. In other words, Arrow emphasizes how it is very simple for subjects other than those who invested in the production of the knowledge to come into its possession and use it without paying any market price. This transferability of knowledge is so much higher that it assimilates knowledge to information, mistakenly supposing that it is perfectly codable.

Given the characteristics of the knowledge as economic good, Arrow considers that its production represents a typical example of market failure: that is the production of knowledge, if left to mechanisms of the market and the initiative of private enterprise, would lead to a sub-optimal situation. The marginal private advantage of the economic subject who makes investments is lower than the social one. For these reasons, the state must intervene and play an active role in the production of knowledge, particularly in the finance and organization of fundamental research. Its results must be placed freely at the disposal of the rest of society as a public good. Certainly, Arrow also predicts instruments aimed at boosting applied research in companies, for example through IPR. Nevertheless, he considers that these instruments are unable to eliminate the gap between social advantages and private benefits, taking into account also the short-run horizon on the basis of which businesses make investment decisions according to profitability. In short, a precise division of labour is established between public-sector and private-sector research: the first provides basic knowledge mainly tied to fundamental research free of charge, like a public good; the second develops applied research in the framework of the large R&D laboratories of the large managerial enterprises. Innovation is internally produced, and resort to the monopoly of intellectual property performs a secondary role.

The norm of open science according to Merton

Merton, the founding father of the sociology of science, actually shares this representation. He completes it defining the *ethos* of the science and the norms of regulation of the public activity of scientists' research according to the principles of *open science*. From this perspective, he defines four "institutional imperatives" (Merton 1973: 270–278):

1 *Universalism*: knowledge and scientific results are judged independently from characteristics inherent to the subject which formulated them, such as social class, political and religious opinions, sex and ethnic origins (Merton 1973: 270–273).

2 "*Communism*": in the non-technical and extended sense of common ownership of goods, is a second integral element of the scientific ethos. The substantive findings of science are a product of social collaboration and are assigned to the community. They constitute a common heritage in which the equity of the individual producer is severely limited [...] The scientist's claim to "their" intellectual "property" is limited to that of recognition and esteem which, if the institution functions with a modicum of efficiency, is roughly commensurate with the significance of the increments brought to the common fund of knowledge.

And it is Merton who states that *common ownership* exactly "of the scientific ethos is incompatible with the definition of technology as 'private property' in a capitalistic economy" (1973: 275). In short, results and discoveries are not the property of a single researcher but a legacy of the scientific community and society as a whole. A scientist does not obtain recognition for their own work unless by making it public and therefore placing it at the disposal of others. The researcher's objective thus becomes that of publishing the results of their own research first and as fast as possible, instead of keeping them secret and/or submitting them to the monopoly of intellectual property, as on the other hand is more and more the case today in the field of scientific research.

1 *Disinterestedness*: each researcher pursues the primary objective of the progress of knowledge, obtaining recognition from their community of peers. This recognition can be translated into reputation and career advancement but not into the possibility of personal enrichment based on privatization of knowledge through, for example, patents or other business initiatives for profit.
2 *Organized skepticism*: this consists of institutional devices, like *Peer Review*, which permit the systematic presentation of scientific results to the critical examination of the peer community.

In brief, according to Merton, the "institutional imperatives" for publication, pooling, and free circulation of research results make it possible to guarantee a system of open science and common ownership, though within a limited community of researchers and people working in those areas. This is a logic that, as we will see, presents some analogies with the model of free software and common ownership set up by copyleft which constitute an original construction.

The development of cognitive capitalism and the crisis of the Arrowian and Mertonian paradigm of knowledge

Whether it is in connection with the representation of the subjects of knowledge production, the regulatory role of the public sector or the *ethos* of the science, the Arrowian and Mertonian paradigm is in crisis today. All these pillars of the regime of knowledge and innovation in force in the age of Fordist capitalism have been profoundly destabilized by two opposing dynamics passing through cognitive capitalism.

Knowledge as a socially widespread activity

The first is about the way in which knowledge production slips away more and more from the traditional places assigned for its production. In short, in contrast with what the Arrow and Merton models postulated,[5] learning and intellectual labour are no longer, as Smith stated in *The Wealth of Nations*, "like every other employment, the principal or sole trade and occupation of a particular class of citizens"(1981: 70). They progressively spread and become manifest within society, even through the development of decentralized and autonomous forms of organization compared to the norms of public research centres and those of large private companies (Vercellone 2013). As David and Foray underline (2002: 10), "a knowledge economy appears when a group of people intensively co-produce (i.e. produce and exchange) new knowledge with the aid of ITC" sometimes establishing genuine knowledge commons. At the centre of this process we find two subjective and structural transformations. In the first place, as previously emphasized, is the success of a widespread intellectuality. It is only the latter that can, in fact, explain the development of knowledge-intensive communities which are able to organize themselves, share, and produce knowledge. It is a new dynamic, completely inconceivable even at the end of the twentieth century by theorists of economy and the sociology of knowledge. A dynamic that can go from the simple creation and sharing of a database, up to complex forms of co-production of intangible and material goods. As in the case of free software, *biohackers* and even more so, the makers, knowledge commons can develop on a technological frontier that challenges the supremacy of the public sector and large private companies on the level of economic efficiency and capacity for innovation.

On this terrain, there is the meeting and hybridization between Merton's science *ethos* model and new forms of *open knowledge* promoted by the practices and cultural models tied to the development of a collective intelligence.

Towards the science paradigm 2.0: New Public Management and the privatization of knowledge

The second dynamic at the base of the destabilization of the Arrowian and Mertonian model is a powerful process of privatization of knowledge that goes hand in hand with the subordination of public research to the short-run imperatives of private profitability. The result is a debate about the concept of knowledge as a public good and the traditional role assigned to the state in its regulation in the Fordist era. The starting point of this evolution is found in the United States between the end of the 1970s and the beginning of the 1980s in a context in which the debate on economic and industrial policy is dominated by the problem of the loss of competitivity of American industry compared to Japan.

This results in the drawing up of a new strategy oriented at moving the norms of international competition ever more to the bottom of the production sphere, on the same level as the results of basic research. Under the thrust of the finance and lobbying of the large-scale enterprises in the pharmaceutic, information technology, and biotechnology sectors between the 1980s and 1990s, this strategy is marked by four main institutional innovations.

The first is constituted in 1980 by the Bayh–Dole Act, which marks the birth of the *Science Model 2.0.* [6] This grants universities and non-profit-making institutions the right to exploit and commercialize inventions made with public research funds in their laboratories. The law equally encourages universities to transfer patented technologies to the private sector, in particular through exclusive licences.

The second innovation refers to the 1980 sentence of the Supreme Court (in the *Diamond v. Chakrabarty* case) which extends protection to any natural product created through genetic engineering, recognizing that genetically modified bacteria are patentable in themselves, that is to say independently of their process of exploitation. Starting from this moment, the instances of obtaining patents on cell lines, gene sequences, animals, and plants have multiplied. The same is true for living organisms that are sufficiently modified to be able to be considered manufactured products. The distinction between discovery and invention is practically erased.

The third concerns the extension of IPR to software according to a process produced through two principal stages. In 1980, following the recommendations of the National Commission on New Technological Uses of Copyright Works (CONTU), US Congress extended the possibility of copyright protection to software. As Mangolte (2013) recalls, it is nonetheless patents that are used initially. The United States Patent and Trademark Office (USPTO) in fact rapidly accepted the introduction of patents in the field of software whether or not they were tied to hardware. However, their validity was strongly fought over on the legal front as the algorithms were still connected to ideas and not to tangible artefacts. Because of this, the copyright route seemed more secure as an ownership strategy, at least until the decision relating to a case in favour of patents on software backed by a 1996 USPTO document.

Finally, in 1994, the agreement on Trade-Related Aspects of Intellectual Property Rights (TRIPS) for the first time in history establishes at world level a regime of IPRs which are binding for all the countries of the globe, in contrast with the United States' essentially national regulation upon which besides the strategy of technological catching-up besides had relied in the past, like all the other countries in course of industrialization. In conclusion, the reorganization of the relationship between public and private sector and

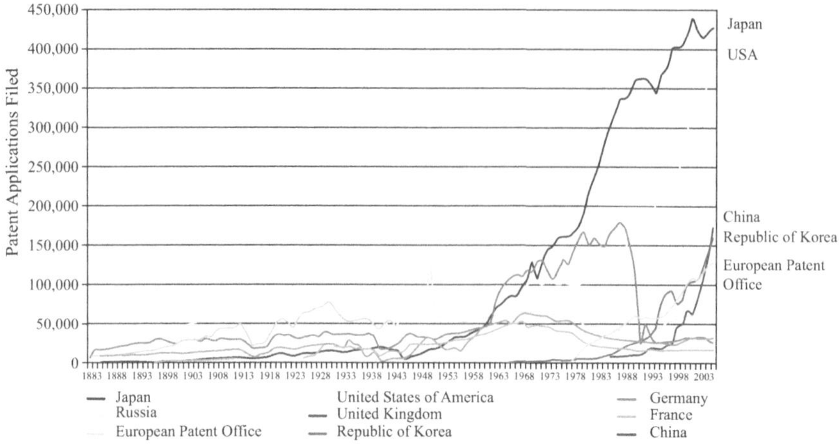

Figure 7.1 Evolution of worldwide patent filings in the long run
Note: WIPO PATENT REPORT: Statistics on Worldwide Patent Activities, 2007
Source: World Intellectual Property Organization (WIPO) statistics database

the IPR regime leads to a real explosion in the process of patenting that is demonstrated through a radical break with respect to the long-dating historic trend regarding the number of patents filed between 1883 and the beginning of the 1980s (Figure7.1).

Patents: a necessary evil or a useless evil?

The excess privatization of knowledge that seems to characterize contemporary capitalism is responsible for creating a tragedy of anticommons. Three key elements will enable us to better understand the signification of this evolution. A first element concerns the extension of the field of patentability. In industrial capitalism, the possibility of resort to the monopoly of intellectual property of the patent was limited to technical devices and products that had to prove their originality, that is to say to be an expression of human creativity and not therefore come from nature but be registered as technological artefacts inherent to the "arts and crafts." The strengthening and extension of IPR that has been produced since the 1980s is not only about the possibility to patent ever more superficial devices, for example Amazon's idea of the "click." It concerns the weakening itself of the traditional frontier between discovery and invention and therefore between basic research and applied research. Algorithms, sequences of the human genome, plants, seeds, genetically modified organisms, even the isolation of a virus,[7] have now entered the range of patentability in fact permitting the privatization of something living and of knowledge as such, of all that is often described in classic texts of Western political thought as a legacy of all humankind to share together (Hardt and Negri 2012; Shiva 2001).

The second element concerns the way in which the obsession for privatization of knowledge at any cost leads to an inefficient use of resources. According to the statistics drawn up by Marc-André Gagnon (2015) in the pharmaceutical industry, for example, the administrative legal costs for obtaining and defending IPRs are higher than those devoted to R&D. This disproportion between unproductive expenses and investment in R&D is even more considerable if integrated with the expenses mobilized on publicity and marketing to promote products and services with an ever more superficial innovative content. The patent then becomes more and more an instrument to renew monopoly rents by replacing, without significant innovations, the *blockbuster drugs* becoming part of the public domain and therefore in the production of generic medicines.

The third element concerns the misleading nature of the traditional argument according to which the patent is a necessary evil, in the framework of a difficult arbitration between static inefficiencies (a patent translates into price increases for the consumer and a lower use of the invention) and dynamic efficiency, tied to the increase of the rate of innovation. As a matter of fact, it is argued that in the absence of a provisional monopoly guaranteed by patents, certain innovations would not come about due to lack of profitability. To demonstrate the weakness of this theory, Boldrin and Levine (2008) have emphasized how in the case of an authentic invention, that is not banal, characterized by a certain level of technical complexity, the advantage of time that the innovator has at their disposal is a competitive factor sufficient to justify and remunerate investment in the innovation. The reason is simple: knowledge does not correspond only to its coded part but rests on a blend of tacit knowledge that requires a long time to be learned before a potential competitor can manage to imitate and improve the innovation in question (Vercellone 2014).

In conclusion, it is possible to maintain that the patent, especially as far as authentic radical innovations are concerned, is not a necessary evil. It is purely and simply a useless evil (Boldrin and Levine 2008), at least if one reasons from the point of view of the dynamics of innovation and not from those of the monopoly rents that large enterprises can obtain thanks to holding these patents.[8] Proof of this is also the way in which the explosion of patent applications that happened in all the OECD countries starting from the 1980s, did absolutely not go hand in hand with a parallel increase of the Total Factor Productivity (TFP) which, according to economic theory, ought to constitute the principal indicator of technical progress. On the contrary, compared to an explosion in the number of patent filings which went, for example in the United States, from an average of 90,000 a year in the 1960s to 345,000 in the 1990s, leaping up again in the first ten years of the twenty-first century (482,871 in 2009; 501,162 in 2013. See Figure 7.2),[9] it is necessary to observe that the dynamics of the TFP in the past fifty years has not shown any tendency to grow (Boldrin and Levine 2008: 79).

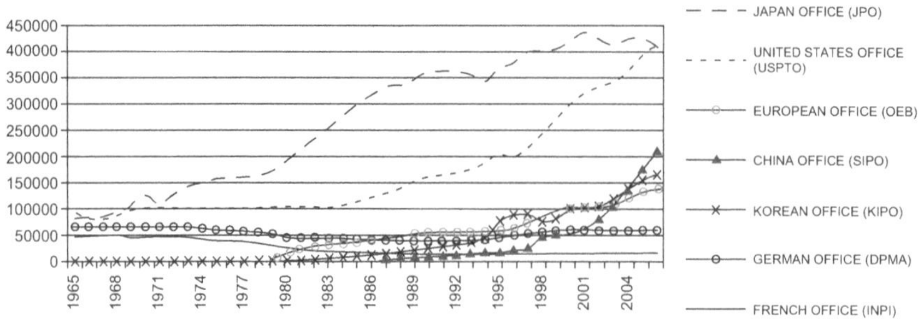

Figure 7.2 Trends in patent filings at selected patent office, 1965–2006
Source: Lallement (2008: 3). Data from *Centre d'Analyse Stratégique*

The second item of empirical evidence is the observation according to which the increase in the number of patents is associated, in the United States, as in Europe, with a strong deterioration of the average quality of the patents in terms of innovation originality (Lallement 2008). As shown in a detailed empirical study by Rémi Lallement for Europe, this evolution goes hand in hand with a use of IPR that, particularly as far as large enterprises are concerned (40.8 per cent of patents), tends more and more to favour the functions of patents as instruments to block competition and not in view of potential innovation.

A last argument that confirms and clarifies the affirmation according to which the patent is often more of a pointless evil than a necessary evil is provided by the long-run dynamics of economic history. In reality, it is in fact very difficult to find an example of a radical innovation in economic history, caused by the existence of the system of patents as an instigative factor.[10] Rather, we notice an inverse causative sequence. The same institution of IPRs is a phenomenon that follows and does not precede a cluster of radical innovations. Proof of this is the same historic genesis of the first structured legislation on patents, developed in Venice in 1474 to then spread to the rest of Europe. In fact, it was produced after and in reaction to the problems of controlling knowledge generated by the invention of movable type printing and by the spread of the information revolution of the so-called *Gutenberg galaxy* (May 2002).

This observation is perhaps even truer for the information revolution in contemporary capitalism which, as Bill Gates himself explicitly acknowledged, could never have happened if at that time we had the arsenal of IPRs that has developed since the 1980s. As shown also by the works of Bessen and Maskin (2000), the re-enforcement of intellectual property regulations in the United States during the 1980s reduced innovation and translated into a decline in R&D in the industries and corporations that were most active in patenting their work, and this in stark contrast with the dynamism and innovative capacity of which the model of open source and copyleft is proof in the same period.

More precisely three logical-historical steps can be distinguished in the development of the information revolution and the new knowledge commons. In the first, the dynamics of the principal radical innovations at the base of the information revolution are driven from the bottom. In this framework, resort to IPRs is still relatively rare and not structured by the new norms of privatization which will gradually come into force starting from the 1980s. It is a process in which the very concept of technological innovation strongly bears the stamp of the dissenting counterculture of the American campus and of what Boltanski and Chiappello (1999) have called the "artistic critique."

In the second, continuation of this dynamic of open-science and open-knowledge innovation must be placed even more explicitly in opposition to the ownership model. In contrast with the development of *biopiracy* and the processes of privatization and standardization of the living, this conflictual logic also concerns more and more the construction of the commons of bio-diversity and agriculture. Two consequences ensue. The movement of the commons has to give itself a more formalized organizational structure and conceive original legal forms of common ownership such as copyleft to protect itself from the "predatory" practices of the private sector. The great oligopolies that have formed in the framework of the information revolution set up strategies that lead to the tragedy of the anticommons of knowledge and to processes of recentralization of the net which, like for the platforms of the well-known GAFA (Google, Apple, Facebook, Amazon) destabilize its open and decentralized structure.

In the third, the protagonists of the ownership model become ever more aware of the limits that the logic of fencing in and secrecy tied to the IPRs implies for their own capacity of innovation. It appears more and more to be a limit in the face of an embittering of the competition in the international division of labour knowledge-based. To compensate for this *impasse* digital and bio-technological capitalism sets up strategies which try to recover the commons model from within, by imitation or co-optation. At the same time, the logic of the knowledge commons spreads more and more to new activities and productive branches, defining, after the model of free software, that of the makers which appears to lay the foundations of a possible new industrial revolution.

The information revolution of the PC and the net: in the beginning was the common

The development of the commons and the principles of free software is often considered to be a reaction to the property excesses of cognitive capitalism. This concept provides an inexact picture of a technological revolution that found its driving force in the system of private capitalist economy and in the role of *Big Science* organized by the public research system.

Thus, in standard presentations of the IT (information technology) revolution, the idealized figure of the great businessmen of success Bill Gates-style often crosses that of the Advanced Research Projects Agency Network (ARPANet), an embryonic form from which Internet was born subsequently in 1983, created in 1969 by Defense Advanced Research Projects Agency responsible for the development of new technologies for military use of the United States.

The part of truth contained in this reconstruction is a little like the tree that hides the forest of creative effervescence of multitudes of hackers and hobbyists mobilized much more by the search for technological virtuosity[11] than by that of personal enrichment and profit. The IT sector is perhaps the best contemporary illustration of the way in which the monopoly of intellectual property is not the cause of innovation. It is rather a consequence that intervenes when the development of a sector, having reached a certain degree of maturity, sees the way to build economic rent and prevent dynamics that could undermine them in resorting to and strengthening the IPRs. The main innovations at the base of the start of the information revolution and the conception of the Internet could not have taken place without the determining role of practices founded on the Common and driven by alternative motivations both to the logic of private and that of public. It is not only the fact that at the dawn of the ICT (information communication technology) revolution, in the 1960s and 1970s, practices of sharing the source code and the gratuitousness of software constituted the norm of co-operation in the work of those employed in IT (Mangolte 2013). It is also and above all the fact that the birth of a new socio-technical paradigm never obeys narrow technological determinism but is the result of a social construction that is engraved in a trajectory of innovation that expresses the interests and visions of the world of the players who are its protagonists.[12] So, unquestionably, on the level of innovative practice, the anti-authoritarian countercultures that developed on American campuses in the 1960s and their meeting with the open-knowledge culture which at the time still innervated the university world in the United States, have been of decisive importance in the history of the IT revolution. As Delfanti (2013a: 30) stresses, "from the bond between activists for the freedom of information who dreamt of using computers as an instrument of communication for the resistant communities and the hobbyists of Silicon Valley [...] the libertarian ethos emerged that partially guided the evolution of computers towards what they are today."

In turn, Michel Lallement (2013) proposes a winning historic reconstruction of the experiences of the counterculture of the hippy community that developed in California in the 1960s and 1970s and in which were embedded personalities such as Gordon French and Fred Moore, founders in 1975 of the Homebrew Computer Club, the first real model of hackerspace. It is right in this club, around the first accessible personal computer, the Altair 8800, they are to produce innovative experimentations and decisive meetings for the conception of our modern personal computer. It is again this libertarian and democratic "ethics" that explain the 'sociology' of principles innovations, as modem, that will lead to the birth of Internet (Cohen 2006). In particular, this ethics of the open knowledge leads Tim Berners-Lee and Robert Cailliau to convince the European Organization for Nuclear Research (CERN) to release in 1993 the web protocols, including the source code of the first navigator,[13] into the public domain. Rapid diffusion is made possible in this way, thanks to the lack of patents on the standard of the net, and this happens while in the United States we witness the rise of software patenting; in France, Minitel's closed pay-for model still predominates.

In short, it is a very precise socio-technical trajectory thought out on the basis of the Common and in function of the creation of the infrastructures of the Common that allows open and original structures to be conceived according to a dynamic that will find two fundamental and closely bound achievements:

- the free-software model with its best-known concrete creations like GNU/Linux, Firefox, Apache, LibreOffice, Thunderbird and VideoLAN Client (VLC);
- the open architecture nature of the Web designed by Tim Berners-Lee like a global hypertext in which all the sites in the world can be consulted and fed by everyone.

In this manner, personal computers put in a network through the internet are, at least potentially, like "a universal tool accessible to everyone thanks to all the knowledge and all the activities that can in principle be put in common" (Gorz 2003: 21 [our translation]).[14] In fact, the information revolution and its emblematic product, the net, are not limited, as is often stated by mainstream theorists of the knowledge economy, to bringing about an extraordinary reduction in the costs of transmission and codification of knowledge itself. It introduces two other greater qualitative breaks compared to previous information revolutions in the history of humankind, in particular, after that of writing, the revolution of movable type printing that gave rise to the formation of the *Gutenberg galaxy*.

The first break consists in the fact that information and knowledge, like all digitizable cultural products, can now circulate independently from a material medium, like, for example, a book. This dematerialization not only drastically reduces the costs of the technical reproduction of intellectual labour making them enter an economy of abundance and at zero marginal cost. It also results in their emancipation from the control mechanisms, censorship and selection that in the past the state and market could exercise over them acting on their material media.

The second qualitative break consists in the way in which the net radically destabilizes the terms of the classic producer/consumer, creator/public, issuer/user dichotomies, that up to today had structured the workings of all traditional media. The Internet, in particular, in fact consents the transition from a classic relationship pattern from *one toward everyone*, usually mediated by a mercantile or administrative/bureaucratic relationship, to an interactive pattern from *everyone toward everyone*. The circulation of information and the production of knowledge can thus become a cooperative process that mobilizes the intelligence of multitudes on a global scale. It is a dynamic of which one of the best exemplifications is without doubt that of Wikipedia, the open encyclopedia that has actually, for the number of terms, but also for the reliability of the content, now definitively won the competition with the noble *Encyclopædia Britannica*.

This decentralized and democratic aspect is undoubtedly the most revolutionary trait of the Internet which makes it the most suitable infrastructure of the Common for the development of a KBE founded on the autonomy of cognitive labour and collective intelligence. Again, for this reason, bringing up for discussion again the neutrality of the net and its open structure is the objective on which the attempts at recentralization of the Internet are focused in order to re-establish the supremacy of mercantile mediation and/or bureaucratic-administrative control of the public. This logic stirs up animated disputes due to its perverse effects on the freedom of citizens and the dynamics of the circulation of knowledge that constitutes one of the key conditions for the development and sustainability of the commons. Around what is at stake here a complex and highly conflictual dialectic is unravelling more and more that opposes the *spirit of Common* [15] from the dawn of the KBE to that of a *new spirit* of digital and cognitive capitalism, which is trying to reabsorb the former within its operational mechanisms.

The spirit of Common: the meeting between the Mertonian culture of open science and hacker ethics

Like Max Weber spoke of the *spirit of industrial capitalism*, relating it to Protestant ethics, it is possible to speak of a *spirit of Common* that has innervated the open nature of IT technologies and the standards of the Web just as the resistance to the growth of ownership capitalism. Like the *spirit of capitalism*, the *spirit of Common* also has a historical and sociocultural base which it is possible to formalize in an ideal-type model.[16] It presents itself as the result of the meeting and hybridization between the *ethos* of open science, described by Merton and the hacker spirit of collective intelligence defined by Pekka Himanen,[17] according to a model that under many aspects is incarnated in the figures respectively of Richard Stallman and Tim Berners-Lee. The new generation brought up on widespread knowledge takes up and reformulates the four fundamental Mertonian principles of *universalism, communism, disinterestedness*, and *organized skepticism*. It integrate them in a new system of values in which the main points are the following:

1 *Universalism* is structured around the criticism of the closure and the claim of official scientific institutions to hold a monopoly on knowledge.

In the hacker spirit and that of the counterculture of widespread intellectuality the values of sharing and cooperation extend to the whole of society, independently of the qualifications and the professional status of an individual: this is a typical aspect of a society based on collective intelligence.

2 *Communism* or *scientific communitarianism*, in which knowledge is considered to be common ownership, takes up the basic imperative again of the publication of results of research and putting them at the disposal of the whole of society. In the hacker philosophy, this need is combined, however, with the awareness that publication, as in the case of an open-source software, as an instrument is no longer sufficient to prevent attempts at private appropriation. From this perspective, legal mechanisms that permit the creation of a protected common ownership, i.e. a non-appropriable public domain, to which each can add something but not take anything away for private benefit.
3 *Disinterestedness.* As in Mertonian open science, the hacker philosophy pursues the disinterested objective of progress of knowledge. It differs however from the *ethos* of scientist which remains largely structured by the Weberian ethic of work as a duty and an end in itself (Merton 1973). Rather, disinterest is associated with a Fourierist concept of work thought of as a creative, even if terribly serious, game. It is about the passion of the cognitive effort, recompense for which, as in the Mertonian model, consists in the recognition of one's peers and the community of users.
4 *Organized Skepticism.* Finally, the hackers as in the science world have adopted the model of organized skepticism and open knowledge as the most functional for the production of new knowledge. However, the hacker spirit differs because of its refusal of academic hierarchy and a structured career of regulated bureaucratic passages.

On this basis, it elaborates two new closely bound principles lacking from the Mertonian universe of open science: the principle of the *do-cracy* (the power of doing) which indicates research of maximal individual autonomy and which opposes any external directive and interference, potentially giving each person the influence that comes out of their own initiatives; and the principle of direct horizontal cooperation intended as a form of self-organization in which individuals co-ordinate themselves, allocating themselves tasks that they carry out taking full responsibility for them. We note that the last two principles are also the most general expression of the culture refusing work directed by others and aspiring to self-management that has characterized the main social movements of widespread intellectuality over the past decades, from the experience of the *social centres* in Italy up to that of the *indignados* in Spain.

Do-cracy, horizontal co-operation and cognitive division of labour: the controversy on the nature of the productive model of free software and open source

This combination between direct co-operation and glorification of individual autonomy in which the individuals themselves allocate themselves tasks and objectives and appeal to others to carry them out gives rise to a particularly effective form of cognitive division of labour.[18] This model of self-management of cognitive labour rests on different strongly autonomous small groups. As Jollivet (2002: 165) stresses, "the work carried out in these hacker communities, like in project Linux, for example, is directly co-operative and voluntary work the structure of which is horizontal" (our translation). These characteristics are important for two reasons.

The first is that they correspond to a form of co-ordination belonging to the commons, in alternative both to the hierarchy and the market, the effectiveness of which made it during the 1990s the most serious competitor to the monopoly of Microsoft and to the logic of the ownership model of the so-called *new economy* (Boyer 2002).

The second is that the explanation for the effectiveness of these models constitutes an important controversial element with some defenders of the standard neo-classic approach of labour economics. In particular, economists like Lerner and Tirole (2000) refute any originality in the model of labour organization in the hacker community of the Linux type. They maintain, in fact, that there is really nothing different in the world of hacking and free software compared to the traditional way enterprises function. Hacking stars, like Linus Torvalds and Richard Stallman, would in fact carry out a role in the productive organization of free software identical to that of a company director. Jollivet (2002), basing himself on Himanen's analysis, supplies numerous elements to refute this theory. He states first of all that the relative lack of organizational structures does not mean that they are missing. The organizational structure is that of a horizontal network that, however, does not profess to be totally flat. In fact, in the free-software project there are prominent personalities who, inside small committees, have an unquestionable influence over certain choices, in particular over the contributions that have to be integrated or not in the programme in question. Nonetheless, there is a fundamental difference between these figures and a hierarchical superior. As Himanen (2001: 80) emphasizes, "the statute of authority is open to everyone." This is a decisive point characterizing the institutional specificness and the production model of free-software projects: the means of production are in fact placed in common, and no one can take advantage of the property right of the software produced under free license. Here there is a substantial divergence compared to the classic enterprise model in which the power of ownership of things (production tools and capital supplied) confers the power of direction over humans and the right to appropriate the product of the labour. So, for example, in the models of the agency theory (Jensen and

Mekling 1976), to which Lerner and Tirole refer, the managers or leaders are, according to the supremacy of private-property rights, agents of the shareholders only. In a classic enterprise—and this is even truer in companies where the main capital is the so-called *human* or *intellectual capital*—this hierarchical structure can lead to recurring conflicts between ownership power and decision-making power of those who hold adequate knowledge (Weinstein 2010). The rigidity of the structures of control and decision-making tied to ownership often interfere with the mechanisms that should guarantee the most efficient forms of organization of a cognitive division of labour (Vercellone 2013a, 2014).

In the free-software model, the absence of ownership instead determines the social conditions which ensure that authority is effectively open and removable, guaranteeing democracy and collective deliberation both as far as the labour organisation and the purposes of the production. For this reason, the free-software model is also more flexible and reactive than the hierarchical model. As a matter of fact, if the decisions taken by one of the micro-structures of arbitration are considered unsatisfactory by a significant number of contributors to the project, nothing is simpler than setting up the process of removal of the leadership of project in hand. Concerning this, it is sufficient for a dissident group to duplicate—which is perfectly legal in general public license (GPL) licenses—the program source codes, set themselves up as a holding group of an alternative project with an internet site appealing to other contributors so that they join the new project (Jollivet 2002). The inappropriability of goods produced in a project of the free-software type (right of duplication and modification) thus constitutes a fundamental incentive to do things in such a way that the traditional schemes of hierarchical authority of an enterprise are not reproducible. This mechanism explains not only why "the statute of authority is open to anyone," but equally why it is "solely founded on results" (Jollivet 2002: 166). In this way, no one can occupy a role in which their work is not subjected to the examination of their peers in the same way as the creations of any other individual (Himanen 2001: 80–82). The individuals to whom authority is delegated temporarily and revocably are those who enjoy the greatest admiration from their peers.

Copyleft and common property in the free-software movement

For certain authors, like Dardot and Laval (2014), common is constituent acting and forms of institutionalization of common property outside a permanent procedure of commoning cannot exist. For other authors, like Coriat (2015) and Broca (2013), the example of copyleft would on the other hand prove it is possible to set up a form of common property that guarantees free access to a stock of resources independently of the activity of commoning. Examination of the free-software model allows us to demonstrate the innate error in both these positions. The case of copyleft rests in fact on a close synergy between a form of common property founded on rights of use, on the one hand, and a logic of cooperative acting belonging to the Common as it is the mode of production organization, on the other hand. There is no disjunction, but a process of reciprocal fertilization between the activity of commoning and the legal regime of copyleft. This process illustrates the way in which labour co-operation, the ontological foundation of the Common, can generate legal forms that promote coherent governance for it and its reproduction (Hardt and Negri 2012). The history of the dynamics through which the free-software movement (FSM) arrived at the formulation of copyleft is a demonstration of this theory. As we have seen, practices of direct co-operation and sharing of the source code and programs were a continuous norm at the dawn of the IT revolution in the 1960s and 1970s. The commons as a method of organization of production, exchange, and circulation of knowledge pre-existed, in short, the institutionalization of the FSM. The latter did not intervene until the logic of Common had to face more and more the development of ownership strategies that marked a turning point in the dynamics of the IT revolution and Internet.

In the 1980s, as Mangolte (2013) recalls, in enterprises in this field, in fact, growing resort to IPR became popular, which the programmers, breaking with historic tradition, were obliged to integrate in their practice, whether they wanted to or not. This is a general reversal of the rules of behaviour that will progressively contaminate the universities themselves and the research centres where the Mertonian norm of publication of research results and making them available in the public domain was still in force. This break-up was particularly unpopular with the community that set itself up from 1974 around the development of the operating system Unix and in which the University of Berkeley performed, together with Bell Labs from the AT&T group, a predominant role, both for UNIX and for the management of the 5TCP/IP networks required for the development of ARPANet. Following the breaking up of the AT&T group, Bell Labs, having become an independent enterprise, developed commercial activities in IT, restricting conditions of access to the codes and increasing the cost of licenses. The conflict between the ownership strategy of Bell Labs and the University of Berkeley users lead to the disintegration of the Unix community which had been working up till then, on an international level, according to principles close to those of open source. The result has also been the multiplication of Unix owners (AIX, HP-UX, IRIX, Solaris 2, etc.). It is in this context that Stallman took the initiative, in September 1983, to promote the GNU project. The aim was to create a group of free software around an operating system compatible with free Unix, with an open-source code, accompanied by very extensive rights of use, rights that the author grants to all users (Stallman 1999). The name "GNU," which means "Gnu's Not Unix," was chosen deliberately, exactly to emphasize the opposition between the philosophy of the new project and the logic that led to the break-up of the original Unix community. From this perspective, rejection of the ownership model is united to the desire to reproduce the model of sharing and horizontal co-operation of the first Unix. This is an important point as well because it shows the unjustified character of certain criticisms levelled at Stallman according to which he was a libertarian tormented exclusively by the matter of ownership, without harbouring any interest instead on the conditions of production in the software world. To dispel any doubt, we need merely remember how Stallman explains with extreme clarity that the birth of the GNU project was above all a way of escaping from "a world in which the higher and higher walls, those of different companies, would have separated the different programmers (or user-programmers), isolating them from each other" (Stallman 1999: 64). We could add that here he demonstrated extreme lucidity on the "negative externalities" that the ownership model, by its nature pyramidal and hierarchical, would have had on the development of the most effective forms of organization of cognitive labour, leading to an individualization of the wage relation and a fragmentation of labour collective. In fact, it is one of the main causes of the inefficiency of the ownership model on the matter of innovation and product quality, particularly if compared to the free-software model of horizontal co-operation. Since the beginning of the FSM, these two objectives, preservation of an open and horizontal co-operative model and the fight against the drift towards ownership of cognitive capitalism, are therefore inseparable. For this reason also, the GNU project sees its number of participants increase progressively, and, in 1985, the Free Software Foundation (FSF) was founded. Its purpose was to defend the principles of free software and to establish norms that made it possible to say clearly if a program is free or not. This was also the sense behind the creation of the GPL. In short, what before was a spontaneous form of co-operation and open-source sharing, now had to organize itself in an institutional way and at the same time formulate forms of ownership that opposed the advance of copyright and the patentability of software. The dynamics of shared production innovation of free software thus gave life to a greater legal innovation. We refer to copyleft, that is to say to the creation of a common property, of an *inappropriable* public domain, "to which each can add something, but not take away any part of it" for their benefit, as the legal professional Eben Moglen,adviser to the FSF, explained (quoted by Mangolte 2013: 1, our translation).

In the light of the same experience lived with the crisis of the first Unix community, Stallman and the members of the FSE were in fact aware of two key elements needed to permit the sustainability of the logic of the free-software commons. On the one hand, in a capitalist system, a simple open-source logic that limited itself to spilling knowledge and information into the public domain was unable to prevent free rider strategies of corporations. The latter can completely legally help themselves to open-source resources (like the source code) released into public domain only to then conceal them in a new product subject to copyright and/or patents. On the other hand, the accumulation of a stock of inalienable common-pool resources implies the formation of institutional forms (rules of governance, incentive norms, and forms of property) that canalize the behaviour of the commoners towards these ends.

To this end, it was necessary to make use of private-property devices in some way, particularly copyright, to turn them against it and to place them at the service of a completely different logic based on the inalienability of resources. Copyleft is in fact a technique that uses the same legal instruments as copyright as a means to subvert its restrictions at the spread of knowledge.

As Stallman states, "copyleft uses copyright law, but flits it over to serve the opposite of its usual purpose: instead of means of privatizing software, it becomes a means of keeping software free" (2002: 22). In other words, in order to guarantee the sustainability of the free-software commons, the private-property devices are astutely used and subverted to create a protected public domain in which "no 'free rider' can any longer operate to strip the creators, which is what was permitted by the absence of rights before software with a GPL license" (Coriat 2015b). In the copyleft, the source code is in effect open and authorizes all users to help themselves to the software, to modify it, and to improve it on condition that they pass on these rights, in turn making all the applications public, freely accessible, and usable. Fundamentally, these rights are the four "fundamental freedoms" that define a free software according to the FSE: (1) the freedom to be able to use a software for every aim; (2) the freedom to be able to gain access to the functioning of a software, to adapt it for specific purposes; (3) the freedom to be able to make copies for others; and (4) the freedom to improve the software and make these improvements as open and accessible as possible for the public good.

We note that the four freedoms at the base of the free-software licences are in general completed by additional conditions meant to eliminate possible impediments for free use, distribution, and the modification of copies. They are what Ostrom (1990) would call the control measures and essential sanctions for governing a commons, like, for example, ensuring that: (1) the copyleft license cannot be revoked; (2) the labour and versions derived from it are distributed in a form that facilitates modifications (in the case of software this is equivalent to requesting both distribution of the source code and all the scripts and commands used for that operation so that the writing the programs can take place without impediments of any sort); (3) the modified labour is accompanied by a precise description to identify all the modifications made to the original work through means of user manuals, descriptions, etc.

For this capacity to closely combine forms of co-operation and alternative ownership, the free-software commons have now become one of the principal reference points of the resistance to a tragedy of the anticommons of knowledge that is spreading well beyond the world of IT.

They present themselves, at the same time, as concrete proof of the possibility to oppose this tragedy and proof of the existence of an alternative model, founded on the Common, capable of giving proof on the matter of quality and rate of innovation of a superior efficiency both to the private model and the public one.

Evidence of this lies not only in the development of the most well-known creations such as Linux, Debian, Mozilla, Guana, etc., but in the more general multiplication of small and large community projects. Besides, the interest of copyleft as a mechanism of protection of the free circulation of knowledge is proven by the extension of this model, beyond the universe of free software or open source, to a whole group of other cultural and scientific practices.

It is exactly to facilitate this process that, in 2001, Lawrence Lessig founded Creative Commons licence (CC) a non-profit-making organization. It proposes to provide all those who desire to leave their cultural content free or partially free from IPRs a way to find an alternative legal solution, through copyleft licenses inspired by the experience devised by Stallman. Apart from Wikipedia, Arduino, numerous journalistic sites or sites of governmental statistical information have registered the protection of their content under the CC license. Under this impulse, the CC license also contaminates the scientific community where a growing number of researchers reject a logic of ownership that denatures the "disinterested curiosity" of learning and prevents the sharing of information.

Nevertheless, in the case of software like in that of the scientific research, it would be simplistic drawing a clear separation between an open science, oriented at sharing and a private science subjected to access restrictions and oriented at the market. As Delfanti (2013a: 50) opportunely stresses, this is more complex and multi-faceted phenomenon. It is what is shown by, for example, the exemplary case of Craig Venter, a symbol of the new figure of a scientist businessman and privatization of research. At first, with the company Celera Genomics, he developed a profit strategy founded on the unscrupulous use of IPRs in the sequencing of the human genome. In this framework, Celera Genomics competes with the Human Genome Project co-ordinated by Francis Collins which respects a more classic logic of publication of the results on Internet. Celera Genomics and Craig Venter do not hesitate to take advantage in a logic of free riding, plundering the results made public by the Human Genome Project. It is not pointless to observe that this predatory strategy probably could not have happened if the results of the Human Genome Project had been protected by a legal formula of the copyleft type. In any case, this fact stirred up massive indignation in the international scientific community and public opinion. Also because of this (reputation is a market value), Craig Venter, in a subsequent bio-genetic project, Sorcener II, has been converted into a business model that integrates the principles of open data and open science. It is not a question of abandoning a profit logic at all but of moving from a strategy based primarily on IPR revenues to a strategy where open access to codes becomes the tool enabling him to sell the services and know-how of his business. This change in strategy is representative of a more global evolution of cognitive and information capitalism. As we will see better below, no longer restricts itself to opposing a logic of ownership to a logic of Common. It is now looking to integrate the same logic of the commons as a resource for the creation of value inside a new form of capitalism. This new form corresponds to what Andrea Fumagalli

(2015) qualifies, with a striking expression, as "cognitive biocapitalism," to indicate exactly, like all life forms, the human common in its most basic form would now be placed directly or indirectly at the service of capital exploitation.

The metamorphoses of cognitive capitalism and integration of the criticisms of the multitudes: can the spirit of Common be diluted inside a new spirit of capitalism?

Fernand Braudel (1979) had already emphasized how the principal strength of capitalism is to be found in its extreme flexibility, in its capacity to adapt incessantly its forms of capture of the surplus. It is in this way that, though still remaining faithful to its systematic principles (the logic of profit and unlimited accumulation of capital) different configurations of capitalism have succeeded each other in the course of history: mercantile capitalism, industrial capitalism, and then cognitive capitalism. And the history of these metamorphoses certainly does not stop there, with the formation of cognitive capitalism in the 1980s and 1990s. Boltanski and Chiappello (2011), in their essay *Le Nouvel Esprit du capitalisme*,[19] insisted on the way in which capitalism regenerates and continually transforms itself integrating the criticisms that have been launched at it, even absorbing "ideas that were initially extraneous to it, if not clearly hostile" (2011: 60, our translation). After having shown, how the transition from Fordism to post-Fordism in France, relied on the integration of the *artist criticism* that had found its climax in the events of May 1968, the authors affirm that this method of analysis can also be applied to a more recent period, that is to the transformations of the regulation of cognitive capitalism.

According Broca (2015), it is necessary to analysing the way in which it is exactly the criticisms aimed at the ownership model by the internet multitudes and in particular from the FSM that contribute to explaining the most recent evolutions of the digital economy. In fact, the neoliberal regulation of cognitive capitalism had rested on a very precise triptych, closely putting in order *commodification, propertization* and *corporatization*, where the last concept designates the development of the power of large multinational corporations and the new oligopolies of the digital economy. Nevertheless from the beginning of the new millennium, this neoliberal triptych seems to come untied giving life to more flexible and original combinations.

The problems of the sustainability and autonomy of information commons: tendencies and countertendencies

The attempt of the large corporations of the digital economy to integrate the logic of open-source software and more in general the mobilization of collective intelligence in a new business model takes on, in fact, ever more important and diversified dimensions. Rapid mapping of the phenomenon is doubtless necessary to better interpret the tendencies and countertendencies that meet there.

First of all, it makes it possible to identify four main and often intertwined tendencies. The first concerns the choice of some of the principal groups of the digital economy to involve themselves actively, both in terms of financial and human resources, in the financing and development of large open-source projects. The exemplary case is, first of all, just that of Linux, which in the 1990s incarnated the only real alternative capable of destabilizing the monopoly of digital ownership capitalism represented at that time by Microsoft. By then 85 per cent of the Linux code would be written by employees of Samsung, Intel, Red Hat, Google, Facebook, or even IBM (Linux Kernel Patch Statistics 2014).[20] Each of these corporations employs programmers to carry out the modifications that it considers strategic for its business, benefitting at the same time from the work of the other enterprises and above all from that of volunteer contributors.

The second tendency concerns the development of companies exclusively specialized in open source. In particular, this is the case of Red Hat, which joined Nasdaq back in 1999 and at the end of the decade 2000 boasted business figures of over $1 billion. This is a company that began its affairs selling an easy-to-install, modified, and personalized Linux system. Though the base system had been obtained free of charge by Red Hat, experimentation and personalization allow the company to sell services associated with the free software. The latter work like almost free appealing products for which it is possible to supply a range of paying services, such as installation, personalization, assistance, training, etc. The business model is thus based on the work of supplying know-how. It does not rely on copyright or patents and is compatible with the principles of copyleft.[21] This type of model constitutes the form of organization between the logic of commons and that of the market that undermines least the philosophy of free software and the autonomy needed for the reproduction of the commons. A very different case is instead that of the profit strategies founded on the spread of software with a system of "multiple licences." In practice, the same software is distributed, both in an ownership version and in a free-software version that has less functionality or is limited to a limited number of platforms. The free software is thus transformed almost by magic into a simple by-product advertising the ownership software. We find here exactly that logic of free exploitation of common goods that copyleft proposed to prevent. It is not by chance that this strategy uses especially the characteristics of the Berkeley Software Distribution (BSD) licence, which allows starting from an open-source software to develop a product that is not free, as long as the merit of the author is acknowledged. Note, however, that the importance of this type of licence must be seen in proportion; for example, in 2009, over the total open-source projects, a BSD licence represented little less than 7 per cent of the total, a percentage that instead rose to almost 62.5 per cent for the GNU-GPL licences.

The third tendency is well represented by the hybrid model of IBM. After having been (and it largely remains so) the business leader in terms of the number of patents registered, IBM has progressively opted for a strategy that tends more and more to combine the IPR proceeds, for the most profitable products, with the revenue from the know-how services for open-source products.[22] To promote this turning point with the public and the image of a large business protecting open source, IBM also announced the decision in 2005 to consent to free access to 500 of its patents as well as its future contributions to the international standards of access to electronic commerce.[23] Despite these announcements, we are very far from an abandonment of the ownership model. The software strategically detained by IBM, as mentioned, remain essentially closed. What's more, IBM continue to make strategic use of patents to affirm a dominant position in the fight for competition with other competitors and start-ups. Like, for example, in 2010, the company TurboHercules, a start-up that had developed an open-source emulator that made it possible to work IBM's OS mainframe (z/OS) on simple x64 servers, it was successfully threatened by IBM with a lawsuit for violation of intellectual property on 173 patents held byBig Blue. In short, collaboration with Linux and other open-source projects has nothing of the philosophical adhesion to the principles of free software. It is based solely on a very precise observation: free access of the partners of IBM to the source code of part of its programs makes it possible to improve them constantly using what is free like a sort of almost free R&D laboratory.

The fourth tendency is written in the sphere of a more general mobilization of the work of the producer-consumer (*prosumer*) and collective intelligence. The development of the Web 2.0 performs an important role in this evolution for different reasons. In particular, the practices of sharing and peer-to-peer of the prosumers have profoundly destabilized the traditional business model of IT, publishing, music, and audiovisual corporations. Response to this technological and cultural challenge has led the "principal Web businesses to invent original forms of creating value. In the new digital capitalism, it is no longer only a matter of making the highest margins possible on the sale of goods produced inside it and protected by IPRs. The logic is to create ecosystems in which the users participate (freely or at a low cost) in the production of the contents whose value increases indirectly through advertising or the sale of services" (Broca 2015: 5), especially databases, as in the Google or Facebook models.

In short, while the first cognitive and digital capitalism had as its main objective that of increasing the price of outputs creating an artificial scarcity of resources thanks to IPRs, these new models try rather to diminish the cost of the inputs, particularly by planning the use of forms of free labour for the creation of value and innovation (Terranova 2000, 2013; Zukerfeld 2014; Broca 2015). Mobilization of the activity, most often free, of the *prosumers* and collective intelligence can take very different forms. They range from the collection and use for commercial purposes of data and the identity of the users, the externalization of simple and repetitive tasks, like the purchase of a ticket online, up to activities of artistic creation (like the videos on YouTube) or that participate fully in what the new knowledge management calls the model of open innovation. On this subject, as well as the volunteers of free software, an exemplary case of the use of the users' creative work in an open innovation model is that of the Lego brand Mindstorms (Vercellone et al. 2017: 191).

Following these evolutions, an important new stream of the criticism of cognitive and digital capitalism is developing: the approach of *digital free labour*, inaugurated by the pioneering work of Terranova (2000), who, with the term *free*, emphasized the character at the same time free and voluntary of these activities creating value for businesses (see also Fuchs 2012). This new stream of criticism can converge with the criticism of ownership capitalism and the FSM. It can even give rise to new forms of integration of this criticism into the dynamics of capitalism, according to a logic of which YouTube has supplied the first outline, installing the Partners Program which permits creators of the most popular videos to receive a share of the advertising revenue (about 55 per cent) that they generate (Carmody 2013).

What will be the outcome of these metamorphoses of cognitive capitalism and, especially, their impact on the dynamics of the commons? In our opinion, two main factors drive this process of integration of the commons into the *spirit* of new capitalism, even though, as we will see, it meets with numerous obstacles and significant countertendencies exist. The first factor is tied to the inefficiencies of the ownership model, in terms of innovation, product quality and, specifically for internet groups, the *impasse* of a strategy of *commodification* of their content. It is to get round these that an ever greater number of large IT and internet oligopolies have become convinced of the need to integrate the information commons or in any case try to reproduce for their own advantage decentralized forms of production of knowledge and innovation. In particular, acknowledgement that innovation escapes more and more from the control inside large companies and calls for the experimentation of forms of so-called *open organization of innovation* is by now a recognized principle of *knowledge management*. More generally, as Marazzi (2010) reminds us, in management theories one clearly talks of externalisation of the production processes based on *crowdsourcing*, that is to say on placing value on the *crowd* and their lifestyle. Turning to resources produced by regimes of open possession and external innovation, allows large businesses to considerably reduce investment in R&D as well, to the point that, as has been spoken of in the past like for the Alcatel case, the model of "a company without factories," today some economists, such as Gagnon (2015), conjure up the possible model of large high-tech corporations without research laboratories. The new business and open innovation models thus seem to allow a certain number of corporations to face a dual challenge more efficiently: (1) stand the pace of a "permanent innovation regime" (Foray 2000; Paulré 2008) regarding which, as Stallman had anticipated, the ownership model is inadequate, both in terms of circulation of knowledge and that of labour organization; (2) invent new profit strategies capable of adapting to an economic structure in which a growing number of knowledges, goods and services are exchanged and produced freely by prosumers, escaping from the rules of intellectual property rarefaction.

The diffusion and sustainability of this model as an alternative to the ownership model founded on the *commodification, propertization*, and *corporatization* triptych, clashes however with greater contradictions tied to what Robert Boyer (1986) would call the Keynesian paradoxes of the shift from a microeconomic scale to macroeconomic scale. At a micro level, in fact, it assures that a certain number of enterprises set up profit strategies less dependent on revenue from IPRs and from the sale of commodities, bartering the gratuitousness of the open source in exchange for know-how services (ICT businesses) and free access to content and services, in return for income tied to advertising. Theoretically therefore, a growing number of businesses should adopt this model, to compensate the lower proceeds tied to IPR with those from advertising, from the reduction in R&D investments and from services providing assistance and marketing of the free software. Nonetheless, at a macroeconomic level, if all businesses were actually to adopt this model, the result would be a progressive expansion of the sphere of gratuitousness which would lead in turn to a proportional fall in the volume of profits.

In this sense, Rifkin (2014) is not mistaken when he suggests that the same process of camouflaged diffusion between businesses of the free and open-source model properly of the commons to make a new source of profit out of it, would end up leading to the opposite result than that looked for. In other words, we would witness more the expansion of what Rifkin calls the zero-price marginal society, founded on the logic of sharing and gratuitousness than, to the success of a new viable business model to give, on a macro-economic and social level, new impulse to capitalism.[24] It is one of the key factors that explain why, in our opinion, the ownership model remains the insuperable horizon of cognitive capitalism. It will continue to remain dominant despite a series of amendments and partial and local sacrifices, more or less significant, of the triptych *commodification, propertization*, and *corporatization.* Awareness of this fact feeds the reflections of distinguished economists besides, like Bradford DeLong and Summers (2001) who right on this basis formulate the justification for the need for further strengthening of the IPR system.

The second factor in the advance of cognitive capitalism on the terrain of the knowledge and information commons depends on the weaknesses and contradictions inside the universe of free software and the hackers. The principle one of these weaknesses is tied to the lack of financial resources. By their very nature commons are an alternative form as much to the public as the private sector and therefore cannot have at their disposal the conditions of financing activities that are in the realm of private enterprise and the state. In particular, in the original spirit of free software, the work of contributors is not a wage relation. It is a free activity, in the twofold sense of gratuitous and free, which consists in producing use values subordinated to a regime of non-appropriable property.

Certainly, these characteristics, as we have seen, contribute to explaining the superior productive efficiency of this model compared to the ownership and bureaucratic one, favouring initiative taking, innovation and horizontal co-operation. But at the same time they make it highly vulnerable on the level of capacity of self-financing, seeing that the commoners cannot benefit from an income generated directly by their activity. This situation explains why one the main obstacles to the development and sustainability of the knowledge commons (from free software to makers) is found in the lack of time that cognitive workers suffer from (Agrain 2005). They must, in fact, find their means of support elsewhere, in particular through wage relation, in activities that require a high level of IT knowledge. Besides, the time at their disposal for the commons is all the more reduced that in cognitive capitalism we witness, for the highest qualified jobs, a stretching of the actual labour time that overflows into all the other times of their life. These economic and temporal constraints also explain why in free-software projects an overwhelming majority of people cannot devote more than a few hours a week to them, while the essentials of the lines of code are the work of a minority of professional programmers (Bonneuil and Joly 2013). The result is that the partnership strategy of the large proprietary groups has been able to slip more easily into this crack. It is like this that in some large projects, as recalled, the majority of the code is now written by employees of large groups who work on it according to the interests of their companies. As far as the regime of ownership of the product continues to respect the principles of the four freedoms defined by the FSE, this situation cannot avoid conditioning both the concept of the software and the way to co-ordinate labour. This results in a loss of autonomy on the side of the free-software commons, the importance of which, in our opinion, is undervalued by the leaders of the open-source movement. Note, on this subject, that the rift between the FSE movement and the open-source one is not in fact, as is often presented, the outcome of the opposition between the rigidity of the ethical principles of a Stallman and the lucid pragmatism of a Raymond or a Torvalds.[25] This division is above all the expression of the converging economic forces that weaken the economy of the commons rendering them vulnerable to the integration strategy of the large IT groups.[26] Even if the commons come out of this unquestionably weakened, one should not however forget a series of elements giving evidence of their resistance and a lasting dynamism: (1) next to large projects like Firefox and Linux which depend more and more on financing from the large players of the IT industry, there exist tens of thousands of independent projects, conducted on a voluntary basis.[27] These preserve, as in the exemplary case of Debian,[28] which counts more than 1,000 voluntary collaborators, the autonomy of the free-software commons from the influence that financial dependency of the large groups exercises over them; (2) free software's market share, in terms of business figures, in the software market remains reduced It does not exceed 10 per cent, even if its rate of growth is much higher than that of the overall market; (3) finally, the most important element is the extension of knowledge-based commons into new sectors of activity and in new productive combinations in which it seems to reconnect at times with the spirit of the dawn of the free-software model, as is the case for very many experiences in the new universe of makers (Lallement 2015). The FSM combines with it and finds today a significant extension in the maker movement that associates the manufacture of material goods and the sharing of means of production: electronic and robotic apparatus, 3D printing, numbered machine tools, etc. The vitality of the maker movement is proven by the growth on a world scale of the number of makerspaces, almost all of which have a non-profit-making memorandum of association. According to the data supplied by the site hackerspaces.org, we apparently passed from twenty or so of these third places of production in 2000 to around 1,700 in 2014. Their geographic distribution in 2012 was prevalently concentrated in Europe with 47 per cent (principally in Germany), followed by the USA with 38 per cent, and ending with Asia with 8 per cent (Lallement 2015).

The term *maker* is used to indicate the culture and counterculture that is acknowledged with the motto, "do it yourself", which designates all the activities of crafting and self-production. The strength of the maker movement is found in the way in which it has managed to translate the potential of a bit, the elementary units in the digital world, i.e. the immateriality of the software, into the capacity to arrive at the atom, that is to the production of material goods. Authors like Gorz even made it the prototype of a new social mode post-capitalistic of production based on the possibility to interconnect craft workshops founded on the common throughout the whole world, to treat software like a common good of humanity, like the FSM does, to replace the market with what it is necessary to produce, how and to what purpose, to fabricate all that is necessary locally and also to make large complex facilities through collaboration with many local workshops. Transport, warehousing, marketing, and factory assembly, which represent two-thirds of current costs, would be eliminated. An economy beyond wage relation, money, and commodities founded on the pooling of the results of an activity conceived of from the beginning as common, is heralded to be possible: an economy of gratuitousness (Gorz 2008: 118–119).

Conclusion

The dynamics of the commons expresses the vital force of a knowledge economy originating from the meeting of collective intelligence, the development of welfare institutions and the ICT revolution. This dynamics often enters into contradiction with the logic of cognitive capitalism founded on the triptych *commodification, propertization*, and *corporatization*. This contradiction brings into the light the alternative between two divergent models of society and regulation of a KBE from which depends crucially the same sustainability and the future of the commons. In this context, it becomes ever more essential and urgent to define the terms of an alternative model of regulation of a society and of a KBE at the centre of which the logic of the commons would perform an essential role.

The analysis conducted in this report brings to the surface three main axes that could constitute the framework of such a mode of alternative development. The first axis is centred on a policy of reinforcement and democratisation of the welfare institutions capable of favouring the transition from a system of a bureaucratic welfare state towards what we have called a system of commonfare. The possibility of this transition rests on the key role that should be assigned to investment in non-mercantile collective services and *production of humans for and by humans* which guarantee at the same time, the satisfaction of essential needs, the reproduction of a KBE and socially and ecologically sustainable development. As we have had occasion to observe more than once throughout this report, *production of humans for and by humans* constitute, moreover, a reservoir of highly qualified jobs in activities in which the cognitive and relational dimension of labour is dominant. *Productions of humans for and by humans* correspond by definition to a co-production of services. This outline would thus favour experimentation of fresh forms of self-government of production, according to modalities that closely involve users in an authentic dynamics of participative democracy.

The second axis of this alternative mode of development, in fact, refers to reforms open to mitigate the elements of weakness of the commons, acting first of all on the precariousness of the labour power and the constraints that limit involvement of the commoners. Sustainability of the commons largely depends on the reinforcement of the logic of the socialized salary by means of the extension of forms of access to a guaranteed income based on citizenship rights opposed to the bonds of economic and subjective dependence moulded through debt. Different proposals have been developed from this perspective: that of an income for collaboration (Stiegler 2015), that of an extension of the model of unemployment benefit of the show business intermittent workers (Corsani and Lazzarato 2008), that of a universal allocation of autonomy (Vanderborght and Van Parijs 2005). Our analysis led to propose a social basic income (SBI), unconditioned and independent from wage relation. This basic income presents itself at the same time as an institution of the Common and a primary income for individuals, i.e. an income directly resulting from production and not from redistribution. An institution of Common, because the SBI does not depend on the public sphere but after all corresponds to the pooling of part of what has been produced in common, deliberately or otherwise (Gorz 1997) and this outside any logic based on a relationship of measurement and proportionality between individual effort and right to an income now made inconceivable by the same development of a KBE (Aglietta 1997). A primary income, in second place, because SBI's proposal, as an institution of the Common, also rests on a re-examination and an extension of the notion of productive labour. From this perspective, the SBI would correspond simultaneously to social validation and to a means of financing this dense network of non-mercantile activities that a society of widespread knowledge and the commons creates, beyond wage labour. In short, it is a matter of asking questions about the historical identification that capitalism has established between labour and wage labour and, with this, between wage labour and right to income. Put another way, it means affirming that work can be non-productive in terms of commodities, but nevertheless productive of non-mercantile wealth and therefore find its return in an income. In this viewpoint, the mitigation of the constraint of a wage relation permitted by the SBI, even more than a reduction of the legal time of work, would permit individuals to recover control over their time and the management of activities that are an end in themselves. Thus it would constitute a real social investment and a liberation of creative energies ensuring, for example, the reproduction of information and knowledge commons, the development of which is noticeably hampered by the lack of time that is a feature of cognitive labour (Agrain 2008).

Finally, the SBI thus presents itself at the same time as an institution of the Common, a primary income for individuals and a collective investment in knowledge by the society. It would allow, together with the growth of collective welfare services, the establishment of a model of development based on the supremacy of what is non-mercantile and on forms of alternative co-operation, as much to the organizational principles of the public as to those of the market. Lastly the third axis concerns the fight against the enclosures anticommons of knowledge and the empowerment of commons property forms.

In this prospective two device are essentials in order to preserve the sustainability of the information and knowledge commons:

- The first device concerns institutional recognition and the spread of copyleft principles as a form of common ownership that establishes inappropriability and a protected public domain. Common property needs legal devices and innovations that, just as for copyleft, must allow the establishment of an inappropriable common-pool resource to which each individual can gain access and/or add something, both by contributing to the conservation of the resource (commons tied to non-renewable resources) and boosting it through shared use (intangible knowledge commons), but not take away any element from it to his/her advantage. Creativity treasures could develop around these principles to apply them to different types of resources taking their characteristics into account.
- The second, which is largely a corollary of it, would imply the ban on patenting informational goods and living organisms. Note well that these would be non-revolutionary changes as they would do no more than take us back to the structure of the IPR which existed before the great reforms begun in the 1980s in the USA. Such reforms would allow the restoration of a relatively clear frontier between discovery and innovation and a mode of regulation of the IPR that from the actual point of view of the

development of knowledge showed itself to be more efficient than the current system. The consequence would be without doubt the inevitable drop in the number of patents. Nonetheless, the explosion of the "speculative bubble" of the IPR, growing from the 1980s and 1990s, would not go hand in hand with a reduction in the pace of innovation, but exclusively with that of the economic rent associated with them.

In conclusion, the three axes of this mode of alternative development expressed here, could constitute a powerful countertendency compared to the triptych commodification, propertization, and corporatization contributing to free the KBE from the weight of the economic rent and from the principal snares of the neo-liberal regulation of cognitive capitalism.

Notes

1 A similar conclusion is also reached by Castel and Haroche when they demonstrate how the principles of the system of social protection established by the councils of the resistance immediately postwar constitute a form of "social property." See: Castel and Haroche (2001); Castel (1995).
2 For example, Aglietta and Brand (2013); Batifoulier (2014); Boyer (2004); Harvey (2010); Stiglitz (2006).
3 Certainly, as well as research centres, Arrow (1962a) recognizes the existence of other non-deliberate mechanisms of knowledge creation. These are tied to learning-by-doing processes for the most part associated with Smithian mechanisms of learning by repetition.
4 Arrow (1962) uses the terms *information* and *knowledge* as synonyms: this represents one of the most serious theoretical defects of his approach. For a discussion of the reasons and theoretical consequences of this assimilation of the two concepts, see Vercellone (2014).
5 Although the latter insisted on the way in which the universality of the science implied as a corollary democratization of the mechanisms of access to knowledge (Merton 1973: 273).
6 About this concept, see Gibbons et al. (1994) and, for a critical approach, Laval et al. (2011).
7 Like that obtained by the US Centre of Disease Control on a particular strain of ebola known as "EboBun."
8 Note that a similar argument has been developed by Eric S. Raymond (2003), the open-source theorist, to assert the pointlessness of copyleft in his dispute against the Free Software Foundation and the GNU GPL license. According to Raymond, having taken into account the fact that the development of free software is more efficient than owned software, the market economy would already carry out all the work of copyleft without discouraging new entrants on the market. In fact it is a position that distorts the spirit of the commons of free software and proposes to back their absorption inside a new business model of the large enterprises in the IT sector.
9 In Europe, applications presented to the European Patent Register grew from about 5,000 in 1978 to around 120,000 in 2003.
10 An observation that already at the end of the 1950s leads the great economist of industrial economics and innovation Fritz Machlup to conclude in a rather disconsolate way, "If we did not have a patent system, it would be irresponsible, on the basis of our present knowledge of its economic consequences, to recommend instituting one. But since we have had a patent system for a long time, it would be

irresponsible, on the basis of our present knowledge, to recommend abolishing it" (Machlup 1958: 80).

11 According to Steven Levy (1984), the term *hacker* takes on exactly this meaning at the Tech Model Railroad Club at the end of the 1950s, an association founded after the Second World War reuniting students with a passion for model trains.

12 In this sense, the development of a technological trajectory is also always an open process which proceeds through conflicts and bifurcations. As Piore and Sabel (1984) have shown, this was, for example, the case of the alternative between the craft made paradigm of flexible specializations and that of mass production at the dawn of the industrial revolution.

13 It precedes Mosaic and is also the first HTML web editor. Without it the subsequent navigators Mosaic, and then Netscape, could not have been created.

14 A similar theory was developed by Hardt and Negri (2000).

15 The term *spirit* is utilized in the sense proposed by Boltanski and Chiapello (1999).

16 The ideal-types are, as intended by Max Weber, constructions of thought that the researcher in social sciences uses to interpret the empirical phenomena analysed. They are abstractions through which it is possible to retrace the infinite variety of reality to a group of conceptual categories.

17 In his elaboration about the *hacker ethic*, Himanen continually positions himself with the pioneering essay by Steven Levy (1984). It differs from it however on two main points: the first stresses the breaking elements between the hacker ethic and the Protestant ethic. The second, the most important, consists in giving a broader definition of the *hacker ethic* that encompasses, beyond the IT sector, all the subjects of widespread intellectuality that "wish to accomplish their passion with others and create something positive for society" (Himanen 2001: 138).

18 We defined the concept of cognitive division in first chapter.

19 By *spirit of capitalism*, Boltanski and Chiappello mean extending Weber's thinking, the representations and implicit and explicit norms put together introjected by the social players that justify the social order of capitalism at a defined time of history.

20 Linux Kernel Patch Statistics 2014, www.remword.com/kps_result/.

21 To better understand this profit strategy, it is necessary to remember that the four fundamental freedoms of GPL licenses for free software do not prevent the sale of a free software. They merely stipulate that the first to buy a free software has the right to redistribute it gratis.

22 Since 1999, IBM has "set free" in open source a significant quantity of the lines of code of its programs and charged a certain number of its employees with the task of collaborating in the Apache and Linux projects. Cf. Tapscott and Williams (2007).

23 A datum which in any case needs to be seen in proportion if you take into account that in only 2004, for example, IBM had registered 3,248 patents.

24 We would get closer and closer to a situation in which the multitude of internet users would benefit from free services financed by growing advertising for a declining number of material and intangible goods. In this way, the attempt of capitalism to make the commons the new support of its logic of accumulation would lead endogenously to the reduction of the sphere in which profit and commodities exercise their hegemony on needs and on labour.

25 In fact, we could state that Stallman is more pragmatic and lucid than many spokesmen of open source when he indicates the unquestionable risks that co-operation with large groups involves for the independence of the software commons. It is not surprisingly that he insists on the fact that the term *free* means especially *freedom*.

26 Certain ambivalences of the hacker culture have also had a role in this rift. Particularly for a spokesman of the open-source movement like Raymond, technical efficiency ends up being considered a value in itself up to inducing him to say that copyleft would be a useless device, seeing that the market itself chooses software and innovations give a competitive advance to open source.

27 Let us also remember that, apart from the important exception of the BSD licenses, the majority of software characterized as open source are recognized as free software in the sense of FSF and reciprocally. Out of this, the widespread diffusion of the acronym Free and Open Source Software (FOSS).

28 For a more detailed analysis of the Debian experience, see www.debian.org/social_contract and Lallement (2015).

References

Aglietta, M. (1997) *Régulation et crises du capitalisme*, Paris: Odile Jacob.

Aglietta, M., and T. Brand (2013) *Un New Deal pour l'Europe*, Paris: Odile Jacob.

Agrain, P. (2005) *Cause commune: L'information entre bien commun et propriété*, Paris: Fayard.

Agrain, P. (2008) "Internet et création: comment reconnaître les échanges hors-marché sur internet en finançant et rémunérant la création?" *In Libro Veritas*,available at www.inlibroveritas.net/oeuvres/12407/internet—creation(accessed 12 March 2018).

Arrow, K. J.(1962a) "The Economic Implications of Learning by Doing," *The Review of Economic Studies*, 29(3): 155–173.

Arrow, K. J. (1962b) "Economic Welfare and the Allocation of Resources for Invention," in National Bureau of Economic Research, Inc. (ed.), *The Rate and Direction of Inventive Activity: Economic and Social Factors*, Princeton, NJ: Princeton University Press, pp. 609–626.

Batifoulier, P. (2014) *Capital santé*, Paris:La Découverte.

Bessen, J., and E. Maskin (2000) "Sequential Innovation, Patents and Imitation," MIT Department of Economics, Working Paper, 00-01, available at www.researchoninnovation.org/patent.pdf (accessed 1 April 2015).

Boldrin, M., and D. K. Levine (2008) *Against Intellectual Monopoly*, Cambridge: Cambridge University Press.

Boltanski, L., and E. Chiapello (1999) *Le Nouvel Esprit du capitalisme*, Paris: Gallimard.

Bonneuil, C. and B. Joly (2013) *Sciences, techniques et société*, Paris: La Découverte.

Boyer, R. (1986) *La Théorie de la régulation: une analyse critique*, Paris: La Découverte.

Boyer, R. (2002) *La Croissance début de siècle*, Paris: Albin Michel.

Boyer, R.(2004) *The Future of Economic Growth: As New Becomes Old*, Cheltenham: Edward Elgar.

Boyle, J. (2007) "Mertonianism Unbound? Imagining Free, Decentralized Access to Most Cultural and Scientific Material," in C. Hess and E. Ostrom (eds.), *Understanding Knowledge as a Commons: From Theory to Practice*, Cambridge, MA: MIT Press, pp. 123–144.

Bradford DeLong, J., and L. H. Summers (2001) "The New Economy: Background, Historical Perspective, Questions and Speculations," *Economic Review*, 86(4): 29–59.

Braudel, F. P. A. (1979) *Civilisation matérielle, économie et capitalisme: XVe–XVIIIe siècle*, vol. II: *Les jeux de l'échange*, Paris: A. Colin.

Broca, S. (2013) *Utopie du logiciel libre : du bricolage informatique à la réinvention sociale*, Neuvy-en-Champagne: Le Passager Clandestin.

Broca, S. (2015) "Les Deux Critiques du capitalisme numérique," *Hal Archives-ouvertes*, available at https://halshs.archives-ouvertes.fr/hal-01137521/document (accessed 31 March 2015).

Bucchi, M. (1981) "Introduzione," in R. K. Merton (ed.), *Scienza, religione e politica*, Bologna: Il mulino, pp. 1–11.

Carmody, T. (2013) "It's Not TV, It's the Web: Youtube Partners Complain About Google Ads, Revenue Sharing,"*The Verge*, available at www.theverge.com/2013/3/4/4062810/youtubepartnerscomplainrevenuesharinggoogleads (accessed 15 February 2018).

Castel, R. (1995) *Les Métamorphoses de la question sociale*, Paris:Fayard.

Castel, R., and C. Haroche (2001) *Propriété privée, propriété sociale, propriété de soi: entretiens sur la construction de l'individu moderne*, Paris: Fayard.

Cohen, D. (2006) *Trois leçons sur la société post-industrielle*, Paris: Seuil.

Coriat, B. (ed.) (2015a) *Le Retour des communs: la crise de l'idéologie propriétaire*, Paris: Les Liens qui Libèrent.

Coriat, B. (2015b) "Qu'est ce qu'un commun? Quelles perspectives le mouvement des communs ouvre-t-il à l'alternative sociale?," *[Attac]—Les Possibles*, 5(winter), available at https://france.attac.org/nos-publications/les-possibles/numero-5-hiver-2015/dossier-les-biens-communs/article/qu-est-ce-qu-un-commun (accessed 4 April 2015).

Corsani, A., and M. Lazzarato (2008) *Intermittents et précaires*, Paris: Éditions Amsterdam.

Dardot, P. and C. Laval (2009) *La Nouvelle Raison du monde: essai sur la société néolibérale*, Paris: La Découverte.

Dardot, P., and C. Laval (2014) *Commun: essai sur la révolution au XXIe siècle*, Paris: La Découverte.

David, P. A., and D. Foray (2002) "Une introduction à l'économie et à la société du savoir," *Revue internationale des sciences sociales*, 1(171), pp. 13–28.

Delfanti, A. (2013) "Geni ribelli: La scienza aperta nell'immagine pubblica di due biologi," *Tecnoscienza: Italian Journal of Science & Technology Studies*, 4(2): 27–29.

Delfanti, A. (2013a) *Biohacker: Scienza aperta e società dell'informazione*, Milan: Elèuthera.

Dockès, P. and B. Rosier (1983) *Rythmes économiques: crises et changement social, une perspective historique*, Paris: La Découverte.

DuTertre, C. (2002) "Services, relations de services et économie immatérielle," in F. Hubault (ed.), *La Relation de service, opportunités et questions nouvelles pour l'ergonomie*, Toulouse: Octares Éditions, pp. 225–235.

Friot, B. (2010) *L'Enjeu des retraites*, Paris: La Dispute.

Friot, B. (2012) *L'Enjeu du salaire*, Paris: La Dispute.

Fuchs, C.(2012) "Dallas Smythe Today: The Audience Commodity, the Digital Labour Debate, Marxist Political Economy and Critical Theory—Prolegomena to a Digital Labour Theory of Value," *Triple C: Open Access Journal for a Global Sustainable Information Society*, 10(2): 692–740. Available at: www.triple-c.at (accessed 2 April 2015).

Fumagalli, A. (2015) *La Vie mise au travail, nouvelles formes du capitalisme cognitif*, Paris: Eterotopia/Rizhome.

Gadrey, J. (2010) *Adieu à la croissance: bien vivre dans un monde solidaire*, Paris: Les Petits matins/Alternatives Économiques.

Gagnon, M.-A. (2015) "Les Stratégies corporatives de gestion fantôme dans le capitalisme cognitif. Le cas du secteur pharmaceutique," Working Paper, Workshop Capitalisme Cognitif, Université Paris 1 Panthéon-Sorbonne, Paris.

Gates, W. H. (1991) "Microsoft Challenges and Strategy," Microsoft Memo, available at www.std.com/obi/Bill.Gates/Challenges.and.Strategy(accessed 1 April 2015).

Gibbons, M.*et al.* (1994) *The New Production of Knowledge: The Dynamics of Science and Research in Contemporary Societies*, London: Sage Publications.

Gorz, A. (1997) *Misères du présent, richesse du possible*, Paris: Galilée.
Gorz, A. (2003) *L'Immatériel: connaissance, valeur et capital*, Paris: Galilée.
Gorz, A. (2008) *Écologica*, Paris: Galilée.
Hardin, G.(1968) "The Tragedy of the Commons," *Science*, 162(3.859): 1243–1248.
Hardt, M. and N. Negri (2000) *Empire*, Cambridge, MA: Harvard University Press.
Hardt, M. and N. Negri (2012) *Commonwealth*, Paris: Stock.
Harvey, D. (2010) *The Enigma of Capital and the Crises of Capitalism*, London: Profile Books.
Himanen, P. (2001) *L'Éthique hacker et l'esprit de l'ère de l'information*, Paris: Exils.
Jensen, M. C. and W. H. Meckling (1976) "Theory of the Firm: Managerial Behavior, Agency Costs, and Capital Structure," *Journal of Financial Economics*, 3(4): 305–360.
Jollivet, P. (2002) "L'Éthique hacker et l'esprit de l'ère de l'information de Pekka Himanen," *Multitudes*, 1(8): 161–170. Available at: www.cairn.info/revue-multitudes-2002-1-page-161.htm(accessed 10 April 2015).
Kendrick, J. W. (1994) "Total Capital and Economic Growth," *Atlantic Economic Journal*, 22(1): 1–18.
Lallement, R. (2008) "Politique des brevets: l'enjeu central de la qualité, face à l'évolution des pratiques," *Horizons stratégiques*, 1(7): 93–110.
Lallement, R. (2015) *L'Âge du faire: Hacking, travail, anarchie*, Paris: Seuil.
Laval, C., F. Vergne, P. Clément, and G. Dreux (2011) *La Nouvelle École capitaliste*, Paris: La Découverte.
Lerner, J. and J. Tirole (2000) "The Simple Economics of Open Source," NBER Working Paper Series (7600). Available at www.nber.org/papers/w7600 (accessed 16 April 2015).
Levy, S. (1984) *Hackers: Heroes of the Computer Revolution*, Garden City, NY: Anchor Press/Doubleday.
Lorenz, E., and B.-A. Lundvall (2009) "On the Role of Social Investment in the Learning Economy: A European Perspective," in N. Morel, B. Palier, and J. Palme (eds.), *What Future for Social Investment?*Stockholm: Institute for Futures Studies.
Lucarelli, S., and C. Vercellone (2011) "Welfare Systems and Social Services During the Systemic Crisis of Cognitive Capitalism," *European Journal of Economic and Social Systems*, 24(1–2): 77–97.
Machlup, F.(1958) "An Economic Review of the Patent System," *Study No. 15 of Comm. on Judiciary, Subcomm. on Patents, Trademarks, and Copyrights*, 85th Cong., 2d Sess. Available at https://mises.org/sites/default/files/An%20Economic%20Review%20of%20the%20Patent%20System_Vol_3_3.pdf (accessed 17 April 17, 2015).
Mangolte, P.-A. (2013) "Une innovation institutionnelle, la constitution des communs du logiciel libre," *Revue de la régulation*, 14(autumn), available at http://regulation.revues.org/10517 (accessed 21 April 2015).
Marazzi, C. (2010) *Il comunismo del capitale: Finanziarizzazione, biopolitiche del lavoro e crisi globale*, Padova: Ombre Corte.
May, C. (2002) "Venise: aux origines de la propriété intellectuelle," *L'Économie politique*, 2(14): 6–21.
Merton, R. K. (1973)"The Normative Structure of Science," in N. W. Storer (ed.), *The Sociology of Science: Theoretical and Empirical Investigations*, Chicago, IL: University of Chicago Press, pp. 267–278.
Moulier-Boutang, Y. (2007) *Le Capitalisme cognitif: la nouvelle grande transformation*, Paris: Éditions Amsterdam.

Ostrom, E. (1990) *Governing the Commons: The Evolution of Institutions for Collective Action*, Cambridge: Cambridge University Press.

Pasquinelli, M. (2008) *Animal Spirits: A Bestiary of the Commons*, Rotterdam: Nai Publishers.

Paulré, B. (2008) "Le Capitalisme cognitif: une approche schumpétérienne des économies contemporaines," in G. Colletis and B. Paulré (eds.), *Les Nouveaux horizons du capitalisme: pouvoirs, valeurs, temps*, Paris: Economica, pp. 23–46.

Piore, M. J. and C. Sabel (1984) *The Second Industrial Divide: Possibilities for Prosperity*, New York: Basic Books.

Polanyi, K. (1944) *The Great Transformation: The Political and Economic Origins of Our Time*, Boston, MA: Beacon Press.

Raymond, E. S. (2003) *The Art of UNIX Programming*, Boston, MA: Addison-Wesley Professional Computing Series.

Rifkin, J. (2014) *The Zero Marginal Cost Society: The Internet of Things, the Collaborative Commons, and the Eclipse of Capitalism*, New York: Palgrave Macmillan.

Shiva, V. (2001) *Protect or Plunder*, London: Zed Books.

Smith, A. (1981) *An Inquiry into the Nature and Causes of the Wealth of Nations*, 2 vols., Indianapolis, Ind.: Liberty Fund.

Stallman, R. M. (1999) "Le Système d'exploitation du projet GNU et le mouvement du logiciel libre," in C. Dibona (ed.), *Tribune libre, Ténors de l'informatique libre*, Paris: O'Reilly, pp. 61–82.

Stallman, R. M. (2002) "The GNU Project," in J. Gay (ed.), *Free Software, Free Society: Selected Essays of Richard M. Stallman*, Boston, MA: GNU Press/Free Software Foundation, pp. 17–32.

Stiegler, B. (2015) *La Société automatique*, vol. I: *L'Avenir du travail*, Paris: Fayard.

Stiglitz, J. E. (2006) *Making Globalization Work*, New York: W. W. Norton & Company.

Tapscott, D., and A. D. Williams (2007) *Wikinomics: How Mass Collaboration Changes Everything*, New York: Portfolio.

Terranova, T. (2000) "Free Labor: Producing Culture for the Digital Economy," *Social Text*, 18(2): 33–58.

Terranova, T. (2013) "Free Labor," in T. Scholz (ed.), *Digital Labor: The Internet as Playground and Factory*, London and New York: Routledge, pp. 33–57.

Vanderborght, Y. and P. Van Parijs (2005) *L'Allocation universelle*, Paris: La Découverte.

Vercellone, C. (2010) "Modelli di welfare e servizi sociali nella crisi sistemica del capitalismo cognitivo," *Common*, 1: 32–39.

Vercellone, C. (2013a) "From the Mass Worker to Cognitive Labour: Historical and Theoretical Considerations," in M. van der Linden and K. H. Roth (eds.), *Beyond Marx: Theorising the Global Labour Relations of the Twenty-First Century*, London: Brill, pp. 417–443.

Vercellone, C. (2013b) "The Becoming Rent of Profit? The New Articulation of Wage, Rent and Profit," *Knowledge Cultures*, 1(2): 25–32.

Vercellone, C. (2014a) *Connaissance et division du travail dans la dynamique longue du capitalisme: une approche néo-marxiste du capitalisme cognitif*. Habilitation à diriger les recherches (HDR), Université Paris 1 Panthéon-Sorbonne.

Vercellone, C. (2014b) "From the Crisis to the Welfare of the Common as a New Mode of Production," *Theory, Culture and Society*, 32(7–8): 85–99.

Vettel, E. J. (2006) *Biotech: The Countercultural Origins of an Industry*, Philadelphia, PA: University of Pennsylvania Press.

Weber, M. (1930) *The Protestant Ethic and the Spirit of Capitalism*, New York: Scribner.

Weber, M. (1991) *Histoire économique: esquisse d'une histoire universelle de l'économie et de la société*, Paris: Gallimard.

Weinstein, O. (2010) *Pouvoir, finance et connaissance: les transformations de l'entreprise capitaliste entre XX et XXI siècles*, Paris: La Découverte.

Zukerfeld, M. (2014) "Inclusive Appropriation and the Double Freedom of Knowledge: On the Capitalist Exploitation of Nonfor Profit Software, Contents and Data Producers," *Sociologia del lavoro*, 133: 145–158.

Postface

Antonio Negri

TRANSLATION FROM ITALIAN BY EMANUELE LEONARDI

It all begins with the "becoming-rent of profit." This process is intrinsic to the financialization of the capitalist mode of production and gets even more complex once cognitive capital turns into the core of the accumulation process. The consequences are remarkable, especially considering neoliberal policies aimed at desocializing the economy. As is well known, the goal of such measures is to enlarge market spaces through an ever-increasing colonization of welfare institutions by deepening both precariousness and individualization of wage relations. Vercellone, Giuliani, and Dughera emphasize that the emergence of cognitive capitalism entails a rupture within the mode of production and regulation of the knowledge economy—a rupture which is particularly based on knowledge and the immaterial becoming the key value source, so that the composition of fixed capital is perturbed. Fumagalli and Lucarelli emphasize that such composition in structurally fragile. This is especially clear once two assumptions are considered: first, knowledge and the immaterial are central features of fixed capital; rhythms and modalities of innovation not only accelerate (to the point of imposing a new international division of labor) but dramatize the productive process by affecting the relationship between capital and labor between fixed capital and living labor. Precarization and individualization, destabilization of collective welfare provisions and privatization of knowledge definitely signal such condition as a character of permanent crisis within knowledge economy.

More analytically in cognitive capitalism, the boundaries between profit and income disintegrate; the role of rent is not only a way of extracting value but constitutes an inextricable mechanism of desocialization of the common and of the politics, through spatial and socio-economic segmentations of the labor force.

From this consideration derives, according in particular to Fumagalli and Lucarelli's essays in this volume, a structural requalification and a spatial recollocation of processes of value extraction. The "becoming-rent of profit" discloses a bio-cognitive capitalism since capital freely benefits from collective knowledge produced by society as if it were a "gift of nature." Bio-cognitive capitalism can, in this case, be seen as an anthropogenetic model of production and accumulation—and (ironically!) an enrichment of "human nature" and of society. This welcome effect is, however, prevented by intellectual property rights (in the context of more general sovereign requalifications of property), which develop a profound effect of privatization, of direct capitalist appropriation, and of financialization of "the common" ("the gift of human nature"). From this Fumagalli deduces (in an economistic reading on which also Vercellone, Giuliani and Lucarelli may converge) that, once the system is faced with such need of "the common," it presents threatening unbalances and is made more and more fragile by the ever-increasing privatization of the common—only a generalized "basic income," he concludes, could bring the system back to a form of equilibrium. Yet, isn't it the case that such arguments (almost a renewal, *mutatis mutandis*, of the Keynesian approach) channel the analysis towards a balanced system when it is known, and politically desired, that this balance cannot be realized? I believe that this first take on cognitive capitalism within the current, financialized mode of production opens up, rather than prevents, a space of contamination with different approaches and points of view. As if insisting on the analysis of bio-cognitive capital represents, at last, a new beginning for the political experience of class struggle.

It is not by chance, thus, that the analysis comes back to the capital–labor relation; better: the link between variable capital and constant capital. What does this cognitive figure modify with regard to the capital relation? And how? How does a conflictual practice get determined—if it still gets determined—within knowledge economy? On this terrain, two options emerge: the first is, so to speak, external. Knowledge which is incorporated and mobilized by labor is described against the background of the technical and social division of labor and of the institutional mechanisms that determine a general level of *Bildung* (education) for the working class as a whole. A second option is, as it were, internal: knowledge (installed on variable capital) is incorporated by capital and somehow essentially presents itself as constant capital. Both Vercellone and Fumagalli and Lucarelli insist on the importance of the external relation: the cognitive and relational dimensions of labor in its relationship with capital (and the relative autonomy of variable capital as well as the autonomy of living labor) are determined by the social conditions and collective productions of welfare policies—namely the ways in which the "production of man by means of man" takes place and develops. More extensively, such externality is repeatedly proclaimed in the volume, especially by Fumagalli and Lucarelli, when bio-cognitive capitalism is said to essentially ground its process of accumulation on the dynamic of network economies and knowledge-learning processes that traverse social spaces, with a fundamental dematerialization of constant capital and the transposition of productive and organizational functions of capital onto the "living body of labor-power."

However, Vercellone and Giuliani attenuate such generically "humanist" conception by underlining the fact that

> The dynamics of the common expresses the vital force of the knowledge economy that comes from the meeting of collective intelligence, the

> development of welfare institutions and finally the ICT of the digital revolution. This dynamic directly enters in contradiction with the logic of cognitive capitalism based on commodification, ownership and industrialization (corporatization = entrepreneurship) of knowledge.
>
> (p. 164)

Also Fumagalli, more cautiously, in Chapter 4 of this volume, attenuates the degree of heterogeneity of the forms of accumulation generated by the separation of the human element from the machinic one; here he rather stresses the hybridization of such realities, of such process.

Yet this line of external relationship between capital and cognitive labor is still fundamental. Its importance is shown by the emphasis on the forms in which welfare provisions constitute a huge space of knowledge production. Exactly such emphasis, however, should bring about a complementary observation: here what gets highlighted is the alternative, internal line. The analysis now assumes as a key factor, beyond the effects of constant and variable capital clashing on the social field, also the appropriation of fixed capital by workers, by living labor.

This determination becomes more and more important in so far as the capitalist mode of production crosses cognitive living labor. Crossing: namely, capital exploits living cognitive labor, extracts value from it, looks for appropriating it but, simultaneously, clashes with it. "We must hear the distant roar of battle," said someone who studied such crossing. If it is true that cognitive living labor, unfolded and spread on the biopolitical terrain, turns into the force that challenges capitalist accumulation (this is the external scenario), it is equally true that constant capital is made more flexible by this clash and is more and more diluted on the social and productive terrain as it confronts the singular performances of productive subjects and the qualitative self-valorization of living labor. On this terrain—namely that on which constant capital seems to dissolve in the battle against living labor, on which capital's productive force seems to be overcome by the power of living labor (variable capital)—the internal line of appropriation of fixed capital by living labor appears to become more and more central, more and more consistent.

Thus, it seems to me insufficient to only pay attention to that process which installs on welfare institutions—namely on the enlargement of the wage-sphere—the paradigm of the current transformation of variable capital. The importance of this form of socialization should not be denied. However, it is still essential to keep into account the appropriation of fixed capital by workers. The anthropological transformation which follows such determination, as shown more than once by Christian Marazzi, seems preferable if the critique of political economy is to be followed by indications for class struggle—in this case, for processes of subjectification. And I believe all of us share the idea of deriving political indications from economic analysis.

Finally, let me elaborate on the central argument of the book, namely the continuity of the process of subsumption through its "formal" and "real" phases until a third form, the "subsumption of the General Intellect." As it is well known, the emergence of the General Intellect corresponds to the structural crisis of industrial capitalism as determined by working-class struggles and by the key qualitative role of knowledge within living labor incorporated in fixed capital. Vercellone and Dughera connect the hypothesis of this third phase of subsumption, marked by the identification of the General Intellect, to the recent development of the Regulation Theory. This latter—according to them—skims over such passage without fully grasping it: this happens because Regulation theorists lack a historically correct analysis of capitalist development and, consequently, do not dispose of adequate concepts. However, Vercellone especially insists that Marx's analysis of rent in volume III of Capital introduces—just as the *Grundrisse*—an adequate conception of the General Intellect. These pages are of great value.

Let me come back to the issue at stake: all the authors share the refusal (with the exception of few economistic passages) of a teleological definition of the subsequent shifts from one form of subsumption to another. Their insistence on the non-teleological nature of phases development is appreciable: history is not a linear process and, rather, proceeds by hybridizations and superimpositions, articulations and subsumptions of different modes of accumulation. In my opinion, however, it should be retained that such process is tendential. What does tendential mean? Tendency does not refer to a determinist direction, a Darwinian movement—although it describes an evolution. Moreover, such evolution—with its interplay of tendencies and countertendencies (as is analyzed in *Capital* more than once)—shows that capital is fragile in its development and that the organic composition of capital always presents itself differently as it registers the impact of social movements and of workers' struggles. From another point of view, in fact, the organic composition of capital should and must be seen as a composition that mutates according to the balance of power between classes. If there is tendency, thus, countertendency invariably arises. For example, referring to the case object of this study, both the appropriation of fixed capital by workers and the possible consideration of welfare policies as an autonomous space for variable capital lower the organic composition of capital. Moreover, as it is well known, both these lines of appropriation of fixed capital and of enrichment of variable capital productive capacity install the "figure of the common" within duration. It is only in this way that the hoary "problem of amortization," which is to say of the productivity of fixed capital over time, can be solved. My hope is that we can come back to discussing this point soon in the future.

What do we learn from this volume? Essentially, we learn that class politics needs to keep together appropriation of fixed capital and welfare provisions, dismantling of capital and de-stabilization of its political system.